Lone Wolf

Walking the Faultlines of Europe

ADAM WEYMOUTH

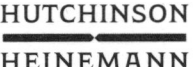

HUTCHINSON HEINEMANN

UK | USA | Canada | Ireland | Australia
India | New Zealand | South Africa

Hutchinson Heinemann is part of the Penguin Random House group of companies whose addresses can be found at global.penguinrandomhouse.com

Penguin Random House UK,
One Embassy Gardens, 8 Viaduct Gardens, London SW11 7BW

penguin.co.uk

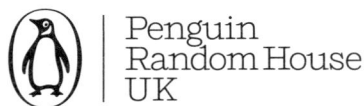

First published 2025

004

Copyright © Adam Weymouth, 2025

The moral right of the author has been asserted

Maps by Ulli Mattsson

Penguin Random House values and supports copyright. Copyright fuels creativity, encourages diverse voices, promotes freedom of expression and supports a vibrant culture. Thank you for purchasing an authorised edition of this book and for respecting intellectual property laws by not reproducing, scanning or distributing any part of it by any means without permission. You are supporting authors and enabling Penguin Random House to continue to publish books for everyone. No part of this book may be used or reproduced in any manner for the purpose of training artificial intelligence technologies or systems. In accordance with Article 4(3) of the DSM Directive 2019/790, Penguin Random House expressly reserves this work from the text and data mining exception.

Set in 13.5/16pt Garamond MT Std
Typeset by Jouve (UK), Milton Keynes

Printed and bound in Great Britain by Clays Ltd, Elcograf S.p.A.

The authorised representative in the EEA is Penguin Random House Ireland, Morrison Chambers, 32 Nassau Street, Dublin D02 YH68

A CIP catalogue record for this book is available from the British Library

ISBN: 978–1–529–15194–7

Penguin Random House is committed to a sustainable future for our business, our readers and our planet. This book is made from Forest Stewardship Council® certified paper.

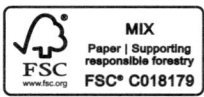

This one's a love story, and it's for Ulli

I will send wild animals against you, and they will rob you of your children, destroy your cattle and make you so few in number that your roads will be deserted.

Leviticus 26:22

Contents

Author's Note   xiii

Prologue   1
Slovenia, Winter   7
Austria, Spring   127
Italy, Summer   225
Epilogue   355

Postscript   361
Acknowledgements   364
Selected Bibliography   367

Dispersal of a young wolf, Canis lupus December 2011 – March 2012

THE ALPS

Bolzano/Bozen

ITALY

Trento

Lake Garda

Lessinia Regional Park

March 2012

Verona

PO VA

Treviso

Venice

Padova

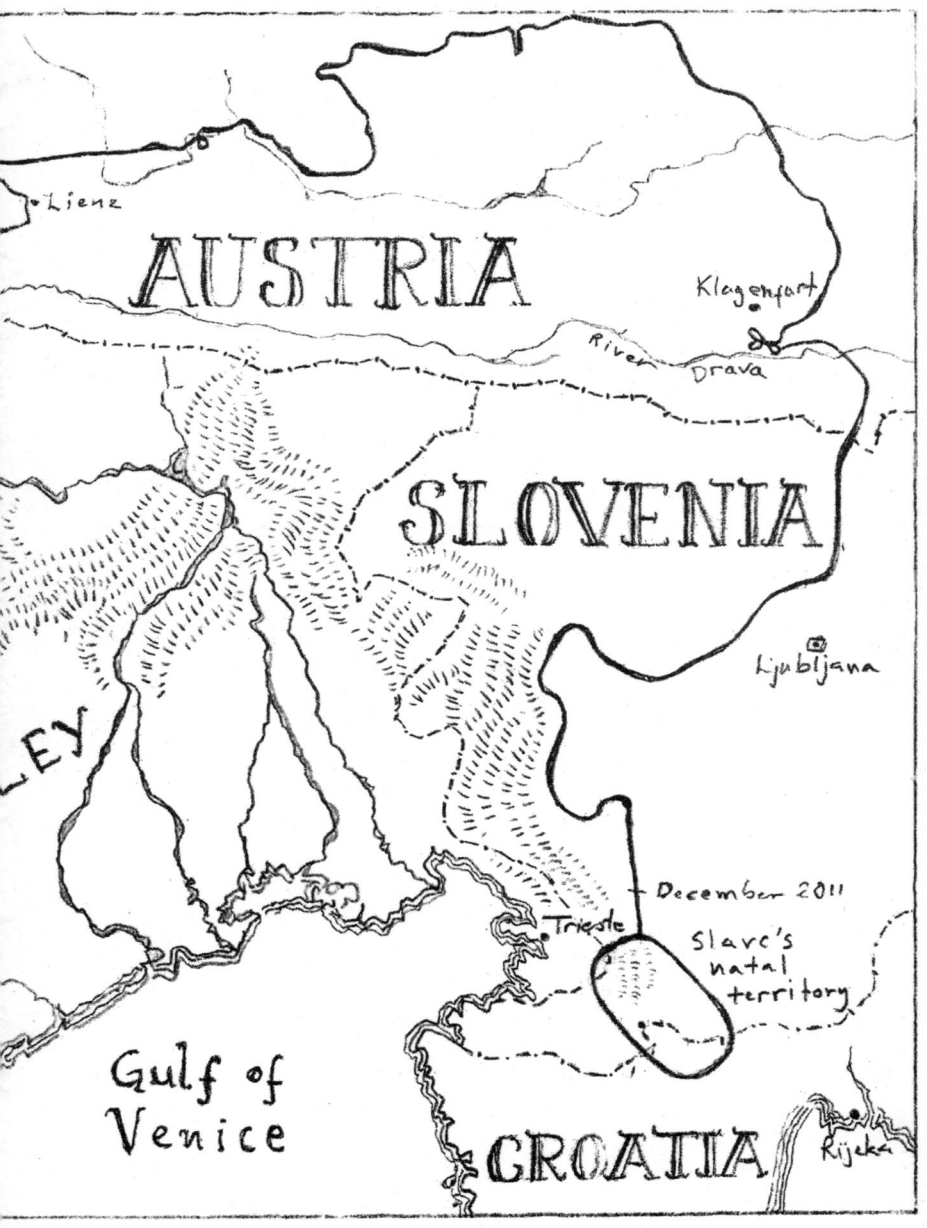

Author's Note

In 2014 I walked across Scotland to research how people living there felt about the mooted possibility of wolves being reintroduced into their country. During the course of that research, I came across a small piece in *The Guardian* by the journalist Henry Nicholls. It was an interview with Hubert Potočnik, Associate Professor at the University of Ljubljana, about a wolf called Slavc who had walked across Europe. Several years later, having returned from Alaska for my previous book, I began thinking about that wolf's journey again.

I first travelled to Lessinia – a Regional Park in northeast Italy where Slavc had set up home – in 2019, but soon afterwards coronavirus made further research impossible. It wasn't until the beginning of 2022 that I made it to Slovenia and met Hubert for the first time. Most of the research for *Lone Wolf* was carried out during that year, although I returned in 2023 to a number of places, often with a translator, to carry out more in-depth interviews than my patchy Italian, or non-existent German and Slovenian, had allowed when I first passed through. Other interviews I expanded with subsequent conversations on the phone. I also travelled to Lessinia several times over the course of those two years.

AUTHOR'S NOTE

Unlike Slavc, I had two small kids by the time I set out to follow in his footsteps, and I was reluctant to be away from home for more than a few weeks at a time. I did the walk in several stages, returning to England in between. I have written about the walk, and my time in Lessinia, as one continuous journey, in order to preserve the flow of the story that I wanted to tell.

Statistics concerning wolf populations and predations, and the current state of European politics, are as accurate as can be at the time of sending the book to print, in late 2024.

Some locations and characters' names have been changed to protect people's identities.

Prologue

Slavnik Mountain, Slovenia, 2011

The wolf left in the winter.

The days are short at this time of year and the nights are very long. Since dawn the light has been held within a fist and now it is close to extinguished once again. The wolf makes his way along the shallow gully, moving counter to its gradient, loose-limbed, his ankles loose and flickering. Were you to balance a glass of water between his shoulder blades, it would not spill a drop. There are no birds, and the bare poles of the beeches recede into the darkening wood, push up into the thin, metallic sky. The snow down here is grey for lack of light. There is nothing moving, no life, except for him.

The wolf moves precisely. Each print that he leaves is the size of a saucer. This small pocket of wood makes up one stretch of the western boundary of his pack; its other perimeters are many kilometres away. He has been moving all day, pacing its border on a southerly bearing, alongside the railway track. Since dawn he has scarcely broken pace. He is an animal built for motion; this is, perhaps, his supreme quality. He has not killed for eleven days, but that does not matter much; he can go for far longer than that. Beneath his fur he is taut and lean, but his coat is as thick as it will get all year, a dense underfur clad by a thick layer of guard hairs, and however thin he gets he will not be cold, not yet, not until he begins to metabolise his muscle. For now he is only keen and focused. His coat is tan and steel and crow-black and snow-white, a palette drawn from the colours of the landscape, and he has black markings that accentuate his muzzle and run the length of his back as though he has been marked by kohl. It is unimaginable that the wolves were once gone from this place because no animal could belong here more completely. His breath clouds in the cold, hard air. An agglomeration of fine blood vessels engorges his toes and prevents his feet from freezing solid.

He moves across land that is very old. Beside a trunk he halts and lifts his leg and urinates, and then he paws at the ground with all four feet to smear the sweat from the apocrine glands between his toes over the snow. This scent speaks of many things. To another wolf that encounters it, it narrates his sex and age (a yearling, male); his subspecies (*Canis lupus lupus*); his social status in his pack (subordinate); his sexual readiness (he is fertile). It gives indications as to his health and diet. To his own pack (which at this moment comprises seven other individuals: his parents, four pups from this year's litter and another older, unrelated male) it is an olfactory fingerprint unique to him. To other wolves it says keep moving; it says this territory is taken, carry on. If it does

PROLOGUE

not snow again, this marker will last weeks. There are other, older scents upon this tree, and most recently a female, dominant, in good health. This is his mother. He shakes himself and carries on. In a couple of minutes he stops to mark again, and then he continues, moving upwards, through the naked wood.

He is still young, he is nineteen months old, but he will not be young for much longer now. Winter is the hard season, but the snow places a finger on the scales in favour of the wolves. The rangy deer punch through the drifts up to their hocks, while he appears to glide over its surface with a deftness that belies his weight and bulk. He is full-grown now, forty kilos and standing seventy-five centimetres at the shoulder. He trots across the snowpack, pausing to sniff, pausing to listen. This track that he follows reeks of deer but they are several days ahead. The balance is weighted in the wolves' favour, but this winter has been hard. The competition for food has been intense. Last winter, when he was a pup, his pack had let him feed. Now there is a new litter to care for. And so increasingly he spends his time alone. Eating a dormouse, eating a fox, eating whatever is left of a carcass once his pack and the pups have had their fill. Poor food.

He pads on. He follows a concertina of twisted razor wire that maps the curvature of the land, still climbing. He knows to avoid its blades; he knows the places that are slack where he can cross. This land has seen the redrawing of borders and the movement of its peoples since the beginnings of recorded time and longer, and the wolf cares for none of this. But sometimes a deer will get hung up on the fence and that is worth something to him. He snaps at a falling leaf, misses it, and surprised by his own silliness, he trots on.

The wolf moves across the landscape and he seems terribly small within it. His species was sharpened on such environments; whetted by mountains and by limber, rangy ungulates, and honed, too, by his relationship of persecution with man. Wolves seem most wolfish when they are in the grip of struggle – in the winter; in human worlds. He climbs the slope with the same true movement and in time he emerges at the crest. The trees thin and he stares out, his eyes resin-yellow, the stone-black pupils interred within them like mosquitoes fixed in amber. All the familiar landmarks: the television mast, the jagged hills, the sea. The hills that drop away in pleats and down there, beyond the shoreline, the many scattered ships and a chill wind scouring the surface of the water.

His territory is sliced by a four-lane highway, and from here he can pick up its incessant thrum. It is the main road from the capital to the coast and the traffic does not let up. Even if you could hear it – you, with your vastly inferior ears – it might still sound like the wind that barrels from the inland slopes and charges for the sea, or like the background drone of the universe. But to the wolf these man-made sounds hold a particular, charged place. The logging trucks downshifting through their gears on the inclines, their air brakes gasping. Since he was young he has learnt how to navigate this road; to find its culverts and the rips in its chain-link fence. Along with how to hunt and his place within the pack, these are things that young wolves here must know. They are the things that their survival is predicated on.

Everything about this land is utterly familiar. The smells, the sounds, nothing out of place. He learns through difference. In essence, the wolf is a conservative species. He retains a sharp memory of the trap, last summer, his forefoot clamped and the utter terror, and of later waking, woozy, and the awful, human scent all over him, and the thing awkward around his neck. Sometimes he is still aware of the collar that he wears. He will not make such a mistake again. His brother was shot. He saw it happen. One-third of them, at least, die before their first year is out. Already he is a wolf that defies odds.

He is conservative, but he is driven, too, by an irrefutable force. A force to eat, a force to breed, a force to live. This, too, his survival is predicated on. And it will be on this same night, 19 December 2011, just after three-thirty in the morning, when for the first time in his life he will set foot outside the boundary of his territory. He will take a bearing north-north-east, following a logging road along the Bukovica ridge, sloping away from Slavnik's summit. Eighty kilometres away, in a room on the second floor of the Biotechnical Faculty in the University of Ljubljana, a GPS point will appear on a computer screen.

PROLOGUE

Did the wolf know, in those first foreign steps, the journey he was embarking on? Was he scared of the newness, the strangeness, the difference? Did he know these were the first steps on a journey of several thousand kilometres, a journey of many months?

Did he know, right there at the beginning, that he would never be coming back?

Slovenia, Winter

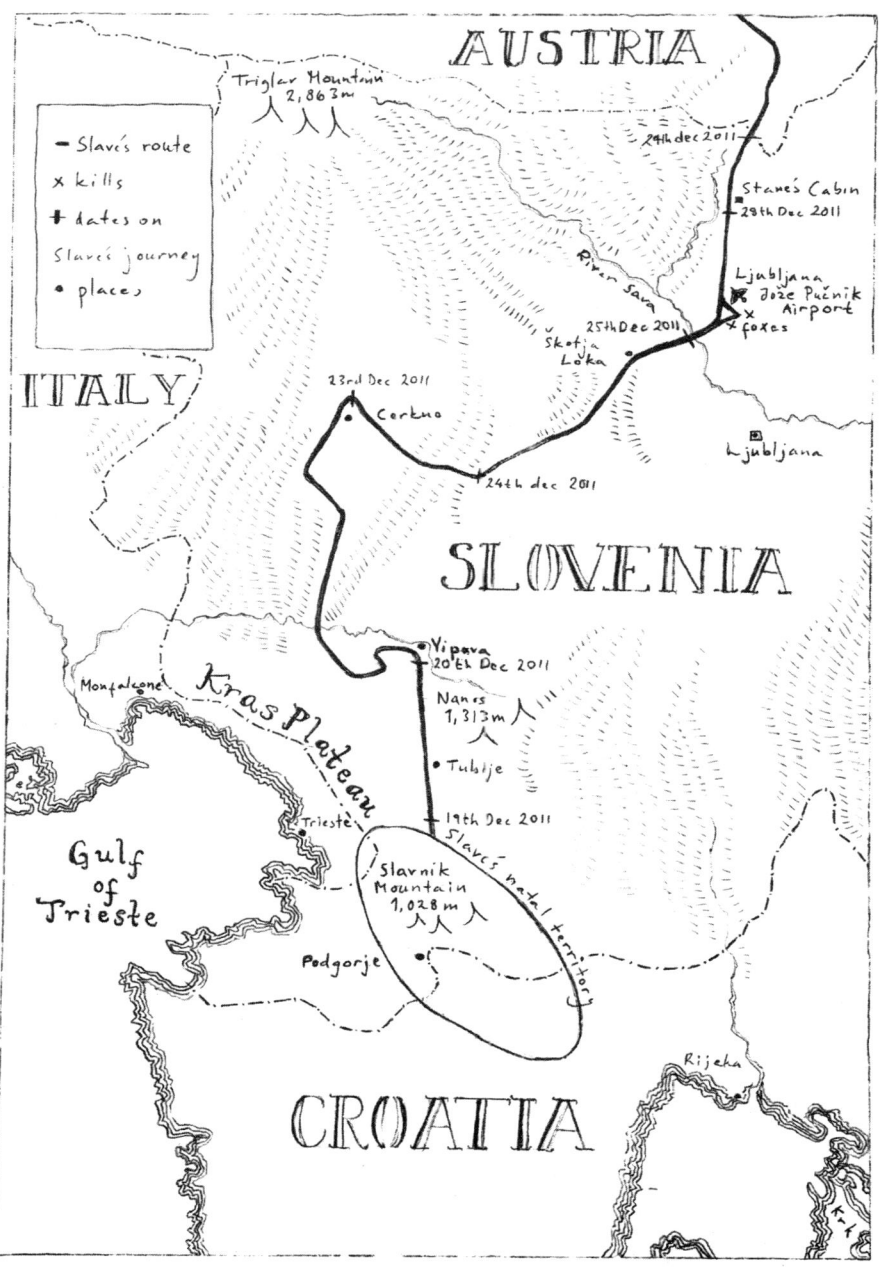

I

Until the lions have their own historians, the history of the hunt will always glorify the hunter.
Chinua Achebe in *The Paris Review*

Last autumn was a poor one for beech mast. Some years there is a carpet of nuts so thick that the forest crackles underfoot; other years scarcely any. The beeches coincide their mast years, so that during seasons of abundance the animals cannot possibly eat them all, and at least some will germinate. But the lean years are hard on the bears, which must double their weight before they den. Now, in the middle of winter, in early 2022, I can see their restless tracks, and wolf tracks too, criss-crossing the forest floor. Hungry bears did more damage than the full ones. There had been two attacks this winter already, on a hunter and a jogger. This is what Hubert Potočnik tells me as we walk side by side, through the silent wood.

I had arrived in Slovenia five days before. I had cleared customs clutching sheaves of Covid documentation, anxious to have remembered everything, and had taken a late-night taxi into Ljubljana. I was uncomfortably hot beneath my mask. People had begun to travel once again.

It was my first time leaving home since the beginning of the pandemic two years before, and all at once I was back in a foreign country, dropped within its foreign sounds and rhythms. I was giddy with excitement, despite the lingering, amorphous threat. During the past two years of strangeness everything around me had become terribly familiar. Now, stepping from the taxi into the city's chill night air and pulling off my mask, I felt shocked just that I was allowed to be here.

The following morning, outside my room on Vodnik Square, the market stalls are piled with Sicilian lemons and persimmons, with oranges and blood oranges and tangerines, with dozens of varieties of apple. Bottles of freshly pressed apple juice, of raw milk, of rakia. There are pickled walnuts and pickled beetroot, crocks of sauerkraut shredded thick or medium or thin, heaps of parsnips, carrots, squashes, cheap clothes made in Bangladesh. Hooded crows sit in the bare acacia trees, black against the nothing of the sky. The whole city smells of snow and cigarettes.

Ljubljana has just experienced a second winter with no tourists and it has not been entirely unpleasant. Without the coachloads, the city's residents have been free to notice the beauty of their streets, instead of fleeing them for the summertime and Christmas. The famous spots – Prešeren Square, the Dragon Bridge – are still deserted. When I buy a postcard to send home, the vendor in his booth congratulates me on my visit as though I am the advance guard of a liberating army, but for myself I feel like a harbinger, the demise of this new normal in favour of the normal.

For now it is still quiet. A busker opposite the Cathedral of St Nicholas, dressed in a black leather waistcoat and knee-high boots, plays the accordion for no one. At night the streets are empty, my footsteps magnified by the icy air. I stop to drink cheap, local IPAs in the sort of bars that you only find in Eastern Europe, in concrete rooms playing severe techno and graffiti scrawled across the walls. Occasionally, on street corners, I come upon small groups of *kurenti*, carnival performers dressed in shaggy costumes like bears conceived in the minds of small children, their red tongues lolling, festooned with cowbells and ribbons. They are all men, and there is something of the stag do about them, clutching large lagers and smoking through their masks, drunk and snug. In a month or so it will be Carnival, and they are making their first forays into the streets. In warm restaurants of varnished wood I eat heavy dinners of stew and dumplings, lining my stomach against the cold.

One day I catch a bus to the University of Ljubljana on the outskirts of the city. I am wrapped up and red-faced. Hubert Potočnik greets me in the parking lot, and after two years of speaking on our computers it is a little bewildering to be in front of him at last. He is in his late forties but he looks not unlike the students that he teaches, his face boyish, a neat thatch of curly, sandy hair, and he is dressed in the sort of greens and khakis favoured by outdoorsy, animal types. As though he could blend into his background at any moment, if his background was the Slovenian bush and not the campus car park. He walks me past the hothouses and into the Biotechnical Faculty and up two flights of stairs to his office.

The room is full of jackal skulls and telemetric equipment. Skis hang from hooks; binoculars; camouflage jackets and caps – all the paraphernalia of fieldwork. Shelves of box files and folders stuffed with papers. Posters of snakes, posters of bats, posters of fish. There is some kind of lizard in a vivarium to brighten the place up a bit, and the office resounds with the chirping of the crickets that it eats, so that the room has the feel of some jungle outpost. Fridges hum. A red deer skull bestrides the back wall, a single paper snowflake dangling from one tine of an antler, the last remnant of last Christmas.

Hubert pours me a coffee from the pot. He asks me about my flight; I ask him about the current Covid regulations, the small talk of modern travel. There is an intense, peculiar smell in the room, which no one mentions, so neither do I. There is a young man at a monitor in one corner, going through videos from his camera traps. Another man is bent over his desk, sorting something unidentifiable. I have always found it intoxicating to be around scientists who are doing what they love, their measured passion quite contagious. Mammals have been Hubert's love since he was young. After high school, after the war, he sat his degree at this university, and he has made a home in its halls ever since. He had thought at first that he might specialise in wildcats. But that was before he saw his first wolf.

He was on a field trip. He had woken at dawn and gone for a walk, as was his habit. 'I had walked maybe two kilometres,' he says. 'And then suddenly I saw them. Sixty metres away. Three wolves.'

He leans forward, hands cupped around his mug. 'I had good weather and a good wind. I had a chance to stay there for twenty, thirty seconds. It was really a long time. They were marking in one place near the forest road. They were marking with urine on a rock on the road. And then they just *disappeared*. I could hear my heartbeat. You know this vein, here in the neck?' He places a finger to show me where. 'I had such adrenaline. Not because of the fear, you understand. Because of the excitement. Because I was able to see a *wolf*.'

Since then he has seen a wolf in the wild perhaps fifteen times, in the twenty years that he has worked with them (not counting those that he has trapped for research). This is someone who is out in the field every day for several months each year, and he is one of the lucky ones. No, it is not easy to see a wolf.

A woman sticks her head around the door, asking for some research paper. 'I'm going to leave this door open,' she says on her way out, 'because it smells really, really bad in here.'

The lab technician grins and looks up from his desk where he is examining samples of what transpires to be wolf shit. The smell is wild and earthy, unpleasant in a dark, licentious way. Prodded at in a Petri dish, they can make out what the wolves have been eating. In the lab, it is possible to extract the DNA to build the genotype to identify a specific individual, and from that they can reconstruct its pedigree and figure out the constitution of its pack, the entire family tree. They collect hundreds of these samples in the field: scat, saliva, urine, hair. The bank of fridges is stuffed with them. The science is not far off being able to scrape a footprint to gather enough genetic material for identification – we are shedding DNA all the time. This data gives a pretty good idea about how Slovenia's wolves are doing. At their most recent estimate there were 137 wolves in the country, spread across seventeen packs (although five of these packs straddle the border with Croatia). In 2010 there were just thirty-four individuals.

The other tool at their disposal is the GPS tracker. The back wall is taken up with a vast map of Slovenia, a stepladder propped beside it to better reach the north. The map is cobwebbed with threads and pins like a police incident board, each thread a different colour, and each bobbin of thread is inked with a name: *Bine. Luka. Jasna. Mala.* Each thread, point by point by point, delineates the movement of a wolf that they have collared.

Some wolves stay local. Their clusters demonstrate the rigid territoriality of their packs. The red and the blue and the cream criss-cross so tightly as to almost weave a blanket, never leaving the confines of a vicinity that lies between two massifs to the east. The brown does the same, ranging around an area to the south of the capital like a ping-pong ball set loose within a space. But other threads do not behave like this at all. There is a white that commences on the Croatian border and sets off in a line resolutely west-north-west, marching across the country, before pausing somewhere to the north of Monfalcone in Italy, zigzagging about a bit, and then coming to a halt. A green starts in the west, in Triglav National Park, before making for the mountains to the north of Ljubljana.

But it is the dark-brown thread that draws the eye. Beginning on the Ćićarija plateau in the south-west of the country, not far off the coast, it arcs across the western ranges of the Alps before descending to Ljubljana's plain, just north of the capital, a few kilometres off from where we stand. From there it turns north, making a beeline for the Austrian border, and vanishes off the top of the map. The last point is pinned where the thread meets the ceiling tiles. The bobbin bears the date 19.12.11. And a name – Slavc.

'Sh-*lough*-ts,' Hubert enunciates for me. 'Try and say it well.'

I repeat his single syllable, imperfectly.

I imagine Hubert is sick of answering questions about Slavc. There is so much important work being done here, not only on wolves but on the trinity of large carnivores, on the bears and lynx as well. It's like a band that can never shake its breakout hit, doomed to play it for evermore. But so be it. It is Slavc that has brought me to Slovenia. It is how I first met Hubert. It is why, after two years of planning, I am here at last. And not unlike the hit song, Slavc was the wolf that got a lot of people into wolves.

I put my coffee cup in the sink. Hubert takes me back down to the car park. Students rush about the campus in the cold. We climb into the faculty's four-wheeler and take the main road south-west out of town, heading towards the Ćićarija plateau, back towards where Slavc was born. Back to where this whole story began.

There is something remarkable happening in Europe.

I wrote my last book about Alaska. I spent five years there, off and on, and five months canoeing down the Yukon. When I came home for the final time, I missed the place with the acuteness of a homesickness. I could not stop thinking about its beauty and its space. I missed the groundedness of people there, the anarchism of their spirit, the way they exemplified both community and self-reliance. I hoped that I could find something similar a bit closer to home. For a time, during Covid, I lived on Scotland's west coast, and if I squinted right I could almost convince myself that I was back there on the Yukon. The geography, the self-sufficiency, the endless summer light. But where were all the animals? The wolf, the lynx, the bear – they all had made their home on our islands once, but they had all been gone for centuries. The badger cull was once more in the news, and for the first time I found it terribly sad that our largest carnivore was about the same size as a skateboard.

I did my reading. In Great Britain we lost our lynx circa AD 500. Our bear at around the time of Jesus. There are various dates for the last wolf, but most stories put it in Scotland at some point in the 1600s. The more I read, the more I understood that this story was not confined to Britain. As in so many other ways, Alaska, with its healthy populations of bear and wolf and walrus, was the exception. Large carnivores had suffered almost everywhere, and the wolf, which people have always found the hardest of animals to love, had suffered the most of all.

I had seen a wolf in Alaska, only once. She was walking a logjam at the river's edge, about her own particular business. Some wizardry of our canoe meant that we drifted past without her seeming to notice us. Her head slung low, that bicycling gait, her coat grey and dun and cream, the same cream as the driftwood. She had paused and blinked and looked about herself, taking a measure of the air. There was a high-keyed hum of alertness. Near the beginning of that journey, it had felt like a good omen.

There was a time when the wolf was the most widespread terrestrial mammal on the planet. Its range spanned the Northern Hemisphere from the tundra to the tropic's edge, from the Arctic to the deserts of Ethiopia and Mexico. Wolves have an adaptability that is comparable to few animals but ourselves. They roamed the conifer forests of Honshū, the grasslands of the Eurasian Steppe, the Essex flats, the Adirondacks, the scrublands of southern India. They are as comfortable at fifty Celsius above as at fifty below. There are thirty-eight named subspecies of *Canis lupus* (although some are now extinct). The petite Arabian, with thin fur and large ears, adapted to the aridity of Oman or Palestine; the huge Tundra, found in Scandinavia's extreme north, and more than capable of pulling down a moose; the coastal subspecies of the Pacific Northwest, which can swim miles with their webbed paws and eat predominantly fish. There are packs in the Himalayas that never descend below 4,000 metres.

And yet, almost without exception, the crusade against them has been merciless. As soon as humans became herders the wolf was cast as thief, and there have been bounties on its head since the coins have existed to pay them in. In Athens, in the sixth century BC, you could get five drachmas for each male wolf killed, one drachma for each female. Charlemagne was the first monarch to throw the full apparatus of the state behind the wolf's eradication, forming the *louveterie* corps in AD 812. That the wolf clung on in France until 1927 suggests something of the nature of the quarry. King Edgar the Peaceful (who ruled AD 959–975) levied 300 wolf skins a year as tribute from the Welsh, and demanded wolf tongues as atonement for certain crimes – wolves were more or less gone from Wales by the end of the first millennium. In England, in 1300, the Reverend William, needing 'four putrid wolves' as a quack cure for the skin condition lupus, was forced to import them from abroad, much to the displeasure of customs. The final definitive record for a wolf in Britain is 1621, a note in the diary of Sir Robert Gordon that 'sex poundis threttien shillings four pennies [was] gieven this year to thomas gordoune for the killing of ane wolf', an exceptionally high sum that suggests that demand was far outstripping supply. Several years later a French ambassador complained on a visit to England that there were no longer any 'fierce animals that require bravery to hunt'. The land had been remodelled in our image. To eradicate them from a country down to the very last animal requires tenacity, a deep familiarity with one's prey, and maybe hatred.

The methods used manifest the full scope of human invention. There were leg snares, neck snares, pitfalls, deadfalls, sprung-steel traps and poisoned bait. In Ireland they were hunted with wolfhounds, their own treacherous descendants; in Kazakhstan they were hunted with eagles. In Russia a dead calf was hauled behind a sled until the wolves gave chase, at which point they were shot. In Spain they were driven by beaters into pits. In Mongolia the hunters mimicked the wolves' own calls; in Scandinavia, they attracted them with squealing pigs. In the Arctic they hid a bent bone inside a frozen bait that would spring when it thawed in the animal's belly, rupturing its insides.

By the time the colonists were pushing west across

America, wolves, forever conflated with the wilderness, were by extension being conflated with its original inhabitants. For the Native Americans the wolf had been a complex compatriot, but now a hatred of wolves spread like the Word of God. The divine was no longer to be found in the earthly and the grounded but in a moral authority that could be rolled out, like carpet, wherever the colonisers went. The wolves were given poisoned meat, the Indigenous blankets impregnated with smallpox. Roads in Kansas were paved with wolf bones. In the 1843 *Trapper's Guide*, Sewell Newhouse described how his eponymous wolf traps were part of a trinity of tools, along with the axe and plough, that were 'pushing back barbaric solitude' to make way for 'the wheatfield, the library and the piano'. Such logic pertained everywhere. As late as 1963 Italian environmentalist Alessandro Ghigi wrote that the continued presence of wolves in the south of Italy was indicative of 'a backward economy and civilization'. It is astonishing to think that in the mid-twentieth century, before advances in technology and field studies, that little more was understood about this shyest of animals than when the medieval bestiaries were written. Had we pushed them to extinction, we might never have known.

In the pursuit of civilisation, wolves were fed glass, strung up, set on fire and ripped apart by horses. Pups were gassed in their dens; cyanide bombs were deployed to eject sodium cyanide into their mouths. A dog in heat was tethered to a stake, and when a passing wolf was caught in the copulatory tie, men set on it and beat it to death. Estimates for the number of wolves killed in North America range between one million and two. 'Such behavior amazed Native Americans,' wrote wildlife journalist Ted Williams. 'Their explanation for it was that, among palefaces, it was a manifestation of insanity.'

Whatever it was, it was effective. Whosoever believes that humanity cannot pull together to effect great change would do well to remember this. By the end of the Second World War, wolves were entirely gone from Central Europe and Scandinavia. There were two small groups left in the Apennines, a few in Iberia and some larger remnants in Eastern Europe. In the United States there were several packs in Minnesota and, but for Alaska, that was it. Outside of the empty expanses of Canada or Russia and some other, isolated pockets, you would struggle to find a wolf anywhere at all. An animal that had dominated almost every habitat of the Northern Hemisphere for three-quarters of a million years was hovering on the brink of extinction.

But this was not to be their final act. Both the wolves and their executioners were to be granted a reprieve. Since the wolf's nadir in Europe, in 1965, their population has increased 1,800 per cent. What had once seemed an extinction turns out to be a hiatus. Their place kept warm, the land holding its breath, until they slipped back in. In 2016 there were 17,000 wolves in Europe, and today the best estimate for the number on the continent (excluding Belarus and European Russia, for which there is no available data) is north of 21,500, putting them as a species of 'Least Concern'. Europe's other large carnivores are on similar, although not quite such stratospheric, trajectories. There are more wolves in Europe than there are in the US, more bears in Europe than lions in Africa. We're not talking about cockroaches or rats here, feral animals thriving on humanity's spread. These are apex predators, the symbolic embodiment of wilderness. And nowhere in Europe have wolves been reintroduced. They have done this entirely on their own.

Slavc, the wolf that I have come to speak to Hubert Potočnik about, is one of the pioneers. In late 2011, at just nineteen months, he quit his natal territory in the south of Slovenia and began a journey of several thousand kilometres. North across Slovenia, west through Austria, south-west into the heart of the Italian Alps. He swam rivers and crossed six-lane highways. He grazed the capitals of Slovenia and Carinthia, Austria's southernmost state. He climbed to passes in excess of 2,500 metres in the middle of a particularly harsh winter. It is impossible to overstate quite how ambitious this was. He was forging a path back into a hostile Europe that had not known his kind for generations. There could have been anything out there, or nothing. I think of those Celtic monks casting off in their coracles, navigating over the horizon by nothing more than faith. A ship sailing off the world's edge.

Wolves are capable of greater distances than any other terrestrial animal on the planet. A male in Mongolia has the record – 7,245 kilometres in a single year, the same distance as from London to Delhi. But what made Slavc's journey so notable was that in the months prior to his departure, and knowing nothing of what he would go on to do, Hubert had collared him with a GPS tracker as part of his ongoing research into wolf behaviour. The map that Slavc produced once he left home – one waypoint every 190 minutes for 100 days, arcing in a rough horseshoe through the mountains of Eastern Europe – gave Hubert and his team a chance to observe a wolf travelling through the heart of the continent, through densely populated human landscapes, with total precision. Each new data point underscored the wolf's tenacity and endurance, the desire for life to thrive.

And then in Italy, in the mountains of Lessinia, north of Verona, Slavc ran into a female wolf on a walkabout of her own. How they found each other is one of the reasons that animals will forever be an enigma. The female wolf, swiftly and inevitably, was christened Juliet by the local press, after one half of Verona's most famous couple. When they bred, they became the first pack in Italy, outside of the Apennines and the border region to the west, for more than a hundred years. A decade on and there are at least seventeen packs back in those mountains.

To defy centuries of persecution, to find one another in the sheer immensity of the Alps, to repopulate the lands that they were banished from – for even the most rational of scientists, it is hard not to see this as a love story. But Juliet's choice of name was also apposite because this was a family union as significant as that of the Montagues and Capulets. Juliet was a member of the Italian subspecies *Canis lupus italicus*, a descendant of the hundred or so wolves that had gone to ground in the Apennines during the centuries of the purges. For his part, Slavc came from the Dinaric population that spanned former Yugoslavia and reached down as far as Greece. The Rhodope Mountains, the Pindus Mountains, the Balkan forests – these were the wilder, less cultivated pockets of south-eastern Europe, places still mined from wars and where the wolves had clung on better. Their meeting was a bridging of dynasties, not just genetically significant, but a symbolic watershed in the wolf's return to Europe. Romania was one thing, but this was Heidi country. And yet, as with Romeo and Juliet, there were those who believed that nothing but bad luck would come from this coupling of the houses.

Today the range of the European wolf reaches from the Black Sea to the Atlantic, from the Mediterranean to the Arctic. Since Slavc undertook his journey, wolves have repopulated many of the areas that he walked through. And they are found not only in the remote forests and mountains where you might picture them, but rubbing up alongside humans: in post-industrial landscapes, in semi-abandoned farming villages, trotting down highways. Greece has 1,020 as of last count; Poland has 1,886; Spain has 304 *packs*. But reading down the list of countries, it is the least expected that really jump out. A Dutch friend of mine who keeps me updated on such things recently emailed that 'the wolf has conquered the whole of the Netherlands', one of the most densely populated, intensively farmed countries in the world. Luxembourg has a single individual, or possibly two. Belgium – Belgium! – has twenty-eight. It is easy to think of Europe as a claustrophobic continent, too long urbanised, logged and tarmacked. If that's the case, then the wolves do not seem much bothered. To see a video of a wolf trotting as bold as brass down a residential street in Holland, or strolling through a herd of cows in southern France, is to experience a moment of profound discombobulation. The wolf appears invoked, summoned from across a threshold, and it upends our quotidian assumptions of how the world can be.

Only five European countries are now without wolves: Malta, Cyprus, Iceland, Ireland and the United Kingdom. Being an island nation lends a different flavour to the debate, giving us a prerogative over what, or who, we choose to let in. If a land bridge still joined Britain to the continent, as it did 20,000 years ago, then we would have wolves by now, and the question would be how we live with them. Max Rossberg of the European Wilderness Society once told me that 'Eventually a wolf will make it to Britain by itself.' What, swim the Channel? 'Otherwise,' he said, 'how the hell did the wolf end up on those Vancouver islands?' This seems a stretch – the furthest distance a wolf has been recorded swimming is twelve kilometres, compared to the thirty-two kilometres between England and France at its narrowest point. And yet, if there is anything the study of wolves is able to tell us, it is that they will forever exceed our wildest expectations of them. I picture her, nose and eyes above the waterline, steely and determined, breathing fast and regular, traversing the shipping lanes, alongside a boat of migrants that is bound for the same shore.

I began thinking about a walk, following in Slavc's steps. I wondered how those living alongside the wolf, touched by its return, were coping with its presence. But there was more to it than that, because the wolf, of course, is scarcely the only change that is happening to Europe. I would follow Slavc during Europe's hottest summer on record, through a year of abject drought that was perhaps its worst in 500 years. Young people no longer wanted to farm and their parents were abandoning the land, driven off by the weather and the impacts of war, the rocketing costs of energy and feed. Those same crises – weather and war – were driving migrants to Europe. And the populist parties that were finding a foothold in this upheaval were endangering the very ideas that held the continent together. I was drawn to Slavc in no small part because he had walked a line through all of this, carving a path through Europe's mountainous hinterlands and some of the places that were feeling these changes most acutely.

Paddling across Alaska, as well as on long walks in the past, I had found that moving slowly, paying closer attention to chance encounters than to a predetermined plan, could afford insights into people and places that I missed when working to a schedule. Following strings of coincidence, choosing the most enticing path, making the time to listen, opened up angles on complex questions that otherwise got lost. Slavc's route gave me a way to get under Europe's skin. Animals live alongside us in parallel worlds that are almost impossible to know, but it seems to me that we run a risk that is not unlike anthropomorphism when we try to explain what is going on inside other people's heads. It can be better to approach such things obliquely. When we speak about the wolf, I would come to learn, we are never speaking only about a wolf. And so I would set out to see what following wolves could tell us about this crossroads in Europe's history, this moment between times.

The wolf may have wondered, in the centuries that it was absent, whether humanity had changed. Humanity has often wondered the same about itself. What is certain is that the wolf has not changed. And that everywhere that the wolf has returned, the fear and hatred have come back, too.

Nowhere in Slovenia takes very long to get to. In an hour Hubert and I are in the small town of Kozina, and from there we take a rutted track south for several kilometres, climbing gently through a scrub of hop-hornbeam and juniper and beech. The truck bounces along while Hubert chats away about the wolf's resurgence. His animation is infectious. For someone passionate about large carnivores, it has been quite the remarkable two decades.

At last we break from the woods and Hubert parks and we get out. Wind rips unimpeded across this bare plateau so that you must stand angular to it, and my eyes stream with the cold. Hubert points out places – to the north-west is Trieste (or Trst as the Slovenes call it, with their snubbing of all vowels); to the west the Adriatic and the Istrian peninsula, its fractured coastline bending away to the south. Stripes of mountains recede in shades of eggshell blue towards Eastern Europe's interior, softening with distance, and the other way is Triglav, Slovenia's highest peak. I can see everything from here. Shrill birds are flying high. The sky is endless and utterly blue.

'We called him Slavc because of Slavnik Mountain,' Hubert says, gesturing to the nearby summit. There is a broadcast transmitter and a mountain hut, still shuttered for the season. The wind has scrubbed the snow from the empty land, but it languishes still in the leeside of the buildings. 'Slavnik, Slavc. But it is also – how do you call it? – a wordplay.' Slavc is a macho variant of Slavko, a common name in Slovenia, and it lends to the wolf a swaggering, tough-guy quality, somewhat tongue-in-cheek. It is hard to get if you don't speak Slovenian, and it is hard to say as well. Sh-*lough*-ts. In Austria they call him Slavko, after Slavko Avsenik, the famous Slovenian accordionist. In Italy they call him Slowz, not even trying, trailing off into a mush of consonants entirely foreign to their tongue.

In the scientific papers wolves get given names that look like flight numbers: O6, OR7, GW950m. To name an animal, runs the logic, is to forgo objectivity. It is, crime of all crimes, to anthropomorphise. Yet once these animals work their way into the public consciousness, they are inevitably baptised. We cannot help but turn them into stories. Subjectivity towards the natural world is, after all, what we are craving.

We return to the truck and drive back down into the trees and pull up at last on the verge of an unpaved logging road. It is dark in here and completely sheltered, the snow still thick on the ground, but look up and the canopy is alive with wind. We walk away from the road, into the trees. The place appears barren, but Hubert sees it differently. He points out dormouse prints and bear prints. ('Dormouse oil,' he tells me. 'Very good for the skin.') He finds the pellet of a Ural owl on the stump of a beech, and he prises it apart to show me all the little bones. It is like walking with some different type of being whose senses vibrate on a separate plane, a glimpse into this place through another creature's mind. A little closer, perhaps, to a wolf.

Hubert's father had stuffed animals. He stuffed the trophy animals of hunters – bear and deer and mouflon – and sometimes he stuffed roadkill. Hubert grew up surrounded by his father's creations, a dead bestiary of wonder. It verged on the divine, his ability to breathe

the life back into them. Hubert wandered the workshop examining each of their intimate forms, their teeth, their claws, their feathers, each one the essence of itself. In another life his father might have been a biologist, but for a young man from the mountains in Tito's Yugoslavia such a thing never crossed his mind; you might as well grow up to be an astronaut. And so he had come to work with animals in the only way he knew. And because he loved animals, he shared that love with his son.

'He taught me how to observe nature,' Hubert says. 'He taught me how to see the things that other people would pass by. He didn't have an academic education, but he had a feeling for observing nature. And this made my own curiosity.'

Before and after school, when the land was flooded with light, the young Hubert would walk out behind his house to where the forest met the fields and sit, watching the animals. He carried a notebook and a camera, and he recorded what they ate and where they went and the relationships they had. Roe deer, badgers, raptors, foxes. He could be out for hours. It became an obsession, in the way that young people become obsessed. The more he wrote in his notebooks, the more he wrote his way into their lives. When adults asked him what he wanted to do when he grew up, he was specific. 'A wildlife biologist,' he said. By then, unlike his father, he had discovered it was a job.

We meet a second logging road. Hubert wants to show me where they trapped Slavc. The place is nondescript, gloomy where the trees grow close. He points out a stand of hazel on the verge. There. The wolves use these roads as people do, as the most straightforward way through a forest, and so it is often where the team set their traps. Slavc was caught on 17 July 2011, in a soft-catch trap, its jaw softened with thick rubber. Gone are the days of snares that cut off the blood supply, so that by the time the team returned the agonised wolf might have gnawed its own foot off and left. Trapped pups can be covered with a blanket, like a budgie, and then tranquillised by hand, but Slavc was fifteen months by then, a strapping teenager, and they darted him from a distance.

There is broad consensus among those working with large carnivores that the wolf is by far the hardest animal to trap. It is more difficult to catch one wolf than a hundred foxes, as the Italian proverb has it. Bears are easy; they are helpless in the face of their own gluttony. Lynx are a little trickier, although being cats they are ultimately vulnerable to their own curiosity. But a wolf. The slightest change to their territory – a misplaced rock, an unexpected smell – puts them on edge. Hubert has seen wolf tracks that change tack a few hundred metres before a trap, only to rejoin the trail on the far side. He has found traps with a tidy shit deposited, impossibly, on top. *Fuck you*. Wolves learn and they teach their peers. If a pack witnesses one of its members being trapped, it is unlikely you will ever catch another. In 2019 the team had up to thirty-two sets out at any one time, from March through to September. Finally, in late September, they caught their first wolf of the season. A wolf can smell if you were there two days ago, even if it's rained. That's the stink we leave behind.

As such, the practice has taken on the nature of some dark art. To say they can smell a trap a mile off is no exaggeration. First, each trap must be buffed with a steel brush to remove all trace of rust. Then, in a large cauldron, make up a rich broth of fallen leaves and rotting wood and soil, and when it is simmering add a good slug of paraffin, which will rise to the surface of your brew. Submerge the traps and cook them, so that they take on the forest's musk, and when the layer of paraffin hits precisely 62°C, remove them with a hook so that the paraffin forms a thin sheen as they emerge. Place them in wooden boxes stuffed with hay, dig a hole and bury them, and then forget about them for the winter. Each team member is responsible for their own equipment, so that if an error is made it does not affect the whole year's work.

Come spring – wolf season – dig them up. Put the traps into sacks that have also been boiled in a forest broth, handling them with leather gloves (likewise boiled) and with a pair of disposable gloves on underneath. On arrival at the trapping site, pull up beside the chosen spot and lay a canvas blanket on the ground. Lie on this while you dig your hole (the shovel, of course, has been boiled). Place the soil on the canvas and, when the trap is set, sieve the soil back on top. Any leftover soil must be disposed of, at least 100 metres away. Cover the trap with a large, flat stone and leave it to take on the fragrance of the forest. Wait for a week or so. Finally drive back and, without setting foot on the ground (and with your gloves on!), move the stone off to one side. The trap is set. Go home and wait for the trap alarm to trigger an alert on your phone. Begin hoping for the best.

'And even if you do all that,' I ask, 'you have never caught the same wolf twice?'

Hubert smiles, a grudging respect, one hunter on the trail of another. 'So far we didn't,' he says. 'So far we didn't.'

A photo from 2011 shows a younger Hubert, bright-eyed with emotion, carrying the drugged Slavc. This was the third wolf that he had ever trapped. Hubert holds the haunches, his colleague has the chest. It is summer and the forest floor is sun-dappled and the wolf's coat is dappled too, black and brown and white and grey, his muzzle and ruff and legs and belly a brindled russet and tan. If you had wished to select an attractive wolf to repopulate the Alps, you could have done far worse than Slavc.

'It is a very strong moment, having a wolf in your hands,' says Hubert. 'It is a very strong concern for the health of the animal. You are full of adrenaline. I only get happy about three days later when the collar starts sending information.'

In the next photo the wolf is laid out on a blanket, sleeping still, the GPS-VHF collar now attached with its prominent EU tag. In the next, Slavc is back on his feet, bearing this new weight, slinking off into the woods and away from this human stench. For the next year of his life his position would be recorded every three hours and ten minutes, broadcast to computers in the University of Ljubljana. Over the course of his career Hubert has handled plenty of large carnivores, but that moment has never diminished.

'I can say it's something like a drug,' he says. 'You think you know wolves, and then, with each new animal, you are always surprised by some new knowledge.'

The collars were intended to aid Hubert's study of pack dynamics. To observe how each individual interacted with the others and how they maintained their territory. That this animal, which he had had his hands on, would go on to undertake such an immense journey, to reclaim lands that had been lost to wolves 200 years before, to forge new dynasties that would long outlive them both — none of this he could have known back then.

We leave the trapping site behind and Hubert sets a path diagonally up the slope. He has not been here for eight years but he makes for the place like a dog on a scent. Our boots break the crust of snow as we slog upwards. At the top we stand there, puffing faint clouds of breath in the weak sun. Squat oaks cling to the hillside, stunted and bent from the winter winds, each bowed to the same angle. On this side of the mountain the land is all but swept clean of snow. Last year's leaves stir at our feet. Through the oaks' contorted branches, far off and far below, I can see the wide, flat sea.

Hubert has stopped talking and is searching. I follow him as he picks his way over the ridge, the wind chivvying us along. We are at the southernmost end of the Kras plateau, which runs north-west for fifty kilometres, delineating the border with Italy, more or less, until that border turns north at Monfalcone. This is the apotheosis of karst landscapes, from which all other karst landscapes take their name. Regions of soluble rock, most typically limestone, that bend and fold in the face of the weather to conjure a glossary all of their own: sinkholes and swallets, clints and grikes. The stone is exposed here, tortured by rain, flayed by sun, and smoothed out by the elements into a fractured world like melted wax.

I follow Hubert, scrambling across its furrowed maze, skirting drops and stepping over fissures, hunting for the place. It is the work of water made visible, paused in time, although water itself is often hard to find, sunk deep beneath the surface. The plateau's subterranean world is a riddle of rock and empty space, like a lung. During the First World War, when this was the frontline, its pliant innards were gouged out to make trenches, chapels, field hospitals. Prisoners of both sides were pushed down sinkholes to their deaths.

'Here we are,' Hubert says, at last. He is pointing to a hole at his feet. The bone-white rock around its rim is polished to a sheen, verdant with moss. This is the den where Slavc was born.

I slither down into the hole until I am several metres below the surface. It is damp, but it is out of the wind and it holds some of the day's weak warmth. The ground is a thick bed of last year's leaves. I peer up at the hole of sky, and at Hubert's head, peering back down at me. There had been a pack on this hill since 2007 or 2008, according to local hunters. Slavc, born in 2010, was from a litter of at least five. Hubert knows this was his birthplace because they found his dead sister on a ledge, halfway up the drop, and later, once they had collared Slavc, they were able to match up the genetics. Based on the autopsy, Hubert's best interpretation is that she was killed by a fox while her parents were out hunting. Soon afterwards the den was washed out by heavy rains and the adults moved the pack to a new site, leaving her body behind.

A wolf pack is not a gang of animals dominated by an alpha. This is the first myth, of many, that needs to be dispelled. A wolf pack is more or less a family. There are as many ways of constructing a wolf pack as there are constellations of the human family, but, also like people, most wolves conform to type. They have been recorded in packs of forty-two and they have been known to live whole lives alone, but typically a pack consists of something like five to ten animals. Usually it comprises a breeding pair and their offspring, perhaps several successive litters, with some older siblings helping with the young. A breeding pair can remain together for many years. 'Their tandem urination convey[s] essentially the same information a wedding ring does,' writes biologist Jane Packard. The young begin dispersing in their second year, and most wolves, both male and female, will have left the familial pack, forced out or gone of their own accord, by the time they hit four years of age.

A solitary wolf is capable of killing large prey alone, but they are far more effective when working as a group. Pack living also benefits the pups as they mature, providing a surplus of food as they learn to hunt for themselves. Wolves mate in winter, their pups born in the spring, coinciding with the birth of the baby herbivores that make for easy prey. Other pack members defend the den site from predators and bring food to the lactating mother, and later they will regurgitate meat for the young when they begin to consume solids. Their eyes open at two weeks, and by five weeks the pups are playing outside the den, tumbling and pouncing, broadsiding one another. The older pack members play with them and mind them. As they grow in ability, the pack leaves the den behind, establishing a well-protected area known as a rendezvous site where the youngsters can continue to play and learn. By four months they are ready to join the pack on hunts. By autumn, by the time the weather changes and things get hard again, they will be almost fully grown.

I climb back up from the den and stand there, looking out. Slavc is over there somewhere on the far side of the sea, 250 kilometres or so as the crow flies, but by land much further than that. To know that, and to be standing where he was born, is particularly intimate. I have never felt closer to a wild animal.

Before me the land falls away to the plain, a featureless expanse full of scrub and little else, stretching out until it meets the sea. A single hill rises up from these flats, lumpy and incongruous. One side has been hollowed by a quarry, and little vehicles creep over its innards. I have a strange jolt of recognition. I can hardly believe it. I know this place!

In 2010 I walked from England to Istanbul. It took me the best part of a year, but I was twenty-six and I wasn't in a rush. 'Walking distance,' it turned out, was however long you gave it. I was seeking an adventure. I was interested in our origins as a wandering animal, and I wanted to experience that constant, rhythmic change. I had never before been in mountains and I loved it, and so, too, the people that I met there, making their lives in these so-called inhospitable places and which turned out to be anything but. I loved the vertiginous feeling of no one knowing where I was. I found people to be kind and welcoming, almost entirely, from my front door to the west bank of the Bosphorus. It made Europe feel vast and complex and connected.

Slovenia was the least significant part of my walk. I emerged from the woods outside Trieste and asked some builders for directions in Italian – '*Siamo in Slovenia adesso?*' – and they replied in another language. It was like a game, to speak a different language from the town just an hour away. I was only in Slovenia one night. I passed a couple fucking in the woods. I passed that quarried hill, the only hill on that wide plain. I laid out my sleeping bag under pines that in the evening still smelt of the heat of the day, and in the morning I rolled it up and carried on. I crossed the border into Croatia at Podgorje, three kilometres to the south of here. I found the border guards in a Portakabin up a narrow road. They pointed out to me, as though they were personally responsible, that this was the first time I had required my passport since leaving England five months before. It was 2010 (12 August, when I check my diary) and Croatia was gearing up to join the EU. The guards were against it, not least because they would lose their jobs. 'Criminals come from the West,' one said, in a telling reverse of what I had been hearing for the previous five months. The Italians had so consistently reminded me that I would find nothing but monsters and psychopaths in the Balkans that I had begun to feel quite nervous. One of the guards poured me a glass of home-made schnapps and we toasted my entry stamp. It was ten in the morning 'Welcome to the East,' they said. 'You will find good people here.'

I wrote in my diary – trekking through those Balkan woods, those tumbling landscapes of karst and beech – how excited I was that there were wolves here: *I imagine I will never see them, but it is enough to know that they are out there. Watching me.* It was an obvious thought, but it spoke to my anticipation at being somewhere else, the East, where things were different, and the animals bigger, and the border guards drank to your arrival. People really did speak about wolves a lot. If they weren't warning me off their mountains, they were warning me off their wolves. They told me not to go out after dark. They told me not to camp. They debated my chances of getting through each night alive. I knew, I thought, that wolves were not particularly dangerous, just as I knew that the Balkans were not full of psychopaths, but you hear this stuff often enough and, alone in the tent after dark, you do start to question it.

Wolves stood in for people, too. I had never been to a place where war sat so close to the surface. The buildings were still pocked with bullet holes, the maps marked with uncleared minefields. In these unsettled border regions, wolves had become a shorthand for people whose neighbours had taken up arms against them a few short years before. 'The Croats are wolves,' the Serbs told me; the Croats said the same about the Serbs. In Bosnia the sentiment was everywhere. No one believed that I would make it through unscathed. 'They will kill you,' they said about each other. 'They will chop up your body, and they will sell you on the market.'

All that to say, as I walked through Eastern Europe a decade ago, that wolves never felt far away. One night in Kosovo I convinced myself that a wolf was outside my tent. I lay there ecstatic, in a paroxysm of fear. I found prints in the morning in the snow, but most likely it was dogs off the leash. The thing is, I desperately wanted to see a wolf. I desperately wanted to be seen by one.

And now, twelve years later, I stand on a limestone boulder above Slavc's den, looking out across the plain that I had walked. 'All this was a wolf playground,'

Hubert says, gesturing about. 'We found bitten sticks all over here. Lots of signs of play.' The summer when I crossed Slovenia, 2010 – a World Cup summer with temperatures in the thirties for what felt like every day – that summer Slavc was a young pup, just a few months old, chasing grasshoppers and mice in the hills above me and beginning to explore his world. Not many people pass through these border regions. Could he have seen me? My bright-red rucksack. Those bright-green shorts I wore until they fell to bits. Flecks of unexpected colour, slogging across the plain below. And not only, maybe, did wolves see me, as I once longed for in that diary, but this one, particular wolf. A wolf I know the name of, and the story, and know where he is now. It is a strange, upending feeling. And I have come here to follow him, more than a thousand kilometres back on his epic journey through the Alps, back the way that as a young man I had come.

2

May we all never be judged by anything so harshly or held to as strict a life or be as unremitting of borders as the ones we try to place on and around wolves.
Rick Bass, *The Ninemile Wolves*

In November 1989 Europe was made whole. I was five years old, the age my daughter is now. Some family friends who had been travelling in West Germany brought me back a small piece of the Wall, a bit of beige rubble in a Jiffy bag. It was an odd souvenir for a kid, but they understood the implications of the moment. The Europe that formed that night became my generation's Europe, a place of open borders and free movement, culturally and ethnically diverse. In no small part what later drew me on that walk to Istanbul was the feeling that the continent was an extension of my home, the whole way from the Atlantic to the Bosphorus.

The fall of the Iron Curtain brought many changes, but one of the more unexpected was that it enabled the large carnivores of Eastern Europe to begin expanding their range west, where they had been practically unknown in the twentieth century. Few large mammals, people included, had been able to cross from East to West before the Wall came down. The mining of 800 kilometres of the border in the early 1960s had resulted in what one East German hunter described as 'cadaver fields' of animals, significantly reducing local populations of deer. Military hunting parties, under the guise of protecting the fences and because replacing mines was dangerous and expensive, killed whatever else they could. From the guard towers they shot the bears for fun.

As the bloc expanded, the vision of a free and open Europe continued to favour the lives of the wolves. They took up residence on abandoned military bases. The Council of Europe had already ratified the Bern Convention in 1979, the first Europe-wide attempt to conserve wild flora and fauna. In 1992, in the wake of the Rio 'Earth Summit', the European Community signed the Habitats Directive, providing stronger enforcement mechanisms within what, as of 1993, would be known as the EU. The wolf was listed, alongside the other large carnivores, as a species of particular interest that required special protection.

The EU also aided the wolf in other ways. Scientists could now share knowledge freely across the continent. The children of pastoralists abandoned their family calling for the newly accessible cultural centres of London or Berlin, and their fathers abandoned the land, forced out by the rigours of the free market and the Common Agricultural Policy. What was left behind – fields going fallow and crowded with browsing deer – was pristine habitat for the wolf's ongoing recolonisation. The lives of wolves have always had a particular way of mirroring human politics. Many of Europe's wolves are descended from Russian ones, whose own population boomed after the collapse of the Soviet Union and the end of state-sponsored culling there. As would become clear as I followed Slavc across Europe, there is no other animal whose behaviour so echoes our own.

Yet even when the fences go, the memories can linger. Like those Japanese men found defending forgotten Pacific islands decades after the end of the Second World War, Czech deer have resolutely stuck to their side of the border since the collapse of communism, the West German deer to theirs. They have passed down this behaviour to their offspring, who never knew a war. On other maps, held by other species, the Cold War carries on.

I wake, disorientated, in a pitch-black room.

I am on the top bunk in a room full of bunks and I lie there, getting my bearings. I am in Tuma Hut, on the summit of Slavnik Mountain. It is the middle of February 2022, two weeks since Hubert first brought me to the den, and the hut is now open for the season. When I push back the shutters of the dormitory the sun is already high, and downstairs the dining room is packed and hot with men in neat beards and technical walking gear, taking their breakfasts of coffee and strudel and schnapps. I wonder what time they must have started out to get here in time for breakfast. Black-and-white photos of the hut's construction line the walls – topless men sitting atop piles of stone, grinning for the camera. It is a Sunday morning, the first decent Sunday of the year, and everyone is out for a walk.

I had arrived at the hut yesterday. Nicolò Giraldi, a journalist I met in Trieste where I had been staying for some days, had dropped me where the tarmacked road petered out on the plain below, and I had climbed the switchbacks, up through the oak forests, to here. I was the only person staying, their first guest of the season, and the feeling was that I was somewhat intruding on the husband and wife who ran the place. I dropped my bag and made myself scarce before dinner. Outside, the light was failing. Birds were flying home to roost and my whole journey lay ahead. Off to the south stood a lone television mast, hazy against the pinking of the sky. That mast, well into Croatia, Hubert had told me, marked the southern limit of Slavc's pack. Their western boundary was the bluff that I had climbed, dropping away half a kilometre to the plain below. To the east, the E61 highway that runs from Italy through to Croatia. *All this.*

This is a place of borders. If you were to pick a place that separated Eastern from Western Europe, there is a case to be made for right here. Every river to my east drains into the Black Sea, 1,100 kilometres away. Everything to the west drains into the Adriatic, sixteen kilometres away, just down there. I can see three countries from where I stand. The Italian border is eleven kilometres to the north-west, the Croatian border two kilometres to the south. The Istrian peninsula, laid out below me, is hemmed in by vast mountains to the north and by the sea on its other three sides, and as such this plateau has been a tussle for millennia – a dynamic flux of Histri, Roman, Goth, Venetian, Hapsburg, Napoleonic, Austrian, Italian, Yugoslavian, EU. And it is not only people who have been guided across here by the logic of the landscape. This has been the funnel, too, for the large carnivores, those other species that require great ranges and are burdened by the imperative to colonise. For as long as people, if not longer, Alpine, Dinaric and Balkan populations of bear and lynx and wolf have loved and fought and forged new bloodlines on this wide, flat land between two worlds.

The territory of Slavc's pack was 442 square kilometres, about average, although the upper and lower ends of how large a territory can be make an average fairly meaningless. In Alaska, the McKinley River pack (ten wolves) had a range of 4,335 square kilometres, while another Alaskan pack of ten covered 6,272 square kilometres in the course of six weeks. At the other extreme, the Farm Lake pack in north-eastern Minnesota (six wolves) had a territory of thirty-three square kilometres. A pack's range depends on several factors, including the other packs in the vicinity and how much food the land provides. For now, Europe is stuffed full of deer that for generations have not known what it is to be prey, and for the advance wave in the wolf's recolonisation there is a lot of unclaimed space. For now, as it has so often been, the primary imposition on a wolf's territory and freedom is that which is placed on it by people.

Wolves have scant concern for people, and yet their lives, like the lives of all wild things, are not permitted to ignore us. Their territories are in sympathy to things that humans make, shaped by a border fence or a highway or a change in the law as much as by a river or a mountain. It is likely that Slavc's mother chose this place for its proximity to borders – precisely because most people stay away, border regions are good places to raise young. In other parts of former Yugoslavia, uncleared minefields have become important refuges for dens.

Once a wolf has a territory then it can focus its energy on acquiring resources, instead of living in perpetual conflict with other wolf packs. 'Territoriality is a very special form of contest competition,' wrote the late biologist Edward O. Wilson. 'The animal need only win once or a relatively few times.' Yet that territory must be maintained, and so it must provide more energy than is expended in patrolling it. Wolves are capable of managing huge ranges because they are such good travellers. 'Their way of life,' said Hubert, 'is running.' They must secure their borders daily, scent-marking regularly with scat, urine and sweat. They howl to broadcast their presence up to sixteen kilometres away – a wolf here could communicate with one down in Trieste. To see the movements of collared wolves overlaid onto a map is to see these invisible borders made real as the animals travel dozens of kilometres a day, sketching out their boundaries, but rarely stepping outside the lines.

To transgress has profound consequences. Wolf encounters between neighbours are rare, because the packs are small and the territories huge, and the consequences often fatal. They meet when they are desperate, which is to say when they are hungry. It is in these lupine borderlands that most wolves kill other wolves, and it is for this reason that deer loiter in the no-man's-lands between wolves' territories, just as wolves use those lands between the humans' borders, finding liminal safety in the places that their predators avoid. As far as Hubert knows, Slavc did not set foot outside his territory from the day that he was born until the night he began his journey. And then he never went back.

It was getting darker but I carried on, following the slope down from the hut. I found the Croatian border in the scrub, snaking through a low fold of the hills, a gravel road shadowing its perimeter. You will find borderlines marked on any map, however scant its other detail. Apparently they are our most noteworthy human constructs, and yet in person they can often seem so flimsy. Stretching into the gloom, as far as I could see, delineating the ideas of Croatia and Slovenia, was a concertina of razor wire. It looked as though a Slinky had become unravelled and then been flung across the landscape. Briars twined through it and grubby snow lingered within its coils. Cast in galvanised steel, the fence will last a good few hundred years, and it was as shiny as if it were laid out yesterday. A sparrow sat atop it, summoning in the dusk. Like the wolves, the migrants, too, come from the east.

This fence was hastily stuck up by the Slovenian government in the dying days of 2015. That year more than 1.3 million people came to Europe seeking asylum. Hungary had erected a fence along its southern border over the summer, and in the rapidly shifting dynamics of that chaotic year, that fence had channelled many of the migrants through Slovenia instead. This became known as the Balkan Route, a path from Greece to Italy, via former Yugoslavia, and culminating on this mountain range before descending to Trieste. The route was dubbed 'The Game' by those who were forced to play it, so-called for the illegal pushbacks that would force them back into the countries they had already passed through, returned to the start to try again. The prize was to reach Western Europe before being made to claim asylum. This fence was initially intended to run the full 670 kilometres of the Slovene/Croat border, but only 200 kilometres were ever completed. It appears entirely unpersuasive to someone who has already made their way here from Syria and is now just shy of Italy, but of course that isn't really the point. It is a statement, a red line.

Until Yugoslavia began to disintegrate in 1991 there was no border here at all. Croatia and Slovenia were both part of the republic, and dialects, friendships, fields and families all flowed between such places. When Slovenia joined the EU early in the new millennium, it found itself with open borders to Italy and Austria, countries that might as well have been different planets under communism, while documents were now required to visit a neighbour in Croatia. To find a fence here was stranger still. Even those who supported the intention were not prepared to see their former neighbours behind a tangle of razor wire. The fence did the additional harm of slicing through the middle of several wolf packs, forcing them into conflict as their own borders were rapidly redrawn. Deer and herons got tangled up in it and struggled themselves to death.

In 2022 the EU Schengen area was surrounded and subdivided by 2,048 kilometres of fences, nineteen separate constructions. They could be found in Spain and Lithuania, Greece and Latvia, Estonia and Bulgaria. Poland had just finished 185 kilometres to keep out migrants coming in from Belarus. Finland was building one to hold back Russia. In 1993, when the EU was first formed, there were none. Back then, border fences felt antiquated, practically medieval. But a couple of decades deep into the twenty-first century and there are plenty of leaders who believe that the old ways were the best. Walls go up when the politics fail.

In Ljubljana, some weeks previously, I had visited the city's last migrant centre. Men sat around in a basement flat in a fug of smoke, playing cards and charging phones. Tacked to the wall were newspaper clippings, flyers for upcoming demos, a list of films people wanted to see: *The Battle of Algiers*, *Schindler's List*, *Police Academy 1–6*.

Zana Fabjan Blažič, one of the centre's activists, was perched on a sagging sofa in a sharp fringe and a vintage dress. She lent people her phone, she lent them cigarettes. 'Slovenia gets so much money for protecting the border,' she said to me. 'It is the best business we ever made. So what does a hundred activists shouting about open borders do? Not very much. Because they are making *billions*.'

The centre opened in 2015 and since then they have not shut for a day. Zana has been here since the beginning. The migrants, for the most part, are from North and West Africa – Morocco, Algeria, Nigeria – and have come via the Balkan Route, have played The Game as far as here. Some had taken weeks to reach Slovenia, some had taken years, with winters spent in camps in Turkey or Serbia or Bosnia. Some depart Ljubljana quickly, on foot or in the back of a car, heading for Italy, for Germany, for England. Others attempt to remain, applying for their papers, languishing in the parade of lawyers' meetings and language lessons, adjournments and appeals. The waiting, the always waiting. We think that migration is about movement, but in truth what it is mostly about is waiting.

'If you want to achieve something, then you have to commit to the long run,' Zana said, rigid on the couch and puffing on a cigarette. 'We got status for three people this year who have been with us since the beginning. One of these guys, we got him off the deportation plane twice.'

Slovenia would have its elections later in 2022 and the left-leaning Freedom Movement would take power, as it was currently polled to do. I asked Zana if she thought it would change anything.

'Now we have this far-right government, and everyone blames the government.' She shakes her head. 'No. It has always been nearly impossible to get asylum here. Slovenia was established under the liberal ideas of democracy and law. People do not believe the police are violent. They do not believe in the violence at the border.'

I helped Patience to cook the lunch. Patience was from Cameroon and we spoke in French. She had been here for several years. Her daughter was elsewhere, back home. I asked Patience, as I chopped greens and she deep-fried small balls of dough, how she coped with her daughter's absence. How she managed the years of waiting for this paper or that hearing.

'Do you read the Bible?' she said.

She told me a story about Joseph, born in Canaan, his father's eleventh son and his favourite. She told me how Joseph's jealous brothers sold him to merchants travelling to Egypt, and tricked their father into believing that he was dead. And of how, when Joseph at last came to Egypt, he was sold into slavery, and that when he refused the seductions of his master's wife, she accused him of rape and had him jailed. And then how, years later, he was freed from prison and became an advisor to the Pharaoh, because God had given him the ability to interpret people's dreams. And how, during the famine that he had foreseen in the Pharaoh's dreams and had warned him to prepare Egypt for, Joseph's father and brothers came from Canaan seeking food because there was none left in their own country. And how Joseph saved them from starvation, and how at last they were reunited. And his father embraced him and said to him: 'Now let me die, since I have seen your face, because you are still alive.'

Patience held this story close, she told me. She read it, every night, before she fell asleep. It helped her trust in the future, when there was little else to hold to.

'*Et ils ont des enfants, et des enfants, et des enfants,*' she said. At the end of the long journey, at the end of all the pain and all the suffering, their family was reunited. And Joseph found a wife, and they had children, and they had children, and more children . . .

Back up on Slavnik Mountain, it was dusk. I could scarcely see the fence now. The warmth had gone with the light and it was suddenly, achingly cold. I walked back to the hut. On the balcony I drank cheap red wine and watched the sun collapse into the sea. The Slovenian flag snapped about on its pole. Inside, the wood burner was lit. The hut keeper and his wife and I sat in an otherwise empty dining room and muddled through our evening in Italian. Over huge plates of gnocchi and wild boar we watched on television the destruction of Ukraine. They went to bed soon after dinner and asked me to turn things off when I was done. I sat up for a time, beside the wood burner, reading about wolves.

I have never been one for early starts. By the time I finish breakfast Tuma Hut has already emptied out. I settle up and shoulder my bag and step outside. The day is bitter and cloudless. A pale, misshapen moon, not far from full, hangs above distant mountains bright with snow. The wind rages, tumbling off the peaks inland and rushing for the coast, scraping off the chimney smoke and hurling it out west. Last night the hut's owner told me that in times past the wind would pick up children and carry them out to sea. I had assumed that he was joking, but now I am not so sure. I trot along before it, down off Slavnik's summit, following a gravel track that supplies the transmitter and the hut. I am on my way at last, heading north, the way the wolf had gone.

The sky is a cold, hard blue. The grass is the colour of lions. But for a few scrubby shrubs there is only this unkempt grass which has sat beneath the snow all winter, exposed now and desiccated, dried by the wind to the bone. The whole land shivers as the wind whips through it. I follow the path over the bare expanse as it bends gradually downwards, the pasture undulating towards the treeline below, brown, naked beeches and thick dark pines. Miles off, ships slice through the Gulf of Trieste. I am invigorated, blasted alive, fairly made of wind.

I have each of Slavc's 635 coordinates, the entire four months of his journey, saved as waypoints on my phone. I have also spent a meticulous couple of evenings back at home with a ruler and a magnifying glass transferring each of those coordinates to the stack of maps that I carry in my rucksack. Those marks lead me more or less along the track that I am following, gradually losing altitude, moving down and east towards the plain. Indelible paw prints left a decade ago, their age determined not by the sharpness of their outlines but by a time-stamp on a screen:

UTC_DATE: 19.12.2011
UTC_TIME: 03:52:19
POINT_X: 420142,287145
POINT_Y: 48940,419665

My plan is to track Slavc across Europe along the trail that he had broken, following the data points that he strewed across the landscape. Yet this could only ever be an approximation of his journey. In between each fixed point there are 190 minutes when he could have travelled anywhere – unlike the Devil, wolves do not move in straight lines. They can travel at eight kilometres an hour for many hours without breaking stride or sweat, and often there is a good deal of country between one point and the next. Drawing a line of best fit, the wolf travelled something like 1,200 kilometres, but Hubert estimates it may have been two or three times that.

Seen as a whole, his waypoints trace a fairly consistent arc from Slovenia to Italy, but home in on the detail and Slavc appears more indecisive. There are detours, dead ends, about-turns. As I transferred each coordinate to my maps I started to intimate his reasons – his proximity to a town, say, or a highway. There was a heavy snow that winter, and there are aborted forays into mountains where he turned back before reaching a pass. Where he made a decent kill he would stick around for days, roaming about, until he was full and there was nothing left but bones. Shadowing each step would take far longer than I had. I was also reluctant to follow him up sheer mountainsides and through impenetrable scrub if a nearby path is more pragmatic. What I think makes most sense is tracing a line that stays faithful to his path as best I can, but avoiding anything too eccentric or too dangerous.

My aim, after all, is not to ape him, but by echoing his journey to see the continent a little more as he did. Slavc has already been well studied, but no one has done a journey like this. It is astonishing that a wild animal can be so flattened into data, and I wanted to breathe the life back into him. What would it be like to be guided across my continent by the choices that an animal had made? What would I see if I situated myself, however clumsily, behind the eyes of a wolf?

Whatever way I play it, several months of walking lie ahead. In every direction the view recedes across bare, brown hills into a distant, pale-blue haze. It is beautiful here, the light fierce, the land spacious. In time the track reaches the beech woods. Thin, naked trees fighting for space, and shaped by this incessant wind into desperate forms that make them look far older than they are. I have been feeling quite frantic, getting so blown about, and now in the shelter of the trees I slow down and look around. A blackbird clatters through the leaf litter. I check the map. Slavc's next mark is a little off the path, away to the east.

Despite my rules, I want to put my feet, at the beginning of our journey, precisely where he stood. I step off the path and immediately know that it is not a good idea. I am not, I remember, a wolf. I blunder my way through the thorny brush, my grandfather's compass clutched in one hand, my phone open to Google Earth in the other. My roll mat, strapped to my pack, is swiftly shredded. I head doggedly north-east. Quite soon, going back becomes as hard as going forward. I nearly step off a small cliff, a cornice of last year's leaves masking its edge. On my screen, the pulsing blue dot that is me approaches the green cross-hairs of the waypoint. I balance along a fallen tree, squeeze through a stand of close-knit saplings and crawl beneath another capsized limb. I stand up and check the phone again. This is it.

I am standing as close as I possibly can (give or take five metres, the GPS's margin of error) to where Slavc stood on 19 December 2011, at 3.52 a.m. Has any living thing stood here since? At my feet is a pale-blue surgical mask, blown in. An early butterfly flits past, primrose yellow. I stand there, waiting for some kind of communion with his spirit, this animal that has led me here and is now reeling me in from several hundred kilometres away. I don't suppose I have given such individual attention to a specific animal since I last had a pet. Perhaps this is the feeling that scientists like Hubert are drawn to – this opportunity to pull the veil back, to take a step across the divide and into the life of another creature.

When I'm done standing there, thinking about this wolf, I look around. I realise I have no idea how to get back to the path. From this point Slavc struck out east, plunging off the ridge, and so I decide to follow, shouldering my way through the undergrowth. I slither down slopes matted with saplings. Day one, and my plans have gone straight out of the window. In places the trees have knitted so thickly it is as though I am walking through a hedge. I am wondering why even a wolf would take such a route when it dawns on me that in fact I *am* walking on a path. It is so overgrown I think I am imagining it, but once I see it clearly it becomes so obvious that I wonder if it has been there all along. Gradually it behaves more like a path, holding to the contours in gentle switchbacks, its verges shored up with stones. It is about a wagon's width, and presumably it was once used to bring livestock and produce off the mountains to the villages below, until it fell into disuse.

The final shepherd on this mountain died last year, eighty-two years old, and with him went the last flock on this range, and centuries of human grit gone with it. Further down the path I pass his place, a cluster of ruined houses and a barn with a brand-new roof. Hubert had told me that for a time the man had fished on the Adriatic, but that he couldn't get on with the other fishermen and so instead he moved up here where there was no one to fall out with but the goats. He never took the compensation owed him for his wolf predations, the livestock that he lost; doing so would have put him in a relationship to the state that he did not need or want. Broken farm tools litter empty, concrete rooms; tins of paint, rusted shut; bags of animal feed that the rats have got to. On the floor in one corner a black-and-white photo of thirteen young women peering out of the past, perhaps the eighties, the only object that makes a concession to something not entirely functional. Inside a caravan, a crumpled sleeping bag still holds the dead man's form. A new toothbrush in a cup, a half-finished packet of crisps, a cheap coat hanging on a rung of otherwise empty hangers. And in the pastures where the animals once cropped the grass and saplings, and in the meadows where he would have cut the hay, bent in the face of the terrible winds, the scrub is beginning to creep back.

Already the land is changing. Just a single ridge back from the Mediterranean and we are moving into a different climate; you are alive to such things on foot. It is a degree warmer, and there is black pine mixed in with the beech, the hills lower and less severe. For an animal that had no notion of what lay beyond the territory of his pack, this would already have been another world.

Where the land flattens I stand where Slavc had stood, looking out across fields towards the small settlement of Tublje. Hay bales dot the meadows. Slavc would have seen people before, but never a place like this. I am reminded of *The Jungle Book* when Mowgli first sees the human village; both of them raised by wolves.

For the rest of that day Slavc hung about the forest, obviously wary. The next few GPS fixes are in a cluster as he paced. He had never been so far from home; he had never been alone so long. It was a Monday, six days till Christmas. The children home for the holidays, snowball fights and barking dogs and decorations going up. Strange smells, strange sounds. He waited for darkness to fall. When it came, he began to move.

The many behaviours that young wolves exhibit on leaving their pack – what is referred to in the literature as 'dispersal' – read like a catalogue of human yearning. 'Disperse from the natal pack, but remain in pack territory.' 'Disperse and establish a new pack adjacent to the natal pack.' 'Disperse and float among the local population, searching for an opportunity to mate and produce offspring.' 'Disperse, pair and split up serially.' And then there are those that 'disperse unidirectionally (i.e. generally in the same direction) for long distances.'

'Each wolf pack can be viewed as a "dispersal pump" that converts prey into young wolves and spews them far and wide over the landscape,' write the biologists David Mech and Luigi Boitani. Wolves disperse for the same reasons as all colonists, because enlarging families eventually demand more resources than the homeland can provide. While some juvenile wolves stay behind to help with raising the pack, others (both female and male) strike out on their own. To do so must grate against their desire for the familiar, but they are helpless in the throes of their pubescent instincts. It is this urge that has made the wolf's reconquering of Europe quite so rapid and effective. If they don't disperse of their own accord, their parents will typically force them out when the amount of care they are willing to provide is outstripped by the demands that their adolescents are making.

Dispersal confers great benefits on the species through the diaspora of its genes, but for the individual it is frequently suicidal. Popular culture has the lone wolf as a Clint Eastwood archetype, fearless, self-sufficient and misanthropic. In reality, a lone wolf has left behind its family and is searching for the same three things we all are: enough food to eat; enough land to make a life; a mate. A lone wolf does not intend to remain as a lone wolf; it has simply not yet found what it is looking for. I think of my own walk to Istanbul and wonder if, rather than being inspired by books that I had read and a desire for self-discovery, which is why I thought I'd done it, I was just one more animal driven to roam the planet for some fairly basic instincts.

For a wolf, there is no more dangerous time. Juveniles do not hunt well alone, and with their prey options reduced to a badger or a hare, they can easily starve. They must navigate the brutal infrastructure of the human world, the railways and the highways, and they must cross the territory of other, hostile packs. Where the wolf is newly arrived it is more likely to be shot than where people are already learning to live alongside them.

Even then, finding and establishing new territory is no guarantee of success. Plenty of wolves reach new lands but die before they can breed. Takaya was a Canadian wolf that swam out to an uninhabited archipelago off the British Columbia coast and lived alone for seven years before giving up, returning to the mainland, and getting shot. In 2012 a lone dead wolf was found in Thy National Park, the first wolf sighted in Denmark for 199 years. A genetic analysis placed his birth pack in Saxony, Germany, 800 kilometres to the south-east. In 2022 a young male, M237, walked 1,927 kilometres from Switzerland to Hungary, the longest journey ever recorded by a wolf in Europe, before disappearing. His GPS collar was found by divers, dumped in a river, and two men have been arrested – it is claimed that one of their nine-year-old sons pulled the trigger. The investigation is ongoing. To read of these dispersals is to be awed not only by the wolves' determination but also by their proximity to tragedy. Slavc is incredible not only in making such a vast journey, but in being so successful.

I had asked Hubert what drove Slavc, and he told me all of this. But I kept on pressing him. It can be fun to do this with scientists, to push them up against the limits of their data and see if you can make them crack.

'Is there something special about Slavc?' I asked. 'Something that made him able to take this journey on?'

'Ah, now you are setting rats!' said Hubert.

'Something about his psychology, maybe?'

Hubert smiled. 'Well, it *is* really intriguing for me,' he consented. 'What is this motivation to move on, to move on. What is the trigger to keep in a certain direction? You are searching for new land. For potential mates. For sure, this is in large part genetically determined behaviour. But as it has a big variation in different animals, it must also be influenced by other things. By environmental factors. And yes, by the individual, too.'

By the individual. We are not accustomed to thinking of wild animals as distinct, as a who instead of a what. Jane Goodall's early work on chimpanzees was dismissed because she gave names, and thus distinct identities, to her subjects. Yet Hubert believes that certain details of Slavc's upbringing contributed, if not to his success, then at least to his willingness to try. Despite the isolation of the den, other parts of his territory would have been busy with hikers and loggers, and he would have got to know their peculiar habits. His pack's territory was bisected by a fenced-in motorway that Slavc crossed often via its over- and underpasses, giving him the experience to navigate the many roads and railways he would encounter. He would have been good at finding gaps in fences. He would have been comfortable with noise. His habituation to the eccentricities of the human race may have given him more of a chance of success than a wolf raised in wilderness.

A 2022 study in the journal *Communications Biology* suggests another take on this. *Toxoplasma gondii* is a parasite that can only reproduce in the stomachs of cats. It is found in their urine and faeces, and if a rodent becomes infected, it has the uncanny effect of making it lose its fear of cats, a sort of mind control. Rather than move away from cat urine, the rodent moves towards it. It is possible that it develops an attraction to cat pheromones. The mouse approaches the cat, the mouse gets eaten, and *T. gondii* completes another reproductive cycle.

Some grey wolves in North America also carry *T. gondii*, probably from eating cougar faeces, as dogs are wont to do. For the parasite the wolf is a dead end, because cats – even cougars – don't eat wolves. Yet the same 2022 study found that *T. gondii* can significantly alter wolves' behaviour, making them, too, more comfortable with risk. Infected wolves are eleven times more likely to disperse, and *forty-six* times more likely to become pack leaders.

'The findings probably represent the tip of the iceberg concerning the parasite's significance to the dynamics of wild ecosystems,' Eben Gering, a biologist at Nova Southeastern University, told *Science* magazine. All sorts of animals carry *T. gondii* – birds, livestock, sea otters – as well as roughly one-third of human beings, often acquired through contact with their pet cats, and also passed on through pregnancy. How it affects us is unclear, although one study found infection to be 'a positive predictor of entrepreneurial activity' – the Wolf of Wall Street. We could choose to see a lone wolf as a courageous, unencumbered individual. Or we could see it as a chauffeur for *T. gondii*, lured into driving its parasitic passenger off into the sunset in search of another cat's stomach.

And what then of the particular animal's nature? Wolves are often described by those who study them as having the sort of distinctive characters – shy or playful, daring or foolhardy – that we have no problem projecting onto dogs. Parasite or personality, is it such a stretch to suggest that Slavc was simply *that kind of wolf*? His brother and sister were killed too young, and we don't know what happened to the other siblings. But Slavc seems to have had the right blend of nature and nurture to enable him to attempt such a vast journey.

And then all he needed was luck.

Slavc moved fast that first night. He moved so fast that Hubert, sitting at home watching the points pop up on his computer, could only assume he had been shot. How else could he show up in the town of Vipava, twenty-seven kilometres in a direct line from where I stand, at 05.12 that same night? The team drove there first thing, expecting to find the animal transmitting from the trunk of a hunter's car. They traced the point to a house on the edge of town, behind a set of grey double doors leading into someone's yard. But as they stood there contemplating their next move another point appeared, three kilometres to the west, in vineyards. They were three hours and ten minutes behind him, and Slavc was on the move again.

At my pace, on two legs, it takes me three days to reach Vipava. The road out of the village of Tublje winds through silent forests and empty meadows. Cars pass, but not often, their drivers eyeing me. I see no one else on foot. There are shrines at every crossroads, mournful Marys spruced up with a few dead or plastic flowers. The villages are small with red-tiled roofs and they smell of woodsmoke and cow shit. Bare fig trees; bare cherry trees; small and watchful cats. A boy on a front lawn, playing badminton with himself.

The views are soft and gentle, the path rolling me along. And then suddenly, at Škocjan, the land collapses, a huge tear in the fabric of the earth. Hundreds of metres below me a river of violent blue, the Reka, plunges into an enormous cave at the foot of the drop. The Romans knew this as one of the entrances to Hades. Much of it is still unmapped and for all we know it really could descend to hell. Olms live down there in the pitch-black, an aquatic salamander devoid of skin pigment, with a fan of external gills and skin covering its blind eyes, and which can go without food for a decade. They were once thought to be baby dragons. What is now known is that the Reka, after flowing thirty-four kilometres underground and passing through caves larger than cathedrals, emerges in Italy south of Monfalcone, just shy of the Adriatic. I sleep a night in a copse at the top of the bluff, a whole world down there beneath me. I wake, chilled, in the morning, and brew coffee and stamp the blood back into my feet, and carry on.

It is a long time since I have gone for a long walk, but already it's coming back. How after a few days it feels as though your body was meant for this. My legs feel stronger, my back stops aching. I develop the encrusted grin and slightly wild eyes that come from several nights outside. Slavc's route leads me over an airfield for light aircraft, a huge, treeless expanse with grass the colour of the prairie. Cows lounge on the runway, chewing cud. I climb barbed-wire fences and nip across a single-gauge railway line, and then I am back in woods again. It is all a very unlikely place for a walk. In the village of Razdrto everything is a grubby white from quarry dust and I leave my ghostly footprints down the road. For two days I have been watching the Nanos massif looming before me, and now, at Razdrto, the path begins to climb.

It is outrageously windy, too windy to think. The path zigzags up through small stands of stunted trees, threading over slopes of scree. There are cables bolted to the rock where the route is most exposed and I cling to them with numb and swollen hands. If I look back I can see the whole way that I have come, back as far as Slavnik and the antenna on its peak. The sun is floundering like a ship going under, the sky is pink and glorious. There are shrines along the path, shrines to the Devil and shrines to God. It is a climb of several hours and by the time I make the summit it is close to dark. There is a new wolf pack up here, as of 2012. I pitch my tent outside the refuge, still shuttered for the winter. There is nothing to drink but melted snow. The sky is a riot of stars, all cloud ripped away. My tent strains against its tethers, and all night my dreams are wild and fractious. In the morning the ground has frozen so hard that when I pull out the tent pegs they snap.

We come down off Nanos, Slavc and I, past Vipava's long since ruined castle and into the town itself. I stand before those same grey double doors that Hubert had been led to and imagine my wolf on the other side, skulking in someone's apple orchard or sniffing through their bins. A clear stream follows the street along one side, and in a recess lit by electric candles is some pastoral diorama – a pious shepherd surrounded by sheep and doves and deer, and certainly no wolves. I take the wide valley north. This is wine country, mile after mile of it, row upon row of bare vines like withered arms. Herons and egrets slide over the fields. I sleep a night in an abandoned shed and then push on to Ajdovščina. Small villages with big churches, red roof tiles and shutters, crumbling alleys and wooden balconies. At Ajdovščina we turn for the mountains once again.

The land is a sieve. There is no water anywhere, except for hundreds of metres below my feet. My whole body is parched and wrung out by the wind. Jays bark. The karst is as thirsty as I am, the brush tinder dry and rasping to the touch. Last year's leaves cling to the beech trees, hissing in the wind. I follow the massif north and come at last to a scatter of houses and barns. There is only one not shuttered. *Lovsko Društvo* is carved in a panel over the door – 'Hunters' Association'. A cement mixer revolves on the front stoop. I knock.

A large man comes to the door. He is dressed in camo pants and a dark-green beanie that has lost all its elasticity and is plonked loosely on his head, and he stands there looking at me like a person was the last thing he expected. I wave my water bottle at him. '*Vodo, prosim?*'

He shakes his head and grins. He leads me by the forearm into the kitchen and hefts a five-litre bottle off the counter. 'Wine,' he says, in English. It is a little after breakfast and I have had nothing to eat. He opens cupboards, rooting around for a container. 'Please,' he says, gesturing to the single table and its vinyl tablecloth. He finds a glass and pours a measure so full that only the liquid's tension holds it within its vessel. I bend my head and lap. He watches me contentedly, like you might watch a pet you've fed.

'It's windy,' I say, when I look up.

'This is nothing,' he says proudly. 'Sometimes, the wind blows three hundred kilometres an hour. Wind big problem.' The bora, that rushes from the inland peaks and out to sea, has been known to flip lorries off the highways. It eviscerates entire mountainsides of trees.

'Everything is very dry,' I say.

'Water big problem,' he agrees. He pours me more wine.

He learnt his English working in the eighties in Iraq. When I have finished my second glass he leads me through into the back room. In the half-darkness, solid wood tables are laid out in a horseshoe. There is a stuffed capercaillie on a shelf, alongside a stuffed bear and her cub. This is where the drinking happens, and the telling of the tales. Lining the walls, like so many coat hooks, are the antlers of hundreds of roe deer. The antlers and a small piece of the forehead, as though they each were scalped, and inked onto the bone are the date and place of death.

Hanging among these antlers are photos of the hunters, the whole gang. There are forty-seven members in what he calls the family. The oldest is ninety-three. The youngest, his son, is twenty-seven. But most of them are over sixty, and that, he says, is a big problem. Hunting is falling out of fashion. He tells me the kids are getting brainwashed that it's wrong to shoot an animal. Video games are cheaper. Yet hunters, he says, provide a vital service for the farmers by keeping deer and boar numbers in check, animals that can wreck a field of crops. For the longest time the hunters were the only predator they had. I wonder if they feel emasculated by the arrival of the wolf, a more effective predator than them by almost any measure.

'Lynx are a problem,' he says. 'We kill ten lynx a year. No problem. Big secret.' He smiles. 'Two hundred wolves here.' This, at least, is a huge exaggeration. There are fewer than 200 wolves in the whole country. 'We kill three or four a year,' he says. 'Wolf big problem.'

He makes the international sign of extermination, a finger drawn across his throat. I make the international sign for handcuffs, asking a question. He makes the international sign for *shhh*.

Hubert had told me that Austria, where Slavc was headed, had problems with poaching, but that Slovenia did better at keeping it in check. To become a member of a Slovenian hunting club you must sit a year's course and take exams. The hunting family here is a diverse crowd drawn from across the political spectrum, a legacy of Yugoslavia's socialism that envisioned local wildlife and environment as being managed by its people. For every hunter who thinks wolves should be shot there will be another in favour of their return. Keeping an eye on one another's behaviour, Hubert said, is a better form of policing than official enforcement. Yet just a few days into my journey and I'm already being told, without much prompting, how the hunters here are conspiring to make this problem go away.

I follow him back through into the kitchen and sit down. There is something on his mind that he wants to ask me. 'Is there any difference,' he says, as he sits across from me, 'now that you are outside the EU?'

This seems to be what people want to talk about when I travel these days. I miss the simplicity of my twenties, when it was only David Beckham. I tell him how difficult it has been for my Swedish partner to secure her settled status in a post-Brexit Britain. I tell him I feel sad that the next generation will not have the same opportunities that I had to live and work and love in Europe. I tell him that I can no longer do this walk as a single hike, because I cannot be in Europe for more than ninety days at a stretch.

'You will see,' he says. 'You will find that life is better outside.'

I tell him that I hope he's right, that we'll just have to wait and see.

'You are better,' he assures me. 'You have less migration now. More money. More jobs. It is better for you. Let me tell you a story.'

He slops another measure of wine into my cup.

'When I was old,' he says, 'ten or eleven years old, I would go down to the river by my house, on my little bicycle, all by myself. And there was in this river the fish that hides under rocks. Today they introduce these American fish because they are good for fly-fishing and politics. But these fish, you could tickle their bellies and throw them on the bank. I would go there and catch two fish. I would wrap them in a leaf. Some pepper and salt. And then I make a fire in the ground. It was an old man told me how, but I worked it out myself. With a hole at one end and a hole at the other, so that the fire comes through and smokes it. And then you leave it there for four, five hours. And when I come back, I eat these two fish. All by myself. Not for hunger, you understand. Just for the pleasure of eating fish.'

He smiles at me. Then he shakes his head. 'The other day I took my son down there. My son is in his twenties now. I get in the river. No fish. I try tickle an American fish. You can't tickle an American fish. We were down there for two days. What the fuck do you do for two days, if you can't fish? We just play cards. No more fish.'

'What happened to the fish?' I ask.

He shrugs. 'How should I know? But I tell you this. When we had Tito, we had fish.'

I cannot quite put my finger on the point of the story. 'It's sad when things change,' I hazard.

He nods. 'Everything changes. You can put that in your book. Everything changes.' He rises to his feet. He has cement to mix. 'Okay,' he says. 'Bye-bye.'

It is understood that I can go. I stumble out into the brightness of the morning. It is still some days to Cerkno, the next town that Slavc passed. The wind is howling and the mountains rise in front of me and the clouds are rolling in. I walk on, climbing slowly, giddy with the lightness that comes from drinking far too much, far too close to breakfast.

3

L'inverno no el la mai magnà el loo — The wolf has never eaten winter.

Italian proverb

Covid rules have only been relaxed this week, and *Laufarija*, Cerkno's carnival, has got its go-ahead last minute. There is a current of liberation coursing through the crowd. At least a thousand people fill the small town square, shoulder to shoulder, before a stage that has been constructed overnight. Families watch from the balconies above and drinkers spill out of the bars. *Kurentovanje*, Slovenia's largest carnival, did not have the time to organise with such short notice, and so people have come to Cerkno from all over the country. They have been shut up at home for two years and they are not missing this one.

The crowd is in wildly divergent states of fancy dress. There are tie-dyed hippies and garish clowns and a couple dressed as rabbits. There are Trump masks, Guinness hats, Spider-Men and Batmen. There is a fiendish wolf, with tusks and horns, made out of duct tape. There is a woman who has come as a carton of milk, her husband as a chocolate bar. There are dinosaurs, witches, cowboys. There are an awful lot of Harry Potters. There is snow on the hills that surround the town and a chill wind blows up the valley, and people shiver in their superhero Lycra.

The music starts. We turn our heads. A marching band steps from a side street – girls on flutes, a brass section, accordionists and drummers. Charging about them, tall and rangy, are three ghoulish figures in wooden masks with blue and sunken eyes. They have great mouths of tombstone teeth that jut at wild angles from red lips, and they are head to foot in loose robes of white tassels so that they look somewhat like mops that have had life breathed into them. These are the *Terjasti*, the Thread Men, the ancestors. They lunge through the crowd, lashing out with hazel switches, carving space for the band to pass. Children squeal, thrilled with horror. They have grown up with these creatures, the fodder for many nightmares. And behind the band, in single file, comes the *Laufarji* family.

The Baker leads. He wears a dour mask with heavy eyebrows and moustache, and he is outfitted in the whites and toque of his profession. He carries a long peel, the sort of thing for sliding loaves out of the oven, and on its paddle is inked *Smrt Pustu* – 'Death to Pust'. Behind him walks the Scabby Man, his mask a crater of sores, playing an old accordion. In times past he would have been wiping his nose and shaking hands with the crowd, but this year that is a little too close to the bone. Then come the Old Man and the Old Woman, and then there is Pust himself, with a great hooked nose and two small, hooked tusks, and from his head stick two great horns. He is dressed entirely in a huge and shaggy coat made out of moss, shaggy hat and shaggy trousers. He is magnificent. Over his shoulder he hefts a small spruce tree, perhaps four metres long. He is bowed by a great weight, both physical and in his soul, and he trudges through the parted crowd towards the stage, towards his reckoning.

Behind him come the others. Pust's brother, the *Smrekov*, in a costume of spruce branches; the Ivy Man in an outfit of 10,000 ivy leaves so that he looks almost reptilian; a girl covered in daisies. There is something distinctly pagan about all this, as though the forest floor has come to life and stood. Others are dressed in the village jobs of former times – the herdsman in sheep's wool with a face burnished by the mountain sun, a cowbell clanging on his back; the innkeeper with his bottle; another clad in thatch; the rich farmer with sacks full of potatoes. The Gentleman and Lady walk arm in arm, keeping their distance. A drunk couple pass a bottle between them and go at each other with a rolling pin. A stooped woman carries her drunken husband in a basket. And some even wilder figures. The *Divji*, dressed in hides, with his matted hair half-covering his face, his hands trembling in fear. *Lámant*, with his face made of goat skin. On and on the procession comes.

I had got into town two days previously. It was Christmas Eve when Slavc passed through, eleven years before that. I took a room in the Hotel Cerkno, an improbably vast building in the centre of town. It had, I was told, somewhat faded. In the evenings waistcoated waiters with combovers hovered in the shadowed corners of an enormous and otherwise empty dining room, presiding over buffets of schnitzel and roast potatoes and buttered spinach. I had the swimming pool and steam rooms entirely to myself. I sat alone in the Jacuzzi, soaking my feet, gazing out of the floor-to-ceiling windows at the mountains that ringed the town. The hotel's construction was paid for, like much of the rest of Cerkno, by ETA, the local factory and the world's largest manufacturer of hotplates. Before the fall of communism, factory profits were funnelled back into the town. ETA had sponsored the handball and skiing clubs. It sponsored Cerkno's brass band. Workers got a week's holiday each year on Slovenia's little strip of coast.

The characters are all up onstage now. Pust is at the front, before five men clad in black.

'Well, Pust,' one man intones. He is dressed in a greatcoat and mortar-board, with a large beard stuck to his face. 'Fool of all fools. You've finally come into the hands of justice. You thought you were going to escape this year, didn't you?'

The *Laufarji* shake their fists, mock Pust and taunt him. The drunk couple are celebrating already, rolling through the crowd.

'Just look around and see how many folks are crowded here,' the prosecution carries on. 'Soon the whole world will know what a rascal you are. But so you won't think you're being wrongly punished, I'm going to tell you everything that is hanging over your head. First of all, let's take a look at how you've prepared the weather this past year.'

The charge sheet is read out, the unfurled scroll ultimately reaching to the floor. Last year, straight after carnival, it rained. It rained and rained, for so many months, that the farmers could not cut the hay, and this winter the animals went hungry. We had never seen rain like it. Don't you know the damp brings on the old folks' rheumatism? The kids didn't have any fun at all. What else? There are so many deer up at Gorenji Novaki that there's no grass left in the meadows. And while we're on it, what's going on with Agata in the butcher's? She is so tired that we have to wait an hour for her just to slice the meat. The Butterfly Bar is so crowded that the publican can only sleep when he passes out in the back. Friends cheer and rib those who have their names read out. At the gas station we could not fill up our cars without a vaccine pass – that was your fault, Pust.

On and on it goes. Pust makes to leave. 'Oh, not so fast,' the prosecutor snaps. 'We're not finished with you yet.'

That container ship that was stuck in the Suez Canal so that Cerkno ran out of baling twine: Pust. Mask regulations: Pust. Corruption in the Ministry of Agriculture: Pust. Putin: Pust. It has not been a good year. Pust's lawyer makes some effort to defend him but he doesn't stand a chance. The *Laufarji* are excited by his imminent conviction. There is nothing else that can restore order to this town. There is no other way to bring back spring. They jump up and down in unison so that the stage boards shake and boom, and through our legs the children chase one another, high on candyfloss. The light is beginning to fade.

'You see, Pust, what you're doing to these poor folks!' It is the judge speaking now, peering over his glasses. 'We've had enough of your wrongdoings. This winter has to end. You deserve nothing less than the worst punishment under the strictest *Laufar* rules. That is death, by wooden mallet. You cannot appeal to anyone.'

The *Terjasti* bind Pust and manhandle him offstage. The prosecutor furls his scroll. The execution has been scheduled for the Tuesday, two days hence. Soon winter will be vanquished. The *Laufarji* begin to dance. The men drift back into the bars.

It does not take long in Cerkno, if you ask around about wolves, to get pointed the way of Ivan Mavri. I give him a call, and one morning Ivan collects me from the hotel lobby and we drive, almost vertically, up one of the several valleys out of town. 'I have been in Berlin,' he says, in English, above the grinding of the gears. 'I was in Paris. I was in Milano. Fuck them. In Slovenian there is a proverb. I cannot directly translate. It says: "I think my place is the best."' Or that is to say, it was. The wolf has invaded this land, and for Ivan there is no greater disaster. Their eradication has become his personal crusade.

Ivan is fifty-three. He has a light dusting of grey stubble. He wears a blue plaid shirt and a furrowed expression and a pair of reflective sunglasses pushed back permanently on his head. We continue to climb and the land opens up, rolling and expansive. Drifts of snow persist in the lee of the hills. A farmhouse, some meadows, a patch of forest, and, in time, another farmhouse. In square footage we are driving through the largest settlement in Slovenia, larger than Ljubljana, with just 400 inhabitants. Nowhere does it feel particularly wild, or particularly tamed.

For many years Ivan was a technical engineer at the ETA factory; now he teaches. In the afternoons, he farms. These small farms cannot support a modern lifestyle so people supplement their income with work in the valleys, but not working the land would be unthinkable. For Ivan's generation, this labour is in their blood. 'You must be a little crazy and you must be born here,' he says. 'People in the cities in the afternoon, they go to the bar. They go to the gym. People here, they come home and they work. They make this land beautiful.'

The land is indeed beautiful. My eye knows how to settle here, like it knows how to rest in a Constable painting. The constellation of elements seems almost self-consciously constructed to achieve a particular aesthetic. An orchard overrun with snowdrops. A disused barn with a single birch clawing out of its roof, breaking into bud. Washing hung from a wooden balcony; smoke curling from a chimney. An ancient tractor overgrown with bindweed. An old dog in a patch of weak sunshine. There is the frontier feel of carving out space, but gently. Not taking more ground than necessary, but not being pushed back, either. And did you ever see a wolf in a Constable? Ivan doesn't think so.

At the mountain pass he stops the car and winds the window down so that I can better breathe the place in. The air is cold and clean. 'Tourists stop here to make pictures,' he says, spreading one of his hands across the view as though encouraging me to sit there. 'They don't stop in the middle of a forest. They stop *here*. They say, "Oh, it's nice, Slovenia." Of course it is! *It's because we work hard.* Goddammit.'

I gaze over a patchwork of farms and woods and meadows. A church, another church. Raptors rise up on the thermals. A car crawls up a succession of switchbacks on the far side of the valley.

'We are the green pearl of Europe, and we want to be,' he says. 'But not the wild pearl. The green, cultivated pearl. We are not Yellowstone Park.' Ivan does not name the wolf as a wolf but instead, always, as a beast. 'Here, the beast cannot move without crossing people's roads and homesteads.'

I try to picture a wolf scuttling from place to place across the valley, the murder of a flock, like a rural *Rear Window*, but it is hard to imagine violence in such a place.

A pack formed here in 2019, perhaps the first in 200 years. Slavc had passed by a few years before, and one lone wanderer came through in 1975 but he was immediately shot. Simpler times. But in May 2019 the wolves came and they stayed. After their first litter, they numbered at least six. As we drive on, Ivan points out the sights. A wolf attacked two horses there. On your left, a donkey. In this village a wolf came down and played with that man's dog, before eating his sheep. Here a wolf was seen outside a school at eleven in the morning. He takes me to meet a young farmer who lost twenty sheep just before Christmas. Then another, who lost a dozen. 'You need to kill them,' this farmer says. 'All of them. No mercy.'

Ivan speaks with the passion of a man who has found his calling. 'People are leaving,' he says. 'The villages become old and empty. The last thing that we need here is beasts. I'm not so much worried about the single sheep or donkey. I'm worried about the hundred sheep that will *not* be in this region because the people will be afraid to lose them. If they put beasts in this country, the small farms will disappear and those people will leave. And then there will be only forests.'

It is a long, depressing day. Beautiful as it is here, these are hard lives in hard places, and the wolf has only made things harder still. Asking whether the countryside needs wolves is like asking if Slovenia misses its war. Ivan had watched with horror during that first year as the farm animals were slaughtered, and he quickly came to the understanding that no one would be coming to help them. He convened a meeting. The resulting petition, to remove large carnivores from the west of Slovenia, was signed by 2,000 people in its first week, close to half the local population. In those first months of the campaign, Marko Gasser was one of Ivan's generals. Marko is the last stop on our tour.

Marko's farm sits at the head of a small valley. We park outside a cluster of houses and barns, some three or four storeys high, built from stone and clad in plaster and roofed with wooden shingles. Marko comes out, walking with the easy grace of someone who owns everything in view. He spent his twenties in politics, in Ljubljana, but it is hard to believe that now. He is dressed in a check shirt and jeans and a green felt hat with a feather in the band, the archetypal mountain farmer, although several decades younger than most. In his forties, he has built a farm and raised four children on this hill where his wife was born.

We gather around his kitchen table. Vanya, his wife, serves us eggs and pâtés and salamis from the farm. There is warm bread and home-made butter. Heat pumps from the *peč*, a great cube of ancient design that takes up one side of the room. A fire smoulders within it and it heats the entire house. The bread is baked inside it and, with its top covered in blankets, it can double as a bed. 'Time has stopped here,' Ivan whispers to me with evident excitement. The whole place feels forged of its past. Icons of Jesus cover the walls, alongside black-and-white photos of their ancestors, smartly dressed young couples gazing with dark eyes at the camera. There is a radio the size of a television. Vanya passes round the beers.

To make a living from a farm you must be creative. They have a business selling milking equipment, Vanya tells me. They sell wood from their forest, and then they have their sheep. Her family has been here for generations and they are determined to make it work, but things are never easy. 'It's criminal that families like these are not supported,' Ivan says to me. 'Goddammit.'

They lost 120 sheep the first year that the wolves came.

Four separate attacks, each time at night. It was terribly upsetting for his kids, Marko tells me, but I think, watching him speak, that he is largely talking about himself. 'The wolf is owned by the state,' he says. 'But the state says it is my fault because I do not protect my sheep. They say I need bigger fences. They say I need dogs. Every year there are new rules.'

The state will compensate for kills if a vet has verified that the predation was carried out by a wolf, ruling out a feral dog. Around eight million euros are paid out annually across Europe, to compensate for the 30,000 to 40,000 farm animals that are predated. But payment can take months, and farmers are only eligible if they have made attempts to protect their livestock. Few people can afford a shepherd, so that means fences. For three summers now Marko has not put his sheep on the high pastures because he has not had the hands or the time to build a fence. What wolves mean is more work. Fenced sheep must be rotated between enclosures. The shit piles up if you don't muck them out. Wires and posts must be maintained. Electric fences must have their batteries charged, their voltages regularly checked. And the sheep behave differently since the wolves came back. They are wilder. They startle at anything. They abort more frequently.

'These guys from Ljubljana tell us how the farmer and the wolf will live together,' Ivan says. 'They say they are ecologists and that they care about the nature. But they do this from behind the computer. People who care about the nature, they *live* there.' He spreads his hands. 'Experts,' he says. 'Fuck them.'

I am keen to speak more with Vanya, but she is clearing the table and I am bustled away with the men. Marko leads us up a flight of narrow stairs into the house's rafters. We wander through rooms of wooden ploughs and wooden sledges, wooden skis and wooden snowshoes and wooden spinning wheels. A wooden stroller for a baby, ancient chainsaws, axes, planes and lathes. A whole museum of rural life, stuck up in a loft at the far end of a valley. Handles polished smooth by centuries of hands.

Ivan points out a wagon wheel, steam-bent and metal-rimmed, the spokes radiating from its centre, functional and beautiful. 'It was made by Marko's father,' he says. 'He had four years of primary school. I have fourteen.' He runs a hand over the hub. 'As human beings, we have become weak,' he says. 'We have become fat. Back then, they were men in the full meaning of man. Seven, eight, nine children. It was not easy, but it was a good way of life.'

'My grandfather had such big hands that he had to have his gun rebuilt for him so that he could get his finger through the trigger guard,' says Marko, by way of corroboration.

'They were very religious people,' Ivan continues. 'They worked together because they had to. In the last thirty years we lose this feeling. We lose this way of life.'

I recall some lines I heard two days ago, when the landlady of a bar in Cerkno showed me around her little attic, stuffed with similar old tools. 'Today, people want everything made yesterday,' she had said. 'Before, you had to wait until tomorrow. That was hard in one way. Now it is hard in a different way. Then was heavy on the body. Today it is heavy on the mind.'

Back outside, the wind has dropped. All the land is on some sort of angle. Gnarled pear trees dot the meadows, and *kozolci* for the drying of hay. They are frames of poles, likewise roofed with wooden shingles, and seem to have grown out of the matter of the landscape. Marko's boy walks with us, maybe ten, in a straw trilby and square glasses, bent forward at the waist, his hands deep in his pockets like the rest of us. I am wondering if he wants to stay here, and whether he always will.

These fields are too small and steep to cut by hand, and so it is the sheep that keep them cropped and stop the trees encroaching. The crocuses are all coming into bloom at once, the fields as yellow and purple as they are green. In a month there will be red clover, hedge bedstraw, forget-me-nots, dandelions, buttercups, vetches, eyebright, dead nettle, ox-eye daisies, orchids, dozens more. They will be hazed by butterflies, chirping with crickets, crawling with insects. These calcareous grasslands are among the most species-rich habitats in Europe. If forests take over these meadows, Marko says, then all this life will be lost with them.

He leads us to where he must now pen his flock at night. The fence is metal and ugly and huge, and looks nothing like it grew out of the landscape. The EU paid for it, but that's beside the point. 'They have to go in at night like children,' Marko says of his sheep. 'It's not logical. In the summer it's hot and animals want to eat at night.'

'Tourists will say what big fences you have,' says Ivan. 'This is not Slovenian culture. It's not *traditional*.'

The men cast their eyes over the animals, and the boy stands beside them, doing the same. The sheep smell earthy, woolly, good. It is a way of life that appears completely in keeping with the rhythms of the world, and I cannot deny, as a tourist, that this is what I'm here for, too. It's apparent just how devastating the killings must have been. It is easy to root for the wolf, but it's less clear, standing here, who exactly the underdog is.

And yet, since 2019, things have not been so bad. By the end of that first awful summer, most of the wolves had disappeared. Three had been killed during a nationwide emergency cull (along with 120 bears). Those that remained have not been seen much since.

'Where did they go?' I ask.

There is a pause.

'We can say that the forest has many secrets,' Ivan says.

And the men share a look and they laugh.

The *Laufarji* gather again on Tuesday at midday. The sun is out, and the snowdrops. A lone great tit is calling, and it really does feel as though winter might soon be vanquished. We follow the characters towards the outskirts of town as they meander in front of cars and heckle the impatient drivers. The Drunk Man carts his wife in a wheelbarrow. The Old Woman sweeps the road. We cross a bridge over a stream and arrive at a parcel of land. This is where they come each year to search for their wooden mallet – the *bòt* – that the judge has decreed for Pust's execution. In Cerkno's museum there are black-and-white photos of the *Laufarji* family digging for it in deep snow, but winter is dying in more ways than one. Today it is almost warm as they wander about, grubbing at the earth with their various implements, pitchfork or baker's paddle. The Scabby Man plays his accordion, a fairground waltz. The Gentleman and Lady keep their distance. The Wild Man quakes.

In the end it is the Old Man who finds the *bòt*, as he does every year, beneath a pile of rocks where he has been poking with his stick. They are all very excited. It is a metre or so in length, the sort of thing a woodcutter would have used for splitting logs. The accordion ups its tempo and they dance down to the stream to wash the mud off. And then they carry it back to town aloft, to await Pust's final act.

Later that day I knock on the door of the *Laufar Kamanda*, the *Laufarji*'s Command Centre, and Miha Bavcon invites me up. Young and bespectacled, in shorts, he leads me through this arcane world. In the dressing room each costume rests on a hanger, its shoes beneath, its various props and mask above – already they seem like old friends. There is the musty excitement of theatres backstage. The ashtrays are overflowing, and the shelves creak beneath a weight of alcohol. Miha points at a framed photo in faded Kodachrome, hung beside a topless Miss February. It shows fourteen of the *Laufarji*, posing in the snow.

'When I was young, my grandfather showed me this picture in his home,' he says to me, in English. 'He said, "Miha, look, I am in this picture. And when you will be old enough to come to *Laufarija*, I will tell you which character I am."'

The young Miha would stare at it, wondering which one was his grandfather. The shepherd? Pust, even? If you weren't part of the *Laufarji*, you could not know who was who. Even your mother should not recognise you. Every ritual was kept secret, 'passed from mouth to ear'. Fathers and older brothers disappearing, night after night, to gather the moss and spruce and sew the costumes. The old words of Cerkno dialect they still used. The hierarchy. It was said, if you did not remove your mask by midnight on the last day of carnival, that you would stay stuck as your character forever. All of it was so alluring. As soon as he could, at fourteen, Miha joined the family. He knows which one his grandfather is now, but of course he won't tell me.

Miha is twenty-two now. He pours me a little schnapps and we toast the carnival. 'You grow with this,' he says. 'This desire cannot be made. It is because my older brother was in *Laufarija*, and my father, and my grandfather. And so I am drawn to the tradition. You simply have it inside, if you have it.'

The carnival's origins are equally mysterious. It may have been brought by German migrants in the thirteenth century, when they came looking for work in the nearby mercury mines. Or it may have been a local ritual that grew more elaborate over time, a means of making it through the darkest months, back when a harsh winter could be a death sentence. It stopped with the First World War, when Cerkno's youth were drafted, and then the Italian occupiers banned the carnival outright as an expression of ethnicity, along with their schools and their sports clubs and their language. On 18 March 1944 a bomb fell on the house where the masks and costumes had been mothballed and the whole lot went up in smoke.

After the war, searching for meaning, Cerkno resurrected *Laufarija*. Gathering the memories of the elders, and working with a local craftsman to make the masks, they brought fourteen of the characters back to life. Since then more have been added to reach the twenty-five of today (via some that have come and gone, such as the Serbian Soldier during the Balkan Wars).

'This is not our property,' says Miha, sweeping an arm around the room. 'This is for the whole community. We just carry it.'

The *Laufarji* are the caretakers of tradition, safeguarding the rituals and resisting the commercialisation of their characters (you cannot buy a mask) while allowing the carnival to evolve so that it retains its vitality. Rumour has it that on occasion a woman has played a character, but no one outside the family knows for sure. What strikes me is that it is the young people driving this; that within this ancient culture there is something still capable of holding a place and its community together. I ask Miha if he would like to always live in Cerkno.

'I think so,' he says. Big families still live together here, the grandparents minding the grandkids and the farm while the parents go out to work. To see it at such a time, the place feels very intact. 'During Covid, in Ljubljana, they were going from work to house, from shop to house,' says Miha. 'Here you could go up to the forest. You could go for a walk. You have a piece of nature for yourself. It is quiet and you can see the wild animals. Not in the zoo, but actually. I like to hunt. I like the mountains. And in the evenings we gather at the bar and we chatter. I do not see myself outside this valley. I hope so. I do my best.'

In the 1930s two families from Cerkno emigrated to South Australia. They purchased two neighbouring farms and lived side by side for generations, the only Slovenians for hundreds of kilometres. Ten years ago, their grandsons returned to Cerkno for a visit. They were speaking a dialect that had long since disappeared. The local museum recorded them, a glimpse into another time. The point is, you have to go a long way to stop the outside world encroaching.

I drive out with Ivan and his son to Zakojška grapa, a deep valley not far from Cerkno. Ivan has things he wants to show me, he says, so that I can understand.

The birds are calling and the morning is cloudless. Ivan's boy is twelve, their last child left at home. The others have all gone to Ljubljana. One of his daughters is reading pharmacology, the other chemistry. In a cruel irony, the chemist's boyfriend is studying biology at the Biotechnical Faculty where Hubert Potočnik works. Often Ivan will argue with the boyfriend about wolves when his daughter brings him home to visit. 'They know hundreds of species of fish but I don't know what else!' says Ivan. 'They study for fifteen years and they don't agree that animals are a problem for our countryside.' He searches for a better way to explain his feelings. 'We will not go on holiday together,' he says.

We park at a farmhouse at the end of a track. There is not much farming going on. This is the house of someone that Ivan went to school with. They called him Little Mouse back then. The yard is a scrapheap of Russian cars and Ivan points them out like old friends, recalling teenage joyrides. A dog is barking, and Little Mouse calls angrily from his balcony until he realises who it is. He comes down to shake our hands. There is schnapps on his breath and he stands at his door and lights a cigarette, smoothing down his thick moustache with a quick finger and thumb. The dog drags itself around the yard, its back legs ruined. They discuss the path ahead. They discuss the wolves. I try to think of them as children, with everything still to come.

Last year's beech leaves are in drifts up to our knees. Ivan's son trots on ahead, swiping with a switch of wood at small rocks on the path, sending them bouncing away to the gully bottom. It is no stretch to imagine wolves here. The path has been hewn into the hillside, clinging to its contours, although much of it has slipped and is almost impossible to make out beneath the leaves. I edge along its brink. Ivan tells me about a group of men he ran into some months back, all with harnesses and ropes. 'If they need all this equipment to walk these paths then they should not be out here,' he says. I do my best to look balanced.

To my untrained eye this forest looks ancient, but Ivan points out tree stumps. When the people go, it is the tree stumps that remain. We pause at a clearing and he brings out a photo, a black-and-white shot of the same view, looking across the valley to Mount Kojca. Before me is unbroken forest, but the view in the photo shows a patchwork of fields and farms. This place once supported more than a thousand people. The maple comes back first, then the birch, then the beech. Bucking the planetary trend, Slovenia is undergoing rapid afforestation; 30 per cent of its land has reverted to forest in the past sixty years. There are big, beautiful trees here, but all Ivan sees is a faltering economy, an untapped resource that should be providing the jobs that would hold this community together.

Walking through these bone-dry woods, I ask Ivan about climate change. Maybe we need the trees? He greets me with a look that I am becoming familiar with. 'Every year with my son we clean the road up to the ski slope,' he says. 'We don't throw plastic in the nature. I have solar panels, I have an electric car. I'm not stupid. But if this planet really was about to heat up two degrees, if the end really was as close as they say, would they not do something? Would they not be making electric cars more affordable? No, they are not.'

Beside the path, Ivan rubs away the dirt from a rock face to reveal names carved in the stone, and dates stretching back centuries. When pallbearers carried a body out of the valley for burial, the names of the deceased were recorded on this rock. If you died in the winter there was no way out until the spring, and you were kept in a cellar, on ice.

'We always want to say what is black and what is white,' says Ivan. 'Here it was very simple. The things that were right were what made you survive. The things that were wrong, they killed you.' I suppose it is possible to romanticise anything. I wonder how many names on this stone did the wrong thing.

Rusting in the stream below us is a hydroelectric turbine that dates from 1895. They had electricity in Zakojška grapa before most of the country. We come upon ruined houses with thick, uninsulated wires hanging from their ceilings like loose threads. Upstairs, mattresses stuffed with hay that are ripped and reek of mice. A leather satchel on a hook; a simple gown. Wooden tools built to outlast their owners. We close the doors behind us and push on, let these places rest again. The house Ivan wants to show me is further up the valley. It is where his grandmother was born.

In 1970 *Planinski Vestnik* (the Alpine Gazette) described his grandmother's place: 'The old couple are numb to life and counting the days ... Deathly silence covered the house and the world around it ... While everyone under Kojca is saying that these old recluses will move away, they themselves know nothing about it. They have no answer to when, where and how. It seems self-evident to the prophets that it is not possible to live here.' A photo beside the article showed their house surrounded by close-cropped pasture. The path that we are on is seen as a clear track, approaching it through the fields.

Today a forty-foot maple sprouts from his grandmother's front stoop, and the buildings are swamped by forest. As the modern world came to Cerkno, it became impossible to find the servants and the day labourers to do the work out here. Once they wanted for little from the outside world besides salt, tobacco and burial plots, but things were different now. Who would aspire to their corpse being kept on ice all winter? The factory opened in town. Farmers downed tools and the forest snuck up. It was too much work for those left behind. The *Laufarija* introduced *Divji*, the character of the Wild Man, to the carnival, recently emerged from the newly grown forests as an old way of life was smothered, terrified of civilisation. A thousand people making way for a hundred thousand trees.

Inside the front door, long off its hinges, is a butter

churn. Ivan tells me that a tourist who had been poking around posted a picture of this object on Facebook, curious as to what it was, and that somehow, via the vagaries of the internet, Ivan had come across it. 'None of his business,' he says.

I sit down in what was once the kitchen, my back against the old *peč*. The names of Ivan's family members are scratched into the walls, back from when this was their home. Piles of leaves and crushed beer cans have drifted in the corners.

'Why is it none of his business?'

'Because they don't know what they are asking for,' he snaps. He runs a finger through the dust. 'There are so many stories here,' he says. 'So many souls. Each of those souls, they leave something.' He lays a hand on his chest. He is scarcely talking to me. 'The grandma would have sat there, the grandpa there. The son would have said, "I am going off to war. Off to protect this land." The mother would have crossed him. The father – I don't know what the father would have done. Crossed him or cursed him. And off he goes.' He trails a hand over the smooth wood that forms a bench around the *peč*. 'You see this wood? How many children's feet? How much laughing, how much tears? How many marriages arranged here? How many deaths? But the world keeps on turning. The sun goes up and down.'

He smiles and turns away. 'I'm becoming an old man,' he says. 'I'm becoming sensitive.' He walks back outside into the light and leaves me sitting there.

How quickly things can fall apart, I think, and back then things were built to last. Sitting here, waiting to die, to be carried out of the valley in a coffin. The table wiped clean. A name carved in a rock. The door closed, one last time.

Ivan leads us up onto a narrow crest with low cliffs dropping away on both sides. We are higher than the canopy. On Sundays the families gathered here. Picture them, flinging their hymns to the horizon. We sit, and Ivan passes out thick sandwiches of home-made salami and home-made bread and home-made butter. I lean back against the wide, cool trunk of a spruce tree. There are four of these trees, in a line, reaching far into the sky. Unlike the naked beeches they are heavy with needles and look wholly out of place. They are a century old, Ivan tells me. They were planted for the folk who died out here, in memoriam. They are all that now remain of the people who once lived hard, full lives out here.

'I have these debates with my daughter and she gets so angry,' Ivan says through a mouthful of salami. 'She does not agree with me. Ever. But I say to her that this is the end of neoliberalism in Europe. I say we have been doing this stuff forever. And now you from the cities, you come here and you tell us how to live. You tell us we must have wolves? Nonsense!' he says. 'Triple nonsense!'

These mountains were in decline, of course, long before the beasts came back. Before the Second World War, 25 per cent of Slovenians lived in the countryside.

Now it is 4 per cent. Seven hundred farms close every year. The expansion of capitalism has meant many things, but one is the death of the small farmer. To walk through these rural villages is to see places largely populated by people well into retirement, out in the fields planting this year's potato crop or tending to the hives. They are locked into this life in a way that means they cannot stop. In a real sense the land is waiting for them to die so that it can claw its way back.

I understand Ivan's nostalgia for a simpler time. I have it too, this terrible longing for something that I have never even known. And it is easier to shoot a wolf than late-stage capitalism or the Common Agricultural Policy. It gives at least an illusion of control. While the wolf as a symbol of rewilding has captured plenty of hearts, such a vision finds itself at odds with those who want to see their countryside re-peopled. I chew my sandwich, looking up into the treetops. I understand the sadness, to see laid out in front of you this withering of your roots. But what I feel more than anything, when I think of my own rootlessness, is a jealousy of at least knowing where you are from. The trees, the stumps, the names scratched in the walls. To have something, at least, to show your children.

'There are many interesting young people who want to stay here,' Ivan says. 'The cities are losing their attraction. They are dangerous. During Covid we were free. We have good possibilities here to keep this countryside alive. What we need to do, I know. But what we must *not* do, I also know. And the beasts, they have no place here.'

Tuesday evening, dusk, the final night of carnival. The *Laufarji* stand onstage and the crowd gathers before them. One village contemplating another, gazing on an archetypal image of itself, ready for its catharsis. Pust is hauled out, with *Lámant* pressing his pitchfork up against his back. For some reason he has on a face mask. Once again, the prosecution runs through his long and diverse list of crimes. The days might be warmer but the temperature still plummets after dark, and the men stand around drinking and smoking to keep warm. I wonder if anyone understands what is going on any better than I do, but then I wonder if it matters. Because behind the topless calendars and the lager and the teenage heroics, there is something ancient occurring here.

Scapegoating was first described in Leviticus. 'Aaron shall lay both his hands upon the head of the live billy goat and confess over it all the iniquities and transgressions of the Israelites . . . Thus the billy goat shall carry on it all their iniquities to an inaccessible region; and the billy goat shall be sent off to the wilderness.' Each year at Yom Kippur, the Day of Atonement, the High Priest would burden a goat with his people's sins and banish it to wander in the wasteland. The Israelites, consciences clean, could go back to sinning all over again.

In ancient Greece the scapegoat was the *pharmakos*, a word derived from 'medicine', and was typically human.

In Athens the ugliest people were sacrificed in droughts. On Leukas a criminal was thrown from the cliffs into the sea during the festival to Apollo. In Abdera a pauper was chased out of town by a mob throwing stones, but only after he had first been given a feast. In Massilia the scapegoat was dined for a whole year before banishment. Invariably those selected were on the fringes of the community, and they took the community's sins with them when they went. The word 'tragedy' comes from the ancient Greek *tragonoide*, 'the song of the goat'. Such ritualised scapegoating has been argued to be the birth of theatre.

I watch the theatre playing out before me. Pust is cowed before the judge and no one can help him now. Channelling our suppressed, collective rage onto an individual is a familiar, if basic, way of achieving harmony. In *The Scapegoat*, French philosopher René Girard describes how the 'old pattern of each against another gives way to the unified antagonism of all against one'. Such a shift can appease a society that actual politics has turned its back on, and it can work, for a time. Often, Girard suggested, the scapegoat is granted mystical power. It is why the Greeks gave them a feast first. It is why these characters come to represent so much more than they are, be they a martyr or a refugee, Pust or a wolf.

'*Laufarji*,' says the judge. 'I leave Pust to you. Execute the sentence.'

The excitement has reached fever pitch. This has been a long time coming, a long winter and two long years of lockdowns. The assembled crowd is hushed. The *Laufarji* family stamps and claps. The *Terjasti* lash their switches on the ground until they splinter. The Old Man raises the *bòt* high above him and brings it down on Pust's horned and mossy head.

Pust collapses onto a waiting cart. Leaping and cavorting, the three *Terjasti* wheel it off the stage and away into the narrow streets, pursued by a gaggle of children.

The Scabby Man strikes up a jaunty polka on his accordion. The family dances in clumsy steps, joining hands and pirouetting. But then the accordion slows right down and finds a minor key, an awful, mournful dirge, and all of a sudden the characters are rolling about the stage in grief, hammering at their chests. The Drunk Man sits in paralytic contemplation, staring down the end of his bottle. It can be hard, sometimes, when you get what you want.

I think of Slavc and all those other wolves, wandering out there in the hinterlands of our imagination. Wouldn't it be so simple if the death of the wolf could restore a community's harmony? If it could hold back the outside world? Yet the yearly cycle of fortune will turn once more, and winter will surely come again. Shoot one wolf and several more return. And perhaps it wasn't all Pust's fault, after all.

It is late. The drinking will go on all night, but it is time for me to head back to the hotel. I am leaving in the morning.

4

Не все, что похоже на волка, является
волком – *Not everything that looks like a wolf is a wolf.*
Russian proverb

East from Cerkno the land eases down towards the plain. Slavc moved quickly, losing altitude, drawn on by the softening of the landscape.

At two in the morning on Christmas Day 2011 he trotted down into the Ljubljana basin, not far from the town of Škofja Loka. Following him, I emerge on wide, flat land. Fields stretch before me, freshly ploughed and awaiting seed. These aren't the mountainous fringes any more, but Slovenia's agricultural and economic heartland. Distant towns and distant spires. Revolving on my axis, I can see mountains at every compass point, far off and blue and hung with cloud, their peaks still heavy with snow. I hoist my bag and set off across the plain.

Roads, small roundabouts, more roads, running straight for miles. Cars pass in a steady stream. On Christmas morning it would have been quieter. Picture him, head bent low and running through an alien world towards where the sun will rise. I long for his uncomplicated swiftness.

Out-of-town stores with tractors in their forecourts, others selling second-hand Škodas and cattle feed and terracotta pots. Kestrels hang cruciform above the traffic. In the fields there are pockets of copse and I see Slavc moving rapidly between them, aware of the impending dawn. Geese, recently arrived, stand about in the furrows. Row upon row of cherry trees, beginning to blossom.

    These are lovely days of walking, full of the hope of early spring. Last night I took shelter from a downpour in a half-constructed house on the outskirts of Škofja Loka, my sleeping bag laid out upon the concrete. But now the clouds have cleared and the sky is a stunning, vertiginous blue. Walking gives you an animal appreciation for the seasons. Winter really has been vanquished, and the day feels taut with promise. There is warmth in my bones and my legs feel strong. I stop in the village of Mavčiče for bread and cheese and then I carry on. A lone dog lopes past me down the side of the road, going the other way.

    By sunrise Slavc had reached a large remnant of forest that straddles the E61 highway. After the exposure of the plain it would have felt like a hallowed place. He stayed in these woods for three days. I sleep here too. While children across Slovenia woke up to their presents, Slavc killed first one fox, then another, and feasted till he was full. It was the first time that he had eaten since he left home a week before. There is an underpass beneath the highway that links the two halves of the forest and there are several GPS fixes here as he wandered back and forth. Hubert came to investigate once Slavc had moved on, and he found the foxes' spines, cleaned of flesh. I cross by the same tunnel and stand there in the half-darkness, listening to the muffled traffic, like a shell held to the ear. Graffiti, and fox prints in the mud. Slavc stood here, right here.

Then he was off again. He waited until midnight; then he left. On 28 December, at 3.11 a.m., he was up against the chain-link fence that surrounds Ljubljana's airport, to the north of the capital. I skirt the runway, walking the same perimeter. A security car passes on the inside of the fence but it does not stop. Imagine Slavc's horror at this artifice, these metal birds taking to the skies with diabolic roars, their rending of the air.

I am not permitted to guess at his thoughts. But the next fix is a huge distance to the north, not far from the Austrian border, high on the western slope of Grintovec. It is an incredible distance to have covered in three hours, crossing valleys, crossing roads, as he made his way back towards the sanctuary of the mountains. As though he were running from something. As though I am navigating by a map of his fear.

To cover this same route takes me days. I pass through Zgornji Brnik, Cerklje na Gorenjskem, Grad. Like Slavc, I search out woods to sleep in, to keep the tent out of sight. And at last my path begins to climb again, first into foothills, then the mountains. In small villages, old wooden barns jostle for space with constructions of concrete and corrugate. An old man in a bee suit watches me pass without acknowledgement, the smoke from his smoker rising lazily in the sharp light. Each of his hives is painted with a crude and disturbing pastoral scene: a hunter shooting an enormous wolf; a donkey strumming a banjo; a bear having sex with a woman. As I stand there looking at these a cyclist passes, Lycra-clad legs furiously pumping, and I wonder what the beekeeper makes of us all, always needing to be somewhere else.

As the hills return, so do the woods. I have never been in woods like the ones I have seen here in Slovenia. Not in Europe, not among familiar trees. It is a part of the national identity. It was W. H. Auden who said that a culture is no better than its woods, and Slovenia has taken this to heart. Outside Scandinavia, it is the most forested country in Europe, 60 per cent of it and growing. It reminds me of the Amazon, but made up of beech and oak. Their trunks tower over me, their leaves brand new and luminescent and casting a stained-glass, spring-green light. As I climb there are expansive views off to more forested hills, and beyond that, ever more. Like Slavc, I played in beech woods as a kid and I have a special affection for them. These are fairytale woods; woods of woodcutters and wolves. I climb hills that are staircases of beech roots, the path beckoning me on, polished where last year's leaves have been tamped down by animal and human feet. At one summit I find a small wooden cupboard built into a trunk containing two shot glasses and a bottle of home-made grappa, as though left by a benevolent sprite. I toast my own achievement and carry on.

In a small clearing I pass a ruined house. The wild garlic is beginning to push out and its scent is on the air. There is a framed sign in Slovenian: *Until 17th April 1944 good people lived here, who offered shelter to partisans.* I wonder what happened afterwards. An electric candle burns among a clump of primroses. I sit with my back against the wall for a while, where it has been warmed by the sun, and listen as the birds readjust to my presence. There is nothing more complicated just now than to eat and sleep and walk. I feel a deep sense of peace.

I carry on. It is getting late. At last I stop and scuff around, searching for a flat place for the tent. By the time I have it up it is dusk beneath the canopy. I get the stove lit and start cooking my usual – a tin of sardines, tomatoes, couscous, whatever greens I have found along the way. Night falls quickly and the wood chatters with different sounds. Something rooting through the leaf litter. The cold hoot of an owl. And then, while I am eating, four loud barks. If I had fur it would bristle. I'm not keen on dogs at night – I learnt that on my last walk. But dogs would not, I think, stray this far into the forest. I cannot understand it. And then they come again.

It is no dog. This noise is throaty, raven-like, but with a tropical lilt, as though a parrot is being stifled. And this time I recognise it, because I have heard it once before.

It was some weeks earlier. I had just arrived in the country and Jaka Črtalič, the youngest member of Hubert's biotechnical team, had taken me to woods south of Ljubljana to check his lynx traps. He had caught no lynx. This was not unusual. We drove around the hills while I dangled from the window of his Toyota waving a telemetry antenna to get their signal, but still we found nothing.

That afternoon we drove to where the computer showed that two lynx had been turning up for several days. It suggested a kill site, that they were coming back to feed. We parked up and scrambled down a hillside so thick with beech leaves that it was like trekking over sand dunes. We fanned out, and for the next hour we paced the same few hundred metres of forest floor, as though conducting a murder inquiry. It was Jaka who found it in the end, although in truth there was not much left to find. She was half hidden in a stand of saplings, a few metres off a deer track. There was no real smell of death – the day was very cold and there was not much meat to rot. Only the hooves and forelegs, still lined with fur, as though the deer was wearing evening gloves. A spinal cord, a skull, some matted hair. The stomach and the bowel, which the lynx avoids so that their ruptured smell does not alert the scavengers. That was it.

'The face has been chewed,' Jaka said. 'The foxes have got to her.'

He reconstructed her last moments for me. Probably she was on this path, and the lynx had been waiting here. There were possible signs of struggle as it dragged the body up the slope. It would have been over very quickly, clamping the deer's throat with its jaw until she suffocated. A lynx is more efficient than a wolf. It was all supposition, but you know an animal as well as this and you have earned the right to make good guesses.

Jaka popped the jaw and one shinbone into a Ziploc bag. The teeth would age her; the shin's marrow would give an indication of her condition. Back at the Biotechnical Faculty there are freezers upon freezers full of death.

And then we heard it. Those same choked barks, distant but distinct. Jaka raised a finger, smiled. They were out there, his lynx. Knowing that was enough.

Just as they are out there now. In a heartbeat I am back to those many nights spent in a tent in Alaska, peering out into the half-darkness, every sense primed, every rustle pregnant with meaning. My instincts had attained a polish that had been hard to relinquish when I got back home, despite having little need for them any more. I cannot pretend that there was not something soothing in being complacent once again. Camping is more relaxing when you don't have to wash up straight after eating, or burn your tins to eradicate the smells, or hang your food from a rope up in a tree.

But comfort kills, does it not, as well as carnivores? Because there was something missing, too, in being home. My longing for Alaska was like a homesickness. I yearned to go back to that place of which our own environment is only a dim echo. To hear lynx out in the woods is to believe that these forests are larger than I ever dared to hope, latent with possibility. In Europe! The feeling is not fear, or not only, because there is nothing, so Jaka told me, to be scared of. But it is my senses charged by different stimuli. It is an awareness of my vulnerability, my own earthy, bodily nature. I understand the problems, and the controversies, and the fear of the large carnivores. But the first thing I feel, sitting here, is deeply moved. Moved that big lives not my own are going on out in these woods. Moved that we share this place tonight, both parts of a bigger whole. And when people say what is the point of having wolves back, really, I think, it is this. This feeling I have, right now.

It rains in the night. I wake in the morning and unzip the tent to a forest washed clean. The great beeches are heavy with water and below me the swollen stream rattles along. I fill the kettle and make coffee and pack my things and carry on. Austria approaches. I have nearly crossed the country of Slavc's birth and ahead of me the high peaks mark the border, perhaps a day away.

I arrive in the village of Kokra at the allotted time for my meeting with Stane Bergant, a contact that Ivan had given me, only to check the map and see that the house I have been invited to is several hundred metres above me. The path charges up almost vertically through the woods with no concession to gradient. I am bent and gasping beneath my bag. Where I meet a track that follows the contour of the mountainside, I take it north. There is only one path marked on the map, but that has absolutely no coherence with what I find before me. There are dead ends and trails that double back or end in landslips. I am hot and late and lost. There is something quite ridiculous about arranging meetings when on foot.

As I tune into my instincts, I think I can pick out a rutted track bearing the way I should be going, so thick with saplings that only a notion of it remains. The track fords a dry river, a small stone dam in ruins further up the gorge. And then I crest a pleat of the land to see Stane's complex of cabins carving out a space within the resurgent forest, and his ancient Mitsubishi four-wheel drive out front.

I find Stane in the garden. He is grudgingly impressed that I have made it. I wonder if this invitation was an initiation test for the city boy, the writer. Stane is a great bear of a man, with great bear paws. He seizes hold of my hand like it's rightfully his. This hand, and everything else in view. Triglav, Slovenia's highest peak, hangs in a haze off to the west, its summit topped by cumuli.

Stane was born in the Kokra valley, below, where land is mostly a vertical proposition. The people raised here grow up climbing mountains. Stane and Maria, his wife, have climbed all over Slovenia, all over the world. They climbed mountains as big as him. He has stood on the summits of Kilimanjaro and the Matterhorn, towering over their peaks. He is interested in the details of my route, its highest peaks and passes. He is stooped now, with a paunch, breathing heavily through his nose and with hearing aids in his great ears. He speaks a decent, enthusiastic English. Hubert had described him to me as one of Slovenia's most prominent anti-carnivore campaigners.

He looks me up and down. 'Okay, you have to change your clothes,' he says. 'You have an excellent opportunity to make a shower, if you want.'

He ushers me inside and talks me through the solar

water-heating system. I stand beneath the scalding water, scraping off the grime. Then he walks me through the vegetable garden to my guest cabin – it is too late now, he says, to get to Austria. There is a soft bed, a reading lamp. I am giddy with gratitude. 'I think you can sleep here very well,' he says.

He leaves me to change into the clean set of clothes that I have been saving for just such an occasion, and then I go through into the kitchen. Maria is in there, pottering over the pans. Religious icons and felt-tip scribbles by the grandkids decorate the walls. Everything is made from wood, like the rest of the country. Maria gets me seated at the table before a plate of home-cured meats. Stane sits beside me and opens up a photo album.

They are sepia photos, light glancing in the lens. Photos of when the cabin belonged to his uncle, when Stane would hike up here as a boy with salt for his uncle's sheep. Those were good days, when the sheep didn't need much more attention than rounding up at the end of the season. Then a photo of this place with trees sprouting from its roof, after his uncle passed. In the next, a bunch of men from the village, grinning in the mountain sunshine astride unroofed rafters, smoking, rebuilding the place plank by plank. 'I could not allow it that every memory, every history, would be forgotten,' Stane says.

The next page shows a group out in the forest. The men are in the checked shirts and green trilbies of the Slovene hunter, the women in scarves and overcoats done up to the top button as though they were going off to market. The dead bear on the ground between them is so huge it does not look real. Most of the men are cocked forward at the hip, a hand placed on their bent leg, a Sunday league team photo. 'That one's my dad,' Stane points. They had lured the bear in with a dead cow of his uncle's. They had a problem, and they fixed it.

Maria serves buckwheat porridge and a dumpling stew and she comes to eat with us. She listens, but Stane does all the talking. Maintaining his uncle's place, he says, meant not only rebuilding but also keeping animals to preserve the pastures, or what he calls the 'cultural landscape'. And for Stane, animals meant horses. Stane, it is clear, loves his horses. He shows me photos of an Austrian breed called a Haflinger. They are beautiful animals, chestnut with a flaxen mane and tail, stocky and muscular. He has bred them for forty years, and now that his granddaughters are learning to ride, he hopes they will take over the business. During the winters the horses are stabled in Kokra, but when the weather breaks they come up here. To roam, to eat fresh grass and saplings, to be free.

Several years ago, one afternoon, he was sitting here when the horses showed up in the yard. That was unusual. They didn't come home unless the weather was on the turn. They were bucking, restive; something had obviously spooked them, and his best breeding mare was not with them. Probably he knew already what had happened. Four of them went out to look. The men found her, and the bear on top of her, pinning her down with one leg as it peeled open her stomach with a single claw as though it were unzipping a jacket. They chased it off and led the mare back to the hut, her insides half out, her skin hanging off of her in flaps. Large carnivores do themselves no favours by killing their prey in ways that are truly grotesque. There was nothing to be done. Stane called the butcher, and that night they dealt with her.

Stane received no compensation because the animal was butchered before an official could assess the kill, but no money could have made up for the loss. 'When you breed, you select over many generations,' he says. 'This is not only one animal. The breeding goal is damaged. *Everything* is damaged.'

Stane shows me a document entitled 'The Dying of the Countryside'. It is from a presentation he gave in Brussels in 2018, when he delivered a petition to the EU signed by fifty-one NGOs, representing a quarter of the country, demanding a reduction in wild game and carnivores. It criticises 'unbalanced European regulation' for enflaming 'social conflict, mistrust in European institutions and . . . Euro-scepticism'.

'The EU pushes this green agricultural strategy,' Stane says. 'Our farm is bio. This I support.' To qualify as organic, he tells me, animals must be outside for at least six months of the year. 'But on the other hand, there is the EU strategy of spreading large carnivores. This is contradictory. If the EU pushes farmers to put animals out of the stables, they cannot also push to make more wolves. The EU cannot claim to support green agriculture while turning pasture-fed animals into prey.' Yet the petition was ultimately powerless to make a difference to policies being decided at a European level.

Before Slovenia's accession to the EU it had the sovereignty to manage its own wildlife populations, including its large carnivores, and Stane says that both sides lived in peace (although the wolves were unavailable for comment). In 1992, when the European Commission chose to protect its carnivores, there were scarcely any left in the Western countries that at that time constituted the bloc. But in 2004 when ten, predominantly Eastern countries (including Slovenia) joined the EU, they brought populations of wolf and bear with them that had never gone away. In these countries, says Stane, the large carnivores were not endangered, although plenty of scientists would dispute this. He does not believe they should now be beholden to regulations cooked up by a bloc of Western countries that had driven their own wolves close to extinction.

'We feel like American Indians when the Europeans came,' he says. 'These Indians were living with their habits and their animals, and then the Europeans came and took their land. We make this country alive. Without the farming, the young people will go out of this valley. And these places will die.' It could equally be Ivan speaking; these feelings are everywhere.

Large carnivore conservation projects are funded predominantly by the LIFE (L'Instrument Financier pour l'Environment) programme, a pot of EU money earmarked for environmental and climate projects. The most recent LIFE WolfAlps project has the stated aim of 'improv[ing] wolf–human coexistence'. It has a budget of twelve million euros, spread across four Alpine countries and various universities, museums, national parks and other institutions.

'These EU jobs are *beautiful* jobs,' says Stane. 'You are walking around, like you are, in the nature. You make some pictures of some prints of the wolf. Take some shit. Make some analysis – which wolf is in relation with which wolf. They get cars, they get clothes, they get shoes. Lots of money. And of course these people will fight for the wolf, because without the wolf they have no future.'

He shakes his head at the absurdity. '*Hundreds* of animals are endangered,' he says. 'Many fishes in our rivers. But no other animal is so attractive to specialists, to politics, to the public. Why? Because of this charismatic nature. You cannot earn money on a butterfly.'

Stane stresses that he doesn't want wolves and bears eradicated entirely. He just doesn't want them here.

'So what's the solution?' I ask.

'Bring back the wolf and bear to the number in 2004,' he says. 'Manage the population like it was before we entered EU. Simple.'

Except, well, it isn't that simple. LIFE WolfAlps estimates that Slovenia had 'only a few individuals' left by the 1980s (bounties on wolves had only been stopped in 1973) and in 2010, when data collection began, there were between thirty-four and forty-two, making the 2004 population somewhere between 'a few' and forty-two. Is that a figure to aspire to? Today there are 135 wolves in Slovenia, and the space for many more. Our difficulty in imagining a world different from the one we grew up in (what gets called 'shifting baseline syndrome' in the scientific papers) does a good job of insulating us from the full horror of what we have unleashed upon the natural world, but it can also make our conservation aims extremely conservative. It is easier to imagine that our elders are addled by nostalgia when they describe the fecundity of the past, because the alternative – to believe them – is unbearable. We started wiping out our planet's megafauna 50,000 years ago. Most of it has been gone so long that we cannot fathom how it shaped the planet. To take 2004 as a baseline feels distinctly unambitious if the aim is to restore the planet's ecosystems.

Despite the wolf's dramatic resurgence, its range across Europe is still only slightly more than half what it was in 1800. Six of the EU's nine transboundary wolf populations have not reached favourable conservation status. Estimating historical populations is imprecise, but 200 years ago there were enough wolves in Sweden that hunters annually killed between 500 and 700. This year the Swedish parliament voted to cap the country's population at 250, while the Hunters' Association continues to lobby for 150. In 1800 France alone had a wolf population estimated at between 10,000 and 15,000 individuals. Today it is approximately 800, and that is approximately 800 too many for the farmers' associations. Only one-quarter of Europeans now live in the countryside, and across the EU a rural area the size of Italy will be abandoned by 2030 – there should be more space for these animals than there has ever been. Yet today even conservationists find it hard to imagine such abundance.

Maria brings us Turkish coffee and a slice of home-made cake and a glass of honey schnapps. Stane flips through his EU presentation, past graphic images of disembowelled, half-dead livestock. On one page is a scale of those who are for and against the wolf, ranging from 'Farmers and Countryside' at the 'Against' end, to 'Experts and Institutions Serving Taxpayer Funded Projects' at the other. He pokes a finger at 'Romantic Nature Conservationists', close to the 'For' end of the spectrum.

'I think you are somewhere here,' he says. 'You cannot convince me otherwise.'

I try to convince him otherwise. I neglect to mention how I felt about the lynx that I heard last night in the forest. Stane looks at me with the faint trace of a smile and waits for me to finish talking about impartiality.

'One question, so that I more understand you,' he says, leaning forward in his chair, the schnapps glass tiny in his hand. 'In which sort of place do you live?'

'Well, right now I live in a town,' I say.

'A town,' he says, already triumphant.

'It's a small town,' I say, lamely. But Stane has found my weakness.

'And do you know what the official services do with the rats in towns?' he says.

'Last year I lived on the Scottish coast,' I mumble.

'The rat disturbs people in towns,' he carries on.

'They come twice a year and they put a lot of poison everywhere. And this is a very *terrible* poison. The rats are dying because the blood comes out of their internal organs. It is a very cruel death. But people in towns don't care about this. They want to live without this predator.'

'Okay,' I say. 'I see your point.'

'This wolf is a predator for us,' he says. 'But we are not allowed to live in a normal way. To kill it. People in towns make *massacres* on mouses, on rats, on pigeons. But on the other side, they would protect wolves, they would protect bears. But not in their towns. They would protect them *here*.' He jabs an enormous finger into the table. 'They think that they have a right to put these animals here. Nobody asks us, do we accept them? They ask people like you are, in towns. They do not know, and they do not feel, the same as we feel here. And they present these very deep investigations, and they say people would like to have the wolf. But people like you are, not like we are.'

'Look, I'm not here to support the wolf,' I say. 'I'm here to listen. I don't want to take sides.'

'But by doing your walk,' he says, 'don't you think you will make more people like this wolf?'

'If we protect the wolf absolutely, then we will destroy the wolf,' Stane said to me later that evening. We had finished our dinner and were still chatting. Maria had gone elsewhere. I was enjoying his company, the way he liked to tease and goad me. 'Hunters and farmers managed the wolf for centuries,' he said. 'That's *why* we still have wolves. The wolf's charisma is what attracts people, but now it's like a dog. They are coming into the streets now, scared of nothing. Wolves and dogs are cross-breeding. We have to protect this nature of the wolf, which was developed during thousands of years. Not cross-breeding *dog*.'

We have always fiddled with the wild, of course. We can't help ourselves. Two thousand years ago Pliny described the Gauls, in a quest for more powerful animals, as tying up their dogs so that passing wolves could impregnate them. Alaska's Indigenous peoples bred hybrids to beef up their sled teams. A man who thinks of himself as the kind of guy who keeps a wolf as a pet will typically own something that has been cross-bred with a dog, to take the lupine edge off. One estimate has it at 300,000 captive hybrids in the United States alone.

Unlike, say, a mule, a wolf-dog hybrid can have pups of its own. The same goes for cats, and in Scotland the true wildcat has practically vanished because of mixing with feral house-cats, its genes diluted by our errant pets. The danger posed to wolves is just as real. When a pack is stable it will generally kill dogs in its territory (the bloody leash outside the kennel, found by one of the kids the next morning, is one of the wolf's worst PR disasters), but where it is recolonising new territory, things are different. When wolves first return there are few potential mates, but what they are certain to run into is dogs. During the nineties, as refugees fled the Balkan Wars, they often left their dogs behind. Aided by the chaos of the moment, wolves recolonised these abandoned territories. Thirty years later and Dalmatia has several packs with high levels of dog ancestry.

If I'm honest, I love the idea of a dog running off with a wolf. It feels very Jack London, very emancipated. In truth, it's not unlike us eloping with a chimpanzee – extremely taboo, and really quite terrifying. It's also terrible news for the wolves. 'Once hybridisation gets ingrained, there is *nothing* you can do,' Hubert had told me. 'You have to shoot them. From a conservation point of view, there is no other way.'

Yet wolves are now so comprehensively protected that even eliminating the hybrids can prove almost impossible. This is compounded by emotional arguments made by those at the romantic end of Stane's spectrum, who see anything that even looks like a wolf as sacrosanct. Since the wolf's return to Italy the current policy has been to sterilise the hybrids' offspring, but sterilising a single pack can cost the best part of a million euros. If the authorities don't sterilise them they will attempt to trap them and stick them in a zoo, because caging an animal feels less morally complicated than shooting it. Yet keeping a wild wolf in captivity can have profound psychological consequences. 'You can see their suffering,' says Hubert. 'All because our society does not accept a death. People worry so much about a single wolf being killed, but if they hybridise with dogs we could lose the entire genus.'

For now, the problem remains small. There is one hybrid pack in Slovenia, and it is a growing problem in the Apennines where wolves have expanded towards suburban areas. A 2019 paper found that in the Swiss Alps fewer than 2 per cent of wolves have a significant amount of dog in them, although in countries with more stray dogs – in Georgia, say, or in Greece – this can reach 10 per cent. 'Scientific evidence is now available to objectively guide the public debate,' concluded the authors of the Swiss paper, optimistically. Yet time and again along my journey, those who stand against wolves will suggest to me that Europe is overrun with hybrids. 'Look at its *face*,' someone will say, getting up a video on their phone. 'Look at its behaviour. That's not a true Austrian wolf.' People who hate wolves can suddenly get terribly worked up about preserving their racial purity. 'Wolf-dog "swarms" threaten to wipe out Europe's wolves,' cried a 2019 *Daily Mail* headline, in language that felt copied and pasted from elsewhere in the paper. The danger is real, but crying 'dog' without due evidence can be more dangerous to the wolf's future than the hybrids themselves. In 2022, for example, a suspected hybrid was shot in the west of Switzerland, yet the post-mortem revealed that the animal was 100 per cent wolf.

In Italy there are wolves with black coats and white claws that are commonly said to be hybrids. These mutations can be traced back to the late 1990s, when the Italian wolf was expanding its range into dog territory. But since then these hybrids have backcrossed into the wolf population so completely that, genetically, there is now very little dog left in them, despite how they might look. How pure should a wolf be? As the tools for analysis become more refined, that question becomes ever more complicated. Dogs and wolves have shared the planet for 15,000 years and it is hard to find a line so untainted that a wolf's great-grandparent hasn't had a fling with someone's dog at *some* point.

Astrid Vik Stronen, a biologist at the University of Ljubljana, believes it is important to focus on how the animal behaves in the wild. To fixate on genetic purity suggests a nostalgia for times past, the most conservative form of conservation. 'Try to think of it not just as preserving wolves,' she said to me, 'but as preserving the ecological function.' At a time of rapid flux, when the only certainty is change, this seems to me a useful way to think about far more than wolves.

After all, the deer doesn't care who's eating it.

Stane wants to show me his horses. One of them wears a collar much like Slavc's, meaning that Stane can locate his small herd using an app on his phone. He pockets a crust of bread from the remains of dinner and we walk outside and get into his truck.

The track curves along the mountain's side, the same way that the wolf went. He gestures to the peaks we pass like he is introducing me to old friends. 'This is Grintovec,' he says. 'Two thousand five hundred and fifty-eight metres. This is Jezerska Kočna. Two thousand five hundred and forty. And over there is where you are going tomorrow.' He points out a range of mountains to the north. Austria is just a few kilometres off, but under communism the border was impregnable. The sun is crashing red below the western peaks and the snow on these slopes burns pink.

'Do you know the moment I moved from the left to the right?' Stane says.

In the passenger seat, in the half-light, I wait for him to continue.

'Maria and I were thirty years old,' he says. 'We took our two sons to Jezersko to ski, in the area that we knew from our youngest years. We were skiers and Alpinists, like I told you.' He points to the slope on the far side of the valley, already lost to shadow. 'There were these Serb soldiers on the border. And they caught us, with these small children, because we did not have our ID cards with us. They took us up to the main station. And we were there for *many* hours, and they asked us a lot of things. They wanted to persuade us that we wanted to escape over the border.' It makes him angry still. He is breathing loudly through his nose. 'I said: my ancestors were *born* here. We were here centuries ago. We *make* this landscape. And now these soldiers from *Serbia* are telling us what to do. My emotions were very disturbed.'

It is hard to imagine it now, the rigidity of those borders. That just a generation ago this place was the frontier, instead of at the heart of Europe. 'And until then,' I say, 'you were on the left?'

'My father was a partisan,' Stane says. 'He fought against Hitler. We were always proud of that. There was nothing wrong with that. What was wrong in Yugoslavia was that these people who loved their countries were abused for the Communist Revolution. We should have kept our democracy after the Second World War.'

We drive on. The dusk is falling rapidly. 'And how are you orientated?' he says. 'What do you think of Brexit?'

Here we go, I think. I say my piece – my partner, my kids, my sadness.

'But what do you think about immigration?' he says.

'I think it's very positive.' Stane smiles. I picture him circling, yet again, 'Romantic Nature Conservationist'. 'Is there lots of migration here?' I say.

'When there was that big wave there was a lot, but they wanted to get to Germany, to Italy. I support people who escape from being killed, but this economic migration is not good. They are changing our way of life. Europe cannot take in half of Africa and Asia. There won't be jobs for everybody, and normally they are not with the right knowledge for working for our needs. If they do not have work, they establish their own way of life with crime and prostitution. In Sweden it is chaos. They have districts that are not under control.'

Wherever I go along Slavc's trail, I will hear such fears of being replaced. This looming presence, coming from the east. The notion that the purity of the European way of life is being reshaped by immigration, an idea that continues to gain currency. Last night, on a campsite, the owner confided to me that blue European eyes are being diluted by the brown of incomers. There are

135 wolves in the country as of last count, and in 2022 Slovenia, a country of over 2 million people, will receive just 6,618 asylum applications. Yet the shadow cast by both wolves and refugees in these rural regions is huge.

Stane is concerned about the coming elections. The left, he says, does not respect the traditional values of the countryside. It preys on the hard work of others. The young people cannot see the danger of the wolves, but his generation remembers how things were forty or fifty years ago. 'They do not recognise the influence of the large carnivores on the social demographic,' he says. 'They are slow processes, but they are happening.'

He checks his phone and pulls up and we get out. We are still in sunlight, but the temperature is not far off freezing. Stane walks out, a little bowed, across the pasture. He reminds me of Atlas, up here on the world's roof. I gaze out on a valley that looks scarcely changed in a thousand years, and that changes with the weather every day.

I follow him to where he is pointing down the slope. Six of his horses are down there, grazing. Several wear bells, that antiquated GPS system, and they ring out in minor keys across the valley. He whistles to them and they raise their heads and amble up the slope towards us. He takes the bread from his pocket and feeds it to the one that comes up first. Haflingers are gorgeous horses, close to mythical, velvet brown with white blazes and stars. He rubs their ears. They mouth at him.

'I don't know where the rest are,' he says. 'Three are

missing.' He points to one of the smaller horses. 'You see this one,' he says. 'For the wolf, no problem.'

'Where are they?' I ask.

He shrugs his great shoulders. 'If this would happen again, I would be forced to stop. You cannot have animals in the stable all the year.' He turns around, peering into the rapidly growing gloom. 'Bonnie!' he calls in a high sing-song. 'Bonnie!'

He walks down the valley's side. 'Bonnie!' he calls, more agitated now. 'Bon-neeee!' He moves stiffly, his knees long gone. I follow on behind.

'Who do you expect will read your book?' he says over his shoulder. 'People like we are, or people from the towns? Will it be the romantics?'

'Both, I hope,' I say.

He nods. 'It will be interesting in which way you will show the people our pain here,' he says. 'The people in the cities, they think that our pain is just part of the improvement of civilisation.'

There is no sign of the horses. Stane stands, stooped and sentinel, gazing out. We listen hard. Crows are flying home to roost, splinters against the sky. He calls again into the silence. And then, at last, there comes a bell. And all of a sudden here comes Bonnie, like an apparition, trotting out of the woods, out of the darkness, leading the other two horses along behind her.

'Okay,' says Stane, the weight falling visibly from his shoulders. 'Everything is okay.'

Austria, Spring

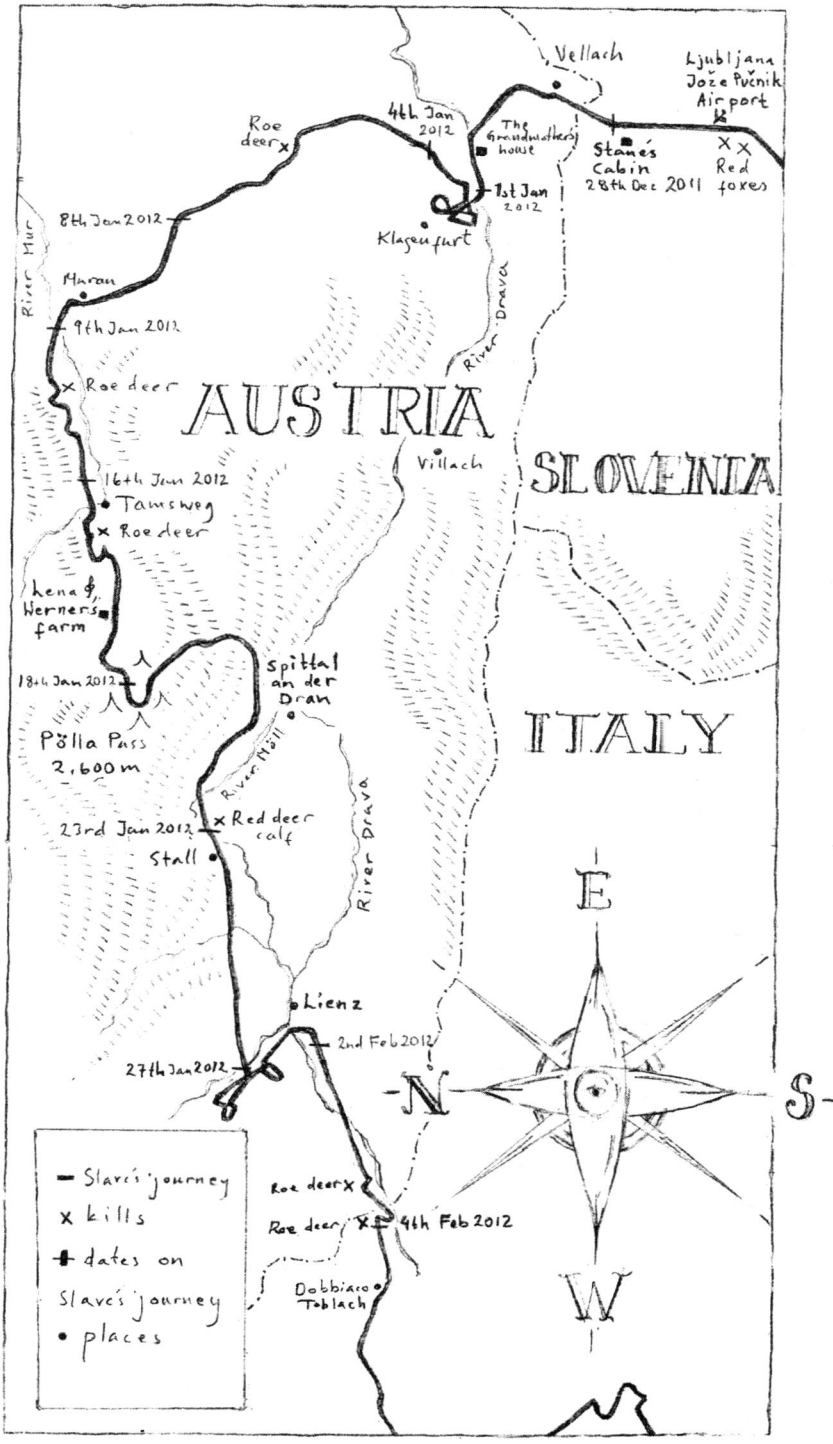

5

> *'Don't you stray from the path, girl. Did you not hear what I told you? Once you stray from the path you're lost entirely. The wild beasts know no mercy.'*
> Angela Carter, *The Company of Wolves*,
> directed by Neil Jordan

There is no obvious way to cross the border into Austria except by road. I tick off the kilometre posts out of Kokra, climbing steadily. All morning I am passed by bikers in their dozens, in their leathers, out practising their hairpins on a Sunday. The mountains pile up ahead. For a time the road follows the Kokra River as it hurries from the peaks, echoing its meanders. It is the first truly warm day of the year and all I really want to do is to lie around and swim. I stop on a small shingle beach to eat the packed lunch Maria made me and soak my feet in the snowmelt. The wild strawberries are out, red flecks in the underbrush, tiny explosions of flavour. The birds are calling, and the sun drips through the trees.

Once there was a bus that ran this route, then later two buses that met at the border. Now there is no bus, and no way of travelling between Kokra in Slovenia and

Vellach, on the Austrian side, without your own vehicle, or your own legs. I cross the border in the early afternoon. *Republik Ö̈sterreich*, it says, on a blue sign ringed by stars. The customs hut is shuttered and looks as though it may have been so for years. All around, everywhere, mountains. At the viewpoint a faded poster warns of the swine-flu epidemic coming from the east, and to dispose of your sausages here. On the penultimate day of 2011 Slavc climbed to this pass up the valley's wooded side, 100 metres above me.

I stop in at the first bar in Austria, a few metres beyond the border. In a fug of smoke a woman rises to serve me in what is, more or less, her sitting room. The lager has changed brand but is otherwise indistinguishable, and I ask for it in the three words of German that I know. Back outside the sky has clouded over, and as I descend it starts to rain. Great fat drops that explode off the road, that catch and bring the blossoms down, so that it looks as though it's snowing. Slavc would have taken the high ground but it is too sheer for me, and so I follow the endless succession of switchbacks down into this new country. The rain comes harder; the air crackles. Half a flattened snake writhes around on the asphalt. For a time, the road smells of the sun.

All down this road are abandoned houses, vast woodpiles stacked beside them in readiness for winters that their occupants never saw, seasoning for how many years now? They are large houses with large wooden balconies, fit for large families. Hard places, cut off in winter, getting the sun for a few brief hours each day. Their owners long since gone to a centrally heated flat in town; their kids moved to Vienna. There are missing tiles, sagging roofs with shrubs exploding out of them, but it would not take much to do them up again. I pass a church, its wrecked graves lost to the sodden grass. The rain comes down in torrents, streaming down the road, and in the end, wet through, I try a house. Rubble has built up in a drift inside and I lean on the door to heave it open. Lino flaps from the floor as though the place has been half-skinned. Everything is gone. The ceiling leaks. Painted over an arch: *Tritt ein bring Glück herein* – 'Come in and bring good luck.' I sit on the floor and eat some nuts and wait for a break in the weather.

That night I stay with Stefan in the Carinthian town of Vellach. He is a biologist by trade, and a mutual friend in Slovenia had given me his address. I knock after dark and undress in his porch, forming puddles on the floor while his cats weave about my legs. He cooks a supper of eggs and sausages and pours me a glass of his home-made apple juice. The house is surrounded by apple trees in blossom, heavy with the rain. Stefan is one of a large Slovene minority whose family ended up here a hundred years ago when Austria finalised its borders. 'Before, it was very bad for us,' he tells me as we eat. 'These populist governments, they find a minority and they target us.' He smiles ruefully. 'But now they target the refugees and it is much better for us.'

I ask him about the empty houses. There were plenty

of jobs here, he says. There were mines for mercury and lead, a paper factory. A railway ran to Bad Eisenkappel carrying people and product, but that became a bike path years ago. There were several spas, because this is the point where the Eurasian plate meets the African and good things bubble from the ground here, minerals and heat. The well-to-do came from Klagenfurt, from Vienna, from Ljubljana, just to soak in what they had in Vellach. They had electricity before Klagenfurt; before the Second World War, even.

But that was all years ago. Vellach's population has declined by 10 per cent in ten years. They moved some migrants here a few years ago to try to stem the tide. The mayor called a meeting and everyone said they didn't want them, but they brought them anyway. They put the young men in an abandoned house a few kilometres out of town. It is hard to be a young man at the best of times, Stefan says. And there they were, in the winter, in the snow, a two-hour walk from town, aimless and traumatised. *Come in and bring good luck.* Stefan and his wife took up bicycles, books, tomato plants. They sat with them, they cooked with them. 'We had a very nice connection with some of them,' he says. As time went on, the men began cycling to town to find work, cash in hand, illegal. Trimming hedges, shovelling snow, that sort of thing. And they turned out to be far more friendly than the people had imagined. Besides, the labour came very cheap.

'The thing was, when they met them, the people

here were not scared any more.' Stefan leans back in his chair, pushing his plate away. 'It is like the wolf,' he says, tapping his temple. 'People are scared of what is in their mind.'

That night I sleep out on his balcony under a half-roof, under a half-moon, under vines.

I am up early. The sun is out again, with a warmth it didn't have even a week ago. The mist is rising from the tarmac. I stop in a shop to stock up on food. Masks are still mandated when inside here, these nuances of borders. My path cuts through Vellach's suburbs, tracking a small stream fat with snowmelt. A kids' playground; a man walking a dog, who laughs when I tell him about my journey as though it is an unfortunate cultural trait. By car I could be in Klagenfurt, Carinthia's capital, in less than an hour, but Slavc was drawn back to the mountains. The countryside bleeds into the town so that it is hard to tell where one becomes the other, but soon I am huffing up paths daubed with red-and-white paint that mark the Alpine routes, and Vellach and Bad Eisenkappel are there below me, and I am back in the woods with Slavc again, on his trail ten years behind.

It is one of those glorious spring days. Chill, and the birds calling precisely. I feel good and alive to be up here. The woods track a narrow ridge that in time bends around to the north. When I pass a mountain hut I am astonished to find it open, the chef smoking at a table outside, contemplating another day with no customers.

I order a large skillet of eggs and potatoes and he rises wearily to cook it. I eat in the thin sunshine, looking back on the way that I have come. Cows stand about, weighty with contemplation. There are swathes of thick, dark plantation all across the hillsides. Chainsaws hum on the wind.

'Cuckoo,' says a cuckoo.

The impact of borders belies their invisibility. Different rules and different fears and different expectations for the future on each side of the line. The woods are different, too. There is a lot more pine now, a lot more plantation, and barbed-wire fences everywhere. After lunch I walk through large sections of forest that have been clear-cut, picking my way over shards of brush and other jackstrawed detritus and through puddles gouged out by heavy machinery like the wallows of wild boar. There are buttercups and nettles and not much else in the understorey, a stark contrast with Slovenia's vibrant beech woods and blankets of wildflowers, and where pesticide use is prohibited in forests. It's no wonder, I think, that Slavc kept moving.

Much of Europe was intensively deforested during the Middle Ages to make way for arable and livestock, the wood turned into charcoal to stoke the continent's booming industries: the smelters, glassworks and potteries. The wolves, with nothing to eat and nowhere to hide, were pushed into direct conflict with people. Much as with the spillover of zoonotic diseases, it's when the line between wild animals and people is eroded that the danger is most acute. Plenty of children left in charge of sheep were eaten. We could have blamed ourselves, but instead we blamed the wolf. They were coming for our animals and our families, and we decided to get them first. Austria did an excellent job. They were gone by the 1870s, and until very recently, that was how it had stayed.

Look at a map from just a few years ago and Austria is an anomaly, a black hole in the middle of the wolf's comeback. Despite having 'high wolf immigration potential', and despite being surrounded by established populations of wolves in Slovenia, Italy, Germany and Slovakia, the country had remained resolutely wolf-free. This was not a coincidence, Hubert Potočnik had told me, but to do with the national psyche. 'Austrians live in nature but they're not connected to nature,' Stefan said to me last night. 'It is not normal to want to kill everything.'

When Hubert realised that Slavc was bound for Austria, he endeavoured to get him as much press as he could in the hope that a celebrity wolf would be less likely to be shot. It is as illegal to kill a wolf in Austria as anywhere else in the EU, but the prevalent attitude here remains the four S's: *Sehen, schießen, schaufeln, schweigen* – 'See it, shoot it, shovel it, shut up.' Stefan told me about a bear killed recently outside Bad Eisenkappel; *murdered* was the word he used. They took the head and paws as trophies and ditched the body – the authorities found it by its tracking collar, dumped in the same hole. Poachers have learnt to use full-metal-jacket bullets, which, rather than exploding on impact and killing the animal instantly, instead pierce it cleanly, causing a haemorrhage. The wolf slinks off to die hours later, in agony, by which time the perpetrator is far enough away that connecting them to the crime is almost impossible.

Yet nature abhors a vacuum, and while wolf numbers remain low here, there are a lot more wolves than none. The country's first pair bred in 2016, and officially there are now seven packs, giving them several thousand square kilometres each. In the right conditions – few other wolves, abundant prey and plenty of space or, in other words, Austria – a breeding pair can produce eight or nine pups a year. The country is at a tipping point, one it has only recently acknowledged; 2022 saw a 230 per cent increase in wolf attacks on livestock. The farmers are furious, villagers are terrified, and there is a general, all-pervasive sense throughout the countryside that all hell has broken loose.

I sleep high, and the night is cold and full of stars. The next day I wake at dawn and follow Slavc's path as it winds back down from the ridgeline, both of us keeping to the forests as best we can. The landscape is messy, a tumble of rock and pine. I pass a torrent of water, flinging itself from the cliffs above and drilling a pool into the rocks below, the pool's banks lush with violets and moss, and a cold mist drifting like smoke among the trees.

At last I step from the trees onto the floodplain of the Drava. Poppies shiver at the edges of newly ploughed fields. Little woods, little villages, church steeples. The sweet, high bullets of the skylarks. Slavc turned his back on the mountains here. Maybe he was weary of the snow, but for the next few weeks he would stay low, his path tracking the valleys of Carinthia and Styria, following the rivers and the roads. He moved fast, so that in scarcely more than a month he had made it to the far side of the country.

Each village bar is shuttered. Faded posters outside, dated March 2020, remind people to wash their hands. Already they feel like artefacts, as do the bars, which have not reopened since. Skinny cats prowl like miniature tigers through the weeds. Small crossroads among fields of dandelions are marked by crucifixes, their Jesuses gaunt and bloody. Late afternoon I stop in a town square for an aperitif. I am tempted to loiter, for dinner and a bed, but I should probably keep on. This is a feeling that I knew from my last walk, of leaving a town at dusk and the sun going down and not yet knowing where I would spend the night. The evening's dew already softening the meadows, the insects swarming, and everything hung with a soft, blue light.

Outside a farmhouse, two kids' bicycles are propped beneath a tree. A light is on, and from the open door comes a woman's voice. '*Ave Maria*,' she sings, '*gratia plena*.' It is a beautiful voice, out here in the dusk, and I stop to listen. It can happen at this time of day that I feel suddenly overcome by the adventure and all the possibilities of the world, or it can happen that I feel acutely lonely, a stranger on the far side of the glass, and those two feelings can change in a heartbeat. A man joins her on the '*Amen*', and then, together, they begin again: '*Ave, Ave, Dominus. Dominus tecum.*' I am bearing witness to something deeply intimate, not meant for me, and suddenly embarrassed, I turn and walk away.

At another crossroads, another crucifix, and a little crowd of people standing, talking. Their shadows are long in this light. They look up at my approach and it is obvious that they are a single family. A boy of maybe seven stares at this approaching stranger and tucks himself behind his grandmother's legs. We all shake hands. The old man says something in German and the younger woman translates. 'My father would like to ask if you are hungry,' she says. It seems that I am always hungry.

Perhaps more than anything else, what I had learnt on my walk to Istanbul was that people are kind. Growing up I had mostly been taught to believe that strangers were not to be trusted, but from England all the way to Turkey that turned out not to be the case. I found people almost desperate to make some sort of connection. I would be walking through a little village in France, or Kosovo, and someone would run out of their house to tell me they were having a barbecue in their garden and please would I like to join them. I was given beds in churches and in mosques. There were times that year when I was terribly lonely, and those kindnesses kept me going. It seemed to make them happy, too.

The family ushers me inside. The grandfather stays

mostly in the kitchen. He has a coiled, taut energy I like, and we warm to each other in that effusive way that people sometimes do when they can scarcely communicate. He serves me up a huge plate of food: bread with caraway seeds; pickles; cheeses; venison salami from a neighbour; tomatoes from the garden; a lager from the fridge. There is a balcony to eat it on, and I sit looking north over the fields that sweep down to the Drava, just a couple of kilometres away. I can't see the river, but I can sense its shape from the way that the land constellates around it. A sprinkler clicks across the garden in the failing light. It is very quiet.

His daughter, in her thirties, comes to sit with me. Lena is a chef in the nearby town. She tells me, searching for common ground, that she follows the Queen on Instagram. Bats dip through the dusk. She asks me if I am a pilgrim. This street is on the *Jakobsweg*, the road to Santiago de Compostela. The next village along is named Gallizien, after Galicia. Before the pandemic they had a pilgrim stay with them – 3,000 kilometres to go – and they had assumed I was another. Perhaps I am not the right kind of wanderer, but she does not seem that bothered whether I am following a god or a wolf. She is a little thrilled to learn that a decade ago a wolf called Slavc stood in her garden.

Of course, in many ways I am the right kind of wanderer, what with my expensive boots and my passport in my pocket. On the way to Istanbul I assumed that all that hospitality was just the way the world worked, if only you opened yourself to it. I have since understood that not everyone on foot is so accepted, or so safe. A safe and simple passage depends on certain privileges of race, gender and class; of having the right documents; of walking by choice and not by force. Slavc is by no means alone in having to slip across borders, unnoticed.

The grandfather makes me a bed up on the balcony and I sleep once again beneath stars. The next day the grandmother joins me while I drink my coffee and helps me to translate the morning paper. She has a kind face and a high bun, a lovely laugh that scrunches up her eyes. The tabloid *Kronen Zeitung* is the country's biggest newspaper. It is Sunday, and at breakfast tables across Austria a wolf glares from the front page into comfortable family homes. It is one of those stock photos, all fang. Inside, across a double page, beneath a headline screaming 'Also our children are in danger!', is a grisly photo of a disembowelled sheep. 'The little ones can no longer play in the forest,' says a farmer. 'Everyone is afraid.'

'I don't like the wolf,' says the grandmother. 'I'm scared of the wolf. We are scared for our children. We have been here forty-three years, and when we came there were no wolves here.'

The grandfather has been up early, digging through boxes in the garage. He comes in now with some rolls of paper and unfurls them on the floor. They are dated 1950. They are the sorts of pictures you might once have found on a classroom wall, back when learning was by rote and morals were hammered home by way of terrifying small children. He has collected more than 200 of these posters, he says, but the two he has chosen to show me are both of *Rotkäppchen* – Little Red Riding Hood.

In the first, she is on a path through the forest – red cap, red skirt, red cheeks. It is spring and the foxgloves are blooming. A red squirrel flits through the branches of an oak tree. The girl is carrying a basket holding a bottle of wine and a piece of cake, intended for her sick grandmother who evidently lives in the cottage in the distance, the smoke curling from its chimney. On the path she has just come face-to-face with the wolf, who is trotting along like a dog far from home. She does not look too startled; he does not look too malevolent. I remember that line, a childhood memory: 'However, Little Red Riding Hood did not know what a wicked sort of an animal he was and was not afraid of him.'

In the second picture we are inside the grandmother's home. Grandmother's chair is ominously empty, her knitting set to one side. The girl is holding the posy of flowers that she has gathered in the woods. (It was by encouraging her to stray from the path to pick them that the wolf was able to reach the cottage first and gobble the grandmother up.) The wolf lies in bed in the grandmother's nightgown and bonnet and glasses, scarlet tongue lolling from his mouth, a goofy expression that is presumably his imitation of the woman he has just eaten. The door is open, and outside we can see the hunter who will shortly be coming in to save them both from out of the wolf's stomach, but not before the wolf has first eaten Little Red Riding Hood as well.

'Do you know this story?' says the grandfather.

I nod. 'Of course.' Who doesn't?

There is no story that has done more to sow our cultural hatred of the wolf. My daughter is five years old, and along with *Peter and the Wolf* and *The Three Little Pigs* and *What's the Time, Mr Wolf?*, she is already well versed in the canon. I tell her that wolves aren't as bad as people say they are, not really dangerous at all, but where's the fun in that? The fairytale wolf carries with it a delicious frisson of fear, the sheer thrill of being devoured.

It is this, the Grimms' version of the tale, that we're all raised on. First published in 1812, *Children's and Household Tales* comes second only to the Bible in Germany as the best-selling book of all time. An earlier French version cast the wolf as a seductive stranger, tricking *Le Petit Chaperon Rouge*, but by the time the story reaches Germany and is set down by the Grimms, it is entirely the girl's fault. In disobeying her mother and straying from the path, she gets her due. The wolf can't help his instincts, and salvation comes only in the form of the hunter reasserting the natural order.

The grandfather has one more poster to show me. Unfurled on the floor, it shows a wolf at the doorway of a house and several small goats cowering inside.

'Do you know this one?' says the grandmother. 'The Wolf and the Seven . . .' She pauses. 'How do you say a baby goat?'

'A kid.'

'Not kids!' she says. 'Baby goats.'

'A baby goat is called a kid.'

'Okay,' she says, although dubiously, like I am teaching her the swear words. 'The Wolf and the Seven Kids. Do you know it?'

I don't know it.

'Would you like to hear it?' And she pushes back in her chair and starts her story.

'Once there was a mother goat,' she says. 'And this goat had seven little kids. And they all lived in a little house in the woods, and she loved all of them the same, and as much as a mother had ever loved her children. But one day she needed to go and get some food from the woods. So she said to her seven children: "I am going into the woods. Don't open the door to any foreigner and watch out for the wolf, for if he gets into the house he will eat all of you up, skin and bones and all. He might come in disguise, but if he comes knocking you will recognise him by his rough voice and his black feet." And her children told her not to worry, so the mother goat went off into the woods. But it wasn't long before someone came knocking at their door.'

The grandmother raps on the table, beside my toast. She is clearly enjoying herself. The grandson is peering in from the kitchen door, not understanding the English, but he has heard it enough times by now he doesn't need to.

'"Who is it?"' bleats the grandmother sweetly. And

then her voice turns deep and gravelly. '"Open the door, little children. It's your mother. I have a present for each of you."

'But the voice was rough and they were scared. "You are not our mother," they said. "Her voice is kind and soft. You are the wolf."

'So the wolf went and got some chalk and ate it to make his voice sweet. And then he came back and he knocked on the door and he said: "Open the door, little children. It's your mother. I have a present for each of you."

'But through the window they saw his black paws and they said: "You are not our mother. Her feet are white. You are the wolf."

'And so the wolf went to the baker and got some flour for his feet, and then he went back to the house for a third time and he knocked and he said: "Open the door, my *dear* little children. Your mother has come home and I have a present for each of you."'

And one more time the grandmother knocks on the table, slow and mean.

'And the kids heard his soft voice and saw his white paws through the window and they said: "Maybe this time it is our mother."'

Her grandson's eyes glimmer. This is his favourite bit.

'So they opened the door and the wolf ran in and ate all of them up!' She looks around at us and pauses, grinning. 'Well. But not *all* of them. Because the seventh kid hid in the clock. And when the wolf was full he went outside and fell asleep in the sun under a tree, snoring so loudly that the branches shook. Soon afterwards the mother came home, and the whole house was turned upside down and none of her children were there. And then the youngest goat came out of the clock and told her mother what had happened, and you can just imagine how she cried then for her children.

'But when she went outside she saw the wolf asleep under the tree, and she saw that there was something moving about in his big belly. And so she sent the little goat to get scissors and needle and thread, and then she took the scissors and cut the wolf's belly open while he slept. And out jumped all six of her children! The wolf has been so greedy that he had swallowed them whole and they were not even hurt. And then the mother sent each of her kids to get the biggest stone they could carry, and they put all of the stones into the wolf's stomach and she sewed him back up. And then they all went and hid.

'At last the wolf woke up, and he was terribly thirsty because of the stones. So he got up and he walked to the well, rattling as he walked. And as he was leaning over the well to drink, the stones pulled him in and he drowned. And the mother and the seven kids ran out of the house and they all danced around the well, singing: "The wolf is dead. Yoo-hoo! Yoo-hoo! The wolf is dead! Yoo-hoo!"'

The grandmother beams at me, singing also. Her grandson is doing the dance. 'This is a nice story,' she says.

After breakfast, before I leave, she stands me in a corner of the living room, surrounded by icons of three of the archangels, Gabriel, Michael and Raphael, guardian of pilgrims, and she blesses me with a bottle of holy water that she keeps on the cat's scratching post. She presses a rosary into my hand, painted the red and white of Austria, and tells me to take care. Her husband teases her, kindly, for her faith, and he shakes my hand with great warmth. And then I am back outside, back on the path through the forest, and no one knows my name again.

The Drava is worked hard, forced through enough dams on its passage across Carinthia to power almost the entirety of the state. Slavc had grown up on the karst, and he would never have seen a river until he left home. Since then he had crossed a few streams and swum the Sava, but the Drava was something else entirely. Like a first glimpse of the ocean to someone from the mountains – an inconceivable feature of the geography. It is more than half a kilometre from bank to bank. Several hundred kilometres downriver, on the far side of Croatia, it will join the Danube, and from there it will flow all the way to the Black Sea.

Slavc had travelled more than 200 kilometres since he had come down off Slavnik Mountain. It was early afternoon on New Year's Eve when he arrived here, the last day of 2011, and he spent its remainder skulking west along the river's southern bank. At midnight he was still pacing. Over the city of Klagenfurt the sky blazed with coloured fire, blue and red and green, like a war, to summon in the new year. Maybe it was emerging unscathed from the bombardment that strengthened Slavc's resolve. Sometime between two and five in the morning, on the first day of 2012, he picked his way down the slope of the bank and dipped his paws to the icy water. At no point in his journey did turning round and going back ever appear to be an option.

Today, when I reach the Drava, it is warm. Men stripped to the waist are fishing from the north bank beside their cars, their boots open, their bellies out and white from winter like snow-capped mountains, wilting in the spring sunshine. Forested hills on both sides climb to bare rimrock above. The river swirls and eddies, a deep and earthy turquoise, and weed billows in its flow. If I didn't have my rucksack I'd be tempted to swim it in the spirit of the project. Not for the first time I find myself thinking of everything I'm burdened with in comparison to the wolf. My stove and bags of food; teeth. Warm clothes and waterproofs; fur. Walking stick; third leg, and fourth. Maps; an innate sense of courage and determination. Swimming trunks; not really.

I have a wash and wash my clothes and dry off on the beach. I find on the map a place to cross a few kilometres to the west, via a hydroelectric dam, and I follow the cycle path along the river. Every few hundred metres are crude A4 posters, a face in a mask and the mask crossed out – *Die pandemi ist Vorbei*, 'The pandemic is over' – distributed by the far-right channel AUF1.

I can see the dam long before I reach it. House martins gust about the structures. I walk out and look over the water, picturing Slavc on his first real swim. Nose and eyes and ears protruding, his rhythmic, rapid breathing, ruddering with his tail. Emerging from the water. Shaking himself dry and pausing, listening, and then trotting off into the scrub in the direction of the city.

I, too, trot off north. I pass Klagenfurt, edging its suburbs, and then I'm back in the countryside again. A few kilometres to the east is the town of Wolfsberg – 'Wolf Mountain'. The cherries are ripening now. I pass wooden barns on shaded lanes, riven with woodworm. Two horses stand in a field with their necks upon each other's backs. Timber lorries barrel through villages so that the wooden buildings rattle. Farmers with white hair, always white hair, buzz around on little tractors, doing the work of those half their age. It all seems self-consciously rural, everything of an aesthetic. Cats everywhere. I cross a four-lane highway via a green bridge meant for animals while the lorries shake the ground beneath my feet.

I rest up in a *Gasthof* on a lake. They have a rowing boat that I can borrow and each evening I go out at dusk, watching the newly arrived swallows dipping to the water's surface. I tell the owner of the guesthouse about my project and ask her if she knows any hunters. She makes some phone calls and Simon comes round for coffee. He is just back from his six months of national service in the military and says he is happy to be home. He seems much older than his nineteen years. Does he like living here? The city makes him stressed, he says; the pace is too much for him. Hunting is what he lives for.

There is no limit to the number of boar that they can shoot, and so that is mostly what they hunt. The farmers depend on the hunters to protect their crops, from both boar and deer. Simon's father first took him out when he was five. He fired his first gun at ten. Got his own gun at eighteen. I think of wolf pups, taught to hunt within the pack before they head out on their own. Now, at nineteen, Simon hunts with his friends. Stakes out boar, talks about girls. 'It's not just about the hunting,' he says. 'It's about everything. It is not a sport. It is not like football.'

I ask him what they would do if they came across a wolf.

He makes as if brushing something under the carpet. 'You have to be very careful,' he says, 'because they have these collars.'

Well rested, well fed, I leave the *Gasthof* two days later. In Austria's interior the fields are virid with new crops, the wheat knee-high. The land would have looked very different when Slavc passed through in early January. The snow thick, the ground frozen solid. In Anglo-Saxon, January was the *Wulf-monath*, when wolves became so famished, it was said, that they dared to enter villages. January's full moon is called the 'wolf moon'. In 2012 it fell on the ninth, and it found Slavc lying up for twenty-four hours in the woods outside Murau. Murau is one of those places that people come to Austria to photograph, clinging to either side of a narrow river that hurls itself through town. There is a castle on a hill, and in the windows of expensive shops perfect families of mannequins pose in lederhosen. I get an ice cream in the central Schillerplatz and sit down on an ornate bench in the shade. Old ladies are taking tea at the pavement cafés. Grand buildings with shuttered windows border the square on every side, plastered in primary pastel shades. It is all very pretty in a highly civilised way. But there is a far darker past beneath the surface of this valley.

I have in my bag a list compiled by the late German journalist Elmar Lorey that gives every werewolf trial in Europe that he uncovered from the archives. It begins in 1407, in Basel, and finishes three centuries and several hundred executions later, about fifty kilometres to the east of here. It mostly covers France and Holland and Austria, a few in Estonia and Latvia. For 300 years the werewolf trials were little brother to the contemporary witch hysteria, during which tens of thousands were murdered, almost all of them women. This list I hold is almost exclusively of men. Alongside the werewolves it includes *wolfsbanners*, men who were said to be able to command wolves to attack, and who occasionally rode on their backs. Styria and Carinthia, these two southern

Austrian states, were the very last bastion in Europe of this particular manifestation of paranoia and hate.

Vastl the Crooked was put on trial as a *wolfsbanner* in Murau in 1705, although the outcome is not recorded. I've stopped here to look for evidence, but there is nothing. Such people are rarely given statues. I climb to the church, where a small robotic lawnmower roams around the grass. Here, I think, there must be something, but there is only a lovely, calming atmosphere, and a noticeboard about a parishioner who is walking to Santiago. In this way, at least, the land heals terribly fast.

I follow the Mur upriver, on up the valley. These valleys groan under their weight of castles. Fish leap in the dusk. To the north the Hohe Tauern Mountains are beginning to stack up, still snowy at their peaks. This is the furthest that Slavc came north. Here he too bent west, persuaded by the landscape. These are quiet villages, empty trampolines on perfect lawns. There are fields where the land is flat, fields of dandelions, fields of clover. There were storms earlier, the thunder barrelling down the valley, but now the evening is fine again and the clouds are light and muddled, the late sun catching on their edges. Men in singlets watch me pass from ride-on mowers.

In the early eighteenth century this valley was experiencing a surge in wolf numbers not dissimilar to now. In 1716, 112 animals were killed by wolves here; in 1717, another sixty-four. These numbers are fairly low (398 animals will be killed in Carinthia in 2022), especially as even the poorest houses would have owned an animal or two. Most likely it was only a couple of wolf packs that had picked up bad habits, but some families were hit hard. Hans Eder lost eleven pigs. On Easter Sunday 1717, Rupp Prantstetter lost twelve of his twenty sheep. With no compensation, such massacres would have provoked an existential crisis. Animals were meat and milk and clothes, and how else were you to get through a winter with eight or ten children at home?

The community organised nine separate hunts and mass participation was expected. Yet the killings continued. It's possible that the entire valley marauding through the forest might not have been the most effective way to eradicate the wolves. Whatever the problem, it became obvious that an alternative strategy was needed. Yet rather than focus on organising a more effective hunt, or questioning the lack of aid for those who had fallen on hard times, in the time-honoured tradition of the human race, they decided to lay the blame on a group that was even worse off than themselves.

Two days later I follow Slavc into Tamsweg, another market town on the Mur. In June 1717, at the height of the wolf attacks, a local bailiff apprehended the beggar Philipp Ebmer here. It wasn't easy to be a beggar in eighteenth-century Austria. Courts were issuing stricter punishments for vagrancy, and it had been made illegal to shelter a beggar in your house. Giving alms had been supported by the Catholic Church as a means of amassing immaterial wealth for the next life, but increasingly beggars were struggling to explain exactly why hard-up peasants should be parting with their money, especially with the wolf now at the door.

Sensing an opportunity, the beggars began selling trinkets to ward off wolves. This in itself might not have meant much, but such expertise in charm-making helped foment the notion that these outcasts held some uncanny sway over the animals, an idea that they saw no reason to dispel. Withholding charity, the beggars insinuated, might be met with some future disaster. A storm, maybe, or a fire, or a depredation by a wolf. A bit of bread and a few coins for a charm would have felt worth it to move the problem on to your neighbour. There were rumours that the beggars could actually transform themselves into wolves and, again, sensing a profit, the beggars did nothing to discourage them. But this was as lucrative as it was risky.

A belief in werewolves was not uncommon. If the local priest was into the idea, chances were the parishioners would be too. The Enlightenment wasn't for everyone. Everyone had heard of Peter Stump, a werewolf who had terrorised Bedburg in Germany for a quarter of a century, devouring fourteen children, including his own son, and two foetuses that he had ripped from the womb and whose hearts he ate 'hot and raw'. When Philipp Ebmer was arrested in Tamsweg he gave the bailiff the names of several other beggars and said that they all had the ability to transform into wolves. The bailiff did not believe him, but clearly it was a matter for the courts. Seven men were arrested and taken to Moosham, eight kilometres down the valley.

Detailed court documents exist for just one of the men, Rupp Gell, forty-eight years old. He was first questioned on 23 June 1717. Most likely he had been begging in these parts for a long time. He denied that he could turn himself into a wolf but events weren't in his favour. He was already unpopular with local farmers, having recently been caught spending the night in a barn, for which he had received fifteen lashes. And besides, the others had already confessed.

Gell maintained his innocence during several interrogation sessions over the course of that summer, and in September they got out the instruments of torture. Raised into the air with a twenty-five pound stone hung from his feet, he admitted everything. The Devil had provided him with an ointment so that he could turn into a wolf, he said (he would wash in urine to transform back into a man). Brought before a court, Gell retracted his confession, but then they stretched him out on a rack for half an hour and he confessed all over again.

Positioned at the border between the human and the animal, the werewolf reminds us that we all have the capacity to regress to the level of a beast, that civilisation is a very thin veneer. This is why it both scares and thrills us. It reminds us that we don't have to be good, that we don't have to stay on the path. During the 300 brutal years in which Europe was gripped by this madness, the ins and outs of whether a human could actually turn into a wolf generated heated debate among religious scholars. Traditionally, lycanthropy was seen as the Devil's work – he would curse an individual or provide a black ointment to be applied to their intimate parts to effect the transformation. But this caused a problem for theologians, because how could the Devil alter what God Himself had made? In his 1599 *Discourse on Lycanthropy*, Jean Beauvoys de Chauvincourt came up with a workaround. Satan, he said, 'thanks to his pure and simple subtlety', was able to make people *believe* that they were 'brutal beasts'. Not only that, but by encouraging them to rub ointments onto themselves, 'the smell and the air [is] so infected by this filth that they ... act on the external senses of the audience, taking possession of their eyes; disturbed by this poison, they are persuaded that these transformations are real'. King James VI of Scotland (later also James I of England and Ireland) went even further. In his *Daemonologie* of 1597 – an otherwise hysterical, misogynistic screed responsible for the deaths of thousands of women accused of witchcraft – he chose a psychological interpretation for the werewolf that actually feels quite modern. Their belief was caused, he said, by a 'naturall superabundance of melancholie', which made people *think* that they were wolves. It was an idea picked up by John Webster in *The Duchess of Malfi* in 1613, in which Ferdinand, the Duke of Calabria, unbalanced by grief and guilt, comes to believe himself to be a wolf.

Just when they had Gell bang to rights, various theologians came by the courtroom to plead for leniency.

While he might think that he could turn into a wolf, they said, that was only because the Devil had bewitched him. 'Haven't we all had enough of experts?' said the privy council, arguing that anyway, the pact with the Devil was reason enough to burn him to death. In the end, thanks to the 'gracious' intervention of the Prince-Archbishop of Salzburg, Gell had his death sentence quashed and was handed over to the Venetians to row one of their galleys for the rest of his life, which probably wouldn't have been very long. If the Venetians were concerned about having a wolf on board, this has not been recorded.

In the modern werewolf canon, in *Ginger Snaps*, say, or *An American Werewolf in London*, the werewolf is typically well known to its victims, lurking just out of sight: the lover, the best friend. But reading down Lorey's list, what stands out are the outcasts: 'beggar', 'mute beggar', 'feeble-minded beggar'. It is a sorry list. In this quiet corner of Austria, far from its major cities, people were still being executed for lycanthropy and *wolfsbanning* into the first decades of the eighteenth century, later than anywhere else in Europe. How was it possible, I wonder, that such beliefs persisted for so long? How did a resurgence in wolf numbers lead to such irrationality and such barbarity? But then I wonder if, 300 years hence, historians will wonder how we managed to spin a story that blamed the disintegration of society on some desperate people fleeing wars in the Middle East.

The werewolf panic was dying down, along with the

wolves, but it wasn't quite over yet. In 1720 another beggar, twenty-four-year-old Simon Wind, was convicted of lycanthropy. He was interrogated in Salzburg, but was returned to Moosham for execution (by sword), so the locals could satisfy themselves that justice had been done. Wind was the last person to be executed as a werewolf in Europe (in 1725 there was one more execution, for *wolfsbanning*, in the east of Carinthia).

As a belief in werewolves faded, a new morality tale was needed. The oral versions of 'Little Red Riding Hood' evolved in an area of the mountains loosely analogous to that which saw the werewolf trials. The wolf, itself now rare to the point of myth, was newly cast in the role of the deviant vagrant, the amoral outcast, the thief of sheep and the destroyer of families. It is a role that it has maintained to this day.

Wolves and woods exist in intimate relationship, and it is from their union that the fairytales were born. As the deep, dark woods have recolonised the pastures, as the wolves have walked back into Europe, so the stories have crept back too. But we live, apparently, in a more enlightened age now. For some audiences the wolf has need of a different narrative, a character arc for the twenty-first century. This time around, it has fallen to science to provide it.

That is not to say that our anxieties, projected onto the wolf and masquerading as biology, have not been a genre of their own for a long time. A thirteenth-century bestiary has the wolf as 'the devil, who is always envious of mankind and prowls around the sheepfolds of the Church's believers, to kill their souls and corrupt them'. O. W. Williams, in *Some Animals of Pioneer Days in Pecos County*, called the wolf 'a specialist in carnage', conceding that 'possibly it has its uses – but it will require a skillful man with a very high powered magnifying glass to ascertain them'. William Hornaday, first director of the New York Zoological Park (later Bronx Zoo), claimed that 'there is no depth of meanness, treachery or cruelty to which they do not cheerfully descend'. Perhaps my favourite comes from the Comte de Buffon's *Natural History*, thirty-six volumes of which he published throughout the eighteenth century. Despite being a remarkable work of scholarship, when it comes to the wolf he cannot resist the following: 'In fine, the wolf is consummately disagreeable; his aspect is base and savage, his voice dreadful, his odour insupportable, his disposition perverse, his manners ferocious; odious and destructive when living, and, when dead, he is perfectly useless.'

How Wolves Change Rivers, four minutes of YouTube narrated by journalist George Monbiot, has clocked up forty-five million views at the time of writing. It is based on a story that Monbiot tells in his book *Feral*, about the wolf's reintroduction to Yellowstone National Park in the 1990s, having been brought down from Alberta in Canada, and the ecological unfolding that this set in motion. It might seem an unlikely video to go viral, but if in earlier times our anxieties were about the state of our souls or how the wilderness might be productively tamed, today there is no concern more existential than whether we have wrecked our planet beyond repair.

Maybe you know the story; maybe it has turned up in your feed. For a century and more, since the wolf's eradication from most of the contiguous United States, the elk in Yellowstone had no predators. Their population had exploded and they were eating all the saplings. The forests were doomed. The wolf's return made a dent in elk numbers, but more significantly, it restored to the park what ecologists refer to as *a landscape of fear*. To understand this, think of how you felt when you left the house during that first spring of Covid. How you wore disposable gloves to the supermarket and plotted your route through a crowded place. How someone coughing on the train sent a collective shudder through the carriage. This is how the herbivores feel. Nothing is obviously different, but every sense is now cued to some amorphous threat. The wolf need not be there in front of you; that is not the point. It is the feeling of *being prey*.

The elk's instincts had in no way atrophied after generations of stagnation. The animals quickly became skittish, and avoided the valleys and gorges where they could not keep watch while they grazed. Willow and aspen started returning along these river valleys, and as they did so, the birds moved back in, and the beavers. The dams the beavers built formed habitat that favoured other creatures – otters, ducks and fish, the reptiles and amphibians. And as the trees' roots shored up the banks, the rivers became more sinuous, forming slower-flowing pools that attracted yet more wildlife. 'The wolves,' says Monbiot, 'changed the behaviour of the rivers.' In scientific terms this is a 'trophic cascade', the indirect influence that a species can have on those more than one level below it in the food chain. In conservationist terms this is a modern wolf, with a value greater than its bounty, and with an integral role in the ecosystem.

When the pro-wolf lobby is asked to justify the wolf's return, it is invariably this story that it points to. There is perhaps no other group of animals on Earth that has been so press-ganged into a symbol of how catastrophically we have misunderstood our planet. Not only as regards their impact on the elk; there have been dozens of books written about the dynamics of the Yellowstone packs, focusing on their humane virtues of courage, loyalty and care, all seeking to demonstrate that we could learn a lot from the natural world. It has the perfect narrative arc, the evil wolf redeemed. But in truth it is hard to find such simple truths in something as messy as an ecosystem.

'The danger we perceive is that all changes to the [Yellowstone] system, now and in the future, will be attributed solely to the restoration of the wolf,' wrote Doug Smith, project leader for the Yellowstone reintroduction. That the wolf is responsible for the changes in elk behaviour, and the knock-on trophic cascade, is hypothesis only, and other hypotheses are available. Concurrent with the wolf reintroduction, populations of other important predators – cougars and grizzlies – were on the rise, and the quota for hunting elk outside the park had just been increased, all of which may have amped up the elk's landscape of fear. Many of the papers responsible for the trophic-cascade narrative were authored by William Ripple and Robert Beschta, but other researchers, using different methods, have got different results for how well the trees are growing. As the climate warms, the growing season in Yellowstone has increased by more than a month since the 1990s, favouring the saplings. During the late eighties 129 beavers were released north of the park, which could, it seems fair to suggest, be at least in part responsible for the increase in beaver numbers. Beaver dams raise the water level, a higher water level is good for the willows, and thus a different cascade begins to tumble. And even if we do allow the wolf to take credit for the changes that have happened in Yellowstone, that does not mean we can map the results directly onto Europe, with its vastly different habitats.

Christopher Wilmers and Oswald Schmitz drew on Ripple and Beschta's Yellowstone work to argue that, by preventing moose from eating saplings in Canada's boreal forest, the grey wolf has the potential to mitigate the emissions of several million cars per year through the carbon that the trees would lock away. Extrapolate for forests worldwide and the wolves' impact would be enormous. In a 2023 paper Schmitz and others did exactly that, calculating that allowing the wolf and eight other species groups – including wildebeests, elephants and baleen whales – to thrive could, through the trophic cascades they set in motion, draw down up to 95 per cent of the carbon needed to give us a chance of keeping global warming to 1.5 degrees Celsius. These are astonishing numbers. The wolf is, quite literally, going to save the world.

Will it? Can we make the data prove it? Science writer Emma Marris suggests that there is a 'beauty in the alternative story: that even ecosystems as well studied as Yellowstone remain beyond our ken'. But it's just so much easier to justify why we need the wolf if we can say how many cars they are taking off the road.

The wolf, as we know, has been misrepresented in the past, and to do so again, albeit in a different light, is not progress. Certainly the wolf's return has affected ecosystems, and David Mech, one of the world's leading wolf experts, who has worked extensively in Yellowstone, does not discount all the claims. But he believes something equally important to be at stake. 'We as scientists and conservationists who deal with such a controversial species as the wolf have a special obligation to qualify our conclusions and minimize our rhetoric, knowing full well that the popular media and the internet eagerly await a chance to hype our findings. An inaccurate public image of the wolf will only do a disservice to the animal and to those charged with managing it.' Once vilified, now deified, the real challenge remains as difficult as ever, to see the wolf for what it is, which is a wolf.

The wolf, as I have said, was once the most widely

distributed, non-domesticated land mammal on the planet. I often wonder whether any animal has likewise dominated the territory of our subconscious. All of us know, one way or the other, whether we have ever seen a wolf or not, how we feel about them. I wish I could tell you that I am able to see it as it is, unencumbered by my needs, but I'm afraid that isn't true either. I am drawn to Slavc, I am following his trail across Europe, because I desperately want to think of him as a beacon of hope in fragile times. The wolf's return urges the question, if wolves can do it, then what else might not be inevitable? At this late hour, if we can learn to love that which was once most reviled, might we not find similar compassion elsewhere? Scientifically, of course, it means nothing of the sort. But then, I think, if we don't let the wolf have its story, will we even be moved to think about it any more?

It is because animals are not driven by story that they will remain forever alien to us.

6

A gaunt Wolf was almost dead with hunger when he happened to meet a House-dog who was passing by. 'Ah, Cousin,' said the Dog. 'Your irregular life will soon be the ruin of you. Why do you not work steadily as I do, and get your food regularly given to you?'

'What must I do?' asked the Wolf.

'Hardly anything,' answered the House-dog. 'Bark at beggars and fawn on the people of the house. In return you will get titbits of every kind, not to speak of kind words and caresses.'

The Wolf had such a beautiful vision of his coming happiness that he almost wept. But just then he noticed that the hair on the Dog's neck was worn and the skin was chafed.

'What is that on your neck?' said the Wolf.

'Nothing at all,' replied the Dog. 'Only the place where the collar is put on at night to keep me chained up. One soon gets used to it.'

'Chain?' he asked. 'You mean you are not free to go where you choose?'

'No,' said the Dog, 'but what's the difference?'

AUSTRIA, SPRING

*'All the difference in the world!' he cried, and away
ran the Wolf to the woods.*

Aesop, 'The Dog and the Wolf'

From the Mur valley, Slavc moved back into the mountains. It was mid-January, early in 2012. Travelling over the compacted snow of Katschberg's ski slopes he would have found the going easy. I follow him up, another season, a decade on. It is early May, and after these weeks of warmth the mists roll in and then the rain begins, heavy and persistent. That night I sleep huddled beneath the awning of a mountain restaurant not yet open for the season, its outside decks still icy with old snow. The fog is so thick below me it is as though I am marooned. When day breaks again it is no different.

That evening it is dark and cold and the rain is still heavy when Lena Schaidl and Werner Ramsbacher usher me in. A friend in Tamsweg, two nights before, had seen the forecast and made a phone call for me. I sit in their farmhouse kitchen devouring chicken and leeks out of the range. I go to bed in an attic room weighted down beneath wool blankets, and all night long the rain hammers on the glass. I am terribly glad to be inside.

By the next morning it has stopped. I shower and wander downstairs. In the kitchen they have left out breakfast for me. Coffee and freshly baked cake, cheese and eggs and ham. The radio is playing English pop. There are framed photos on the walls showing the two of them, before kids, with friends at the summits of mountains. I eat and then I walk outside into the yard. The clouds are thick and close and mist is rising from the valley. Down below is the small town of Rennweg, and the mountains rearing up behind, the direction that I have come.

Lena and Werner have been up since half-past four. Lena is tall and wiry from hard work, dressed in a pink headscarf and green wellies, and she has Ronja, who is two, perched on one hip. I follow her into the barn. It is cool, ecclesiastical, the thick, sweet stench of slurry. Each cow has her name above her stall, like the place settings at a wedding. Ozeane, Iris, Britta, Freida, Beauty, Annabelle, Vanessa, Maja, Anja, Blume, Inka, Amelie, Veilcha. Flies revolve. Vanessa chews on Maja's ear. Lena walks the length of the stable with Ronja clamped under one arm, throwing down hay with the other. The cows bend their heads to eat, as though at prayer. Lena points to a shovel and as we talk I scrape the night's shit out through the grate.

'Once there were a lot of people on a farm,' she says in her excellent English. 'Big families. Day labourers. But now you have just a couple. Dairy farmers quit every year. They grow up as kids never having had a summer holiday. I know what it means to have a holiday. I know what it means to have a *weekend*.'

The farm has been in Werner's family for 300 years, give or take. Generation after generation eating in the kitchen, passing through this yard. One morning, two years ago, Werner's father fell six metres from the hayloft to the concrete floor where we are standing. For a month they kept him in an induced coma; then he died. He had done all those little jobs that now there wasn't time for. With Ronja, Lena can only do so much, and Werner is not yet used to working by himself. Friends ask him why he does it when there are better-paid jobs down in Spittal that clock off at five o'clock on a Friday, but being last in line of so many accumulated generations is a hard weight to shrug off.

'The collar around the neck of small farmers is getting tighter,' Lena says. 'Cow food is much more expensive with the war in Ukraine. Milk prices are okay, but who knows. The vegans are saying that dairy milk is only for children. They are saying that milk is full of infections and pus. And now the wolf comes along. It isn't the wolf that makes people stop, but the wolf is so *emotional*. People don't blame the EU or the war. They blame the wolf.'

Lena sets Ronja down and pours feed into the troughs. 'Everything is exhausting,' she says. 'I read about young families doing great things in the farming papers, but where do they get the money from? Where do they get the *energy* from? I'd be interested to go back in five years and see how things have worked out. It's not the romantic lifestyle you hear about. When I worked at the Wolf Center, I thought that was a lot of work. It's nothing like this.'

I follow her through into the dairy. Everything sparkles, chrome and clean. 'The Wolf Center?' I ask.

She pulls on a white apron and uncoils the hose and sets to work scrubbing the floors. Lena, it turns out, has a welly in both worlds. In her past life she was a wildlife biologist, and her wildlife was wolves. She worked at the Wolf Science Center, just outside of Vienna, one of the leading institutes worldwide researching wolf behaviour. She did her thesis on the comparative spatial awareness of wolves and dogs, under one of its founders, Kurt Kotrschal. Wolves, it seems, are much better able to remember where they left stuff. 'Dogs,' Lena says, 'have lost a lot of these abilities, because they no longer need them.'

Ronja wanders into the dairy dragging a lump hammer behind her.

'I got to know the wolf from the other side,' says Lena. 'Eye to eye. I don't like the approach that the Earth is only here for humans.'

Wolves were her passion. She had assumed they would be her career. She came here first on holiday, renting the cottage on the property. Then she met Werner, and so it goes. She started helping him with the animals because she preferred it to staring at a computer. The romance of hard graft to city academics. But it didn't take long before her past was catching up with her.

'I didn't do farmer training,' she says. She is bent now with the hose over the milk churns, cleaning them to a sheen. 'But I did do a five-day intensive course. And on the course a Carinthian politician got up to speak, and everything she said was so wrong. She said that wolves are nasty. That they kill for fun. And in the end I couldn't sit there any longer. I said, "Excuse me, but I have to say something here." I kind of outed myself.'

She straightens up, a hand at the small of her back. 'I understand it,' she says. 'If I'm a farmer, give me one hard reason why I should like wolves. If half my sheep are eaten then I'm not interested in balance. But here's what I don't understand about farmers. If you keep animals, you should understand animals. You should understand that if you shoot one wolf, another one will come.'

A US study bears this out. For each wolf killed, the chances of livestock getting predated the next year rose by 4 per cent for sheep and 5–6 per cent for cattle. This continued until a quarter of a state's wolf population was shot, at which point predations did decline. But as soon as the kill rate sank below 25 per cent, predations ticked up again. Why this happens is unclear, but it is thought that a pack is weakened if its most experienced members are removed, making them more dependent on domestic animals, not less. If the main breeding pair is killed, the pack may splinter into smaller units, each of which can have its own pups. Just as human birth rates rise in the aftermath of war, so shooting wolves can encourage them to breed.

Yet the local farming papers advise against other livestock protection measures. To keep guardian dogs or to build fences is framed as an act of capitulation, an acceptance that the wolf is here to stay. 'They build these fences at country fairs to show people what the countryside will look like, but it's completely over the top,' Lena says. 'It looks like they are trying to keep *refugees* out.'

'Is it possible to live with the wolf?' I say.

She shrugs. 'They haven't tried. I would like to try. I don't think the farmer should disappear for the wolf. But if my animals are attacked and I have done nothing to protect them, the first thing I am thinking is not stupid wolf, but stupid me.'

Unlike their neighbours, Werner and Lena are building fences. Rather than watch their livestock get picked off (and, I presume, under Lena's influence) they have fenced an area of two and a half hectares on the mountain, large enough to hold the handful of young cows born this past winter. To qualify for EU subsidies they must keep their animals out of doors for 150 days in a year, with sixty of those days up on the *Alm* – the mountain pasture. Werner's grandfather would have been up there minding the animals at seven years old, but cowherds don't come so cheap these days. Building the fence has been a huge amount of work. Every winter they will have to drop the wires so the winter snows don't snap them, and every summer they must erect them again. There hasn't been time to fence near the house, so for spring the cows are still stuck in the barn. They lost one cow to a wolf before the fence went up, but they have not lost any since.

'What does Werner think?' I ask.

'He's angry that the wolf is here, because it's causing so much trouble,' she says. 'It's not just the workload. He's angry that it's made people so strange.' The reaction to their fence was far worse than she had expected. 'If you try to protect your animals, you're a traitor.'

'Have you lost friends?'

'Not friends,' she says. 'All the farmers help each other. But I'm not sure if they trust us, and if you can trust them. The things they say about our family have definitely changed.'

Because of Lena's background there have been rumours since the start. 'They say that I am bringing the wolves here, and keeping them in the basement or something. And that's the reason we're building fences. They come and tell me when a sheep was killed, like I am the wolf's representative.' Local leaders have been only too enthusiastic to oxygenate the rumours.

'I live here with my little daughter, and I'm really afraid that people—' She pauses, unsure whether to finish the thought. 'I'm afraid that people will burn down our farm. I mean, it's extreme. But I'm really not sure what people are thinking and how angry this can get.'

We head back outside. House martins dip through the yard and now the sun is burning off the cloud. From somewhere their dog is barking. It gets out through a hole in the fence that they have not had the time to find or fix. Lena shakes her head. 'You're not my therapist,' she says. 'But you did ask. To be honest, if the wolf disappeared overnight, I wouldn't even be sad any more.'

Werner appears, pushing Ronja along on a pile of hay with a pitchfork, in games unchanged for centuries. She is giggling heartily. Ronja is the same age as my own son, and I think about her growing up here. Knowing where her food comes from, and how to provide, and the true things of the world. A life with animals beneath the open sky and a yard full of dirt and dogs. Is there anything more important than feeling grounded when the world lacks other constants? But I look at Ronja on her pile of hay and I wonder if she will want this life. Will her parents want it for her? Or is this more urban romanticisation of the sort that also likes the idea of having wolves back?

'Do you make a living from this?' Werner asks me as I stand there, watching, scribbling my notes. He is off to spend the day hammering fence posts into the ground; I am off for a walk.

'I'm always wondering why people are so intensely *emotional* about this topic,' Lena says to me once Werner has gone off to the pasture. 'At the Centre, Kurt was always saying that the wolf and the human are so closely bonded because of their style of living. How they share the same space. How they live socially in groups. How they look after their children.' She picks Ronja up from where she is sitting in the grime and pops her back on a hip. 'That's why wolves became dogs. I don't know if it's true, because everyone's talking about the wolf in such a negative way here. But maybe this really is the reason why it's so emotional. Because it's the animal that has been so important to us for so many thousands of years.'

She urges me to visit the Wolf Science Center before I continue with my journey. After all this time, the prospect of seeing wolves in the flesh is tantalising. Later that morning, I make a phone call.

I step off the train at Vienna's Hauptbahnhof with no idea of how to find Kurt Kotrschal, Lena's former supervisor. But as the platform clears there is a man coming towards me with a dog on a short lead, both of them at a prim trot. The dog is brown and foxy, a Eurasier, and she carries herself in a way that suggests she is *exceptionally* well trained. Kurt himself has a little of the lupine – thick grey stubble creeping high up on his cheeks, slabs of eyebrow and moustache, a neat thatch of grey hair. We shake hands, say hello. The dog stands poised beside him, like an extension of his mind.

He bustles me through the station and underground into the car park. He opens the boot and the dog hops neatly in and he closes the boot and we get in ourselves and he drives up and out into the city. The radio is dialled to opera. He has just arrived himself, from his house out in the country where he has lived since he retired, but he still keeps his apartment from when he used to lecture at the University of Vienna.

He points out landmarks as we crawl through the weekend traffic. The State Opera, the Museum of Natural History. It is a bit of a shock, all these people going places, after so long in a tent. We pass the parliament building, covered in scaffolding and hoardings. 'Currently under renovation,' Kurt says. 'A little like our democracy.'

We park in the street outside his apartment. It was the right distance from the University to give the dog a good walk each morning. Then it would snooze in a corner of the lecture theatre as professor and students discussed its species' development and nature. Kurt has arrived with five gallons of water from an Alpine stream to top up his aquarium, and I lug it up the crumbling flights of spiral stairs. He has kept fish since he was five years old, his first non-human love. The flat is a magnificent place, on the building's corner, so that from the room he puts me up in I have a view down two boulevards. Some huge plant grows directly from the aquarium, shading one half of the lounge, the fish swimming among its roots. A bookcase takes up an entire wall, filled with natural histories and leather-bound classics and copies of his own works, in German: *Wolf, Dog, Man: The Story of a Millennia-Old Relationship; Wolf and Us: How He Became Our First Pet, and Why His Return Offers Opportunities.* On one cover Kurt and a vast wolf sit side by side, both of their furs turning to silver, their eyes both held by the same distant point.

We go out for dinner. We sit on a wide street on a close, warm night and Kurt orders the liver and I have a stew of dumplings and goulash. It is several degrees warmer than in the mountains and Austrian food feels entirely unsuited to this weather. The wine is so acid it makes me pucker. And Kurt tells me about his life's work.

'We know that *Homo sapiens* came to Europe forty-two thousand years ago,' he says, with that charming way of saying 'we' as though all scientists were engaged in some great, collective endeavour. 'We know that they found Neanderthals here, and that within a thousand years they had driven them to extinction. They would have found an incredible diversity of grazers. The aurochs. The woolly mammoth. The steppe bison. The European hippopotamus. They would have found an incredible diversity of carnivores. The cave bear. The cave hyena. The cave lion. Highly social animals. It was not a pleasant place to live. But they had a big brain, they worked it out. And who runs into each other? Wolves and humans. That's pretty funny, don't you think?'

A couple on their evening stroll see Kurt's dog tucked neatly beneath his chair. She is one of those dogs that people are drawn to and the man reaches down to pet her. She is thoroughly disinterested. It is a little awkward, in the way that such things are. Kurt ignores him too.

'The point is,' says Kurt, as they wander on, 'we didn't just get together with wolves forty-two thousand years ago. We *stayed* together.'

I wonder why we sought out that relationship, but he admonishes me for my utilitarian thinking. 'These people were animists,' he says. 'They believed in brotherhood and sisterhood with animals. I wouldn't be surprised if first contact was between shamans and wolves.' No one set out to domesticate a wolf, he means, any more than someone harnessed fire with the intention of smelting metal. Human progress has lurched forward through random experiment, a series of fortuitous missteps.

And yet the benefits of wolves to *Homo sapiens*, once enlisted, would have been obvious. 'I know from my own experiences, if you spend all night with socialised wolves, that no one could surprise you,' Kurt says, like knowing this was the most normal thing in the world. Socialised wolves would have kept wild wolves at bay, as well as other predators. That would have allowed us to move through the world with less fear, rather than skulking about in caves. Originally humans were cursorial hunters – running down our prey until we exhausted them through our superior endurance – and wolves hunt in the same manner. We would have worked well together. Mammoth hunting might have only become viable when we began to collaborate. As time went on, wolves became more embedded in our lives. They played with our kids. They kept us warm at night.

But just how a wild wolf became first colleague, and ultimately pet, is one of science's enduring mysteries. There are plenty of theories but few hard facts, very few bones. The Campfire Theory imagines wolves being drawn to the fires of early *Homo sapiens*, lured in by roasting meat. They would have scavenged for bones, nosed through the middens; maybe a curious human tossed one a scrap of fat. In time the wolves began to feel territorial about their newly adopted humans. According to this view it could be said that wolves, in making the first move, domesticated themselves. Realising the benefits, humans kept the more friendly wolves around, intentionally feeding them. Friendly wolves begat friendlier wolves. And eventually, so the story goes: dogs. It does not seem implausible.

Except that Kurt does not believe a word of it. 'Everybody who knows wolves knows this doesn't work,' he says. 'Not being in a social relation from the beginning is dangerous. You must make a wolf respect your children and not consider them as prey. Otherwise, one day or another, the wolf will try to test this strange animal. If wolves had eaten children we would not have dogs today. To engage in true cooperation you need to hand-rear a wolf.'

Kurt, who by his own estimate has hand-raised thirty wolves – perhaps more than anyone else on the planet – has a good idea about this. The work at the Wolf Science Center is experimental archaeology; he is sceptical of academics who theorise from the library. 'It means beginning at younger than ten days,' he says, which is before the eyes have opened. 'This is a *sine qua non*. For hunter-gatherers, this would have meant breastfeeding.'

'Pardon?'

'Well, they didn't have bottles,' he says.

And indeed, when I look into it, I find definitive accounts of women breastfeeding canines well into the twentieth century. Australian Aborigines breastfed the young of wild dingoes they had killed. Women have been recorded as nursing dogs on the Malay Peninsula, the Pacific Islands, in New Guinea and South America.

It was less common in Europe, although there is a reference from ancient Greece in Euripides' *The Bacchanals*:

> Some in their arms held kid, or wild-wolf's cub,
> Suckling it with her white milk; all the
>   young mothers
> Who had left their new-born babes, and stood
>   with breasts
> Full swelling.

It's a neat inversion of Romulus and Remus, and those other tales of abandoned children who were suckled and saved by nursing she-wolves. Interspecies breastfeeding feels taboo, although quite why, when the UK gets through fifteen billion litres of cow's milk annually, is unclear. And as a means of taming animals, it does appear to be effective. Worldwide, there are anthropological accounts of women suckling not only dogs, but also goats, pigs, monkeys, bears, bison, possums and elephants. One anthropologist, writing in the 1970s, observed that 'in spite of . . . harsh treatment the [Aboriginal] dogs appear to be so successfully imprinted on their owners at the puppy stage that they remain devoted and faithful'. Various cases in the literature document the mother favouring the animal that she is nursing over her own child, and in exceptional instances killing her baby so that 'the puppies might not be robbed of their food'. Such imprinting would have lasted long after the animal was weaned.

Except that there are those who don't believe a word of that, either. 'We like dichotomies,' the evolutionary geneticist Greger Larson would say to me in the School of Archaeology, in Oxford, some months later. 'We don't like continuums. And what's more one-off than going into a cave and grabbing a wolf puppy and bringing it back for *reasons*, and then going: "Right, if we continue to select this thing and bottle-feed it, that's going to turn into dogs?" Fuck off. It's Kipling all over again, only without the creativity. It's boring Kipling. In which case, what are we even talking about?'

Greger is fast-talking, affable, American. I had gone to visit him after my return, as I had hoped he might be able to shed some light on the various hypotheses. I was wrong.

'Dogs can't exist,' he says, throwing up his hands. 'They just don't exist. If you can't explain it, it must not exist.'

Greger has spent the last decade of his career trying to explain it. He has gathered shards of dozens of ancient wolf bones from museums throughout the world, ground each to a powder, and sucked out the DNA to sequence their individual genomes. The latest research suggests that the modern dog is more closely related to Asian wolves than to European ones, and thus that dogs would have been first domesticated in the East. Greger hazards at Siberia, around something like 20,000 years ago, but it's all just informed guesswork. If there was a missing link – a wolf on the way to becoming a dog – then some of this might be easier to figure out, but no one has ever found such a skeleton.

'It might as well have been shot here out of a cannon from Mars and just landed in Siberia,' he says.

Twenty thousand years ago was the last glacial maximum. A challenging climate and very little available protein – did these two species form a partnership rather than both go extinct? 'It sounds fantastical,' says Greger. 'But, you know, in the absence of anything else . . .' Much of the fossil record was scoured from the earth as the glaciers retreated, and maybe this explains the lack of bones.

What *is* certain is that dogs were domesticated long before we domesticated any other animal or, for that matter, ourselves. Austrian scientist Wolfgang Schleidt suggests that rather than bringing the wolf into the *domus*, or home, which early hunter-gatherers did not have, that instead the wolf introduced to us the notion of the den. With 250,000 wolves worldwide, but up to 900 million dogs of 360 different breeds spanning every continent, it's clear that, from the wolf's point of view, getting domesticated has been a devastatingly successful strategy. Forget the wolf's ongoing recolonisation of the Alps. From this perspective, the wolf has already regained its foothold as one of the most widespread mammals on the planet, and it has done it disguised as a dog. For humans, taming the wolf was the first step in a chain of events that freed us from our own animal constraints. It led to the domestication of the other animals and the crops, the spread of agriculture, the liberation of humanity, and all the beauty and all the mess that we are surrounded by today.

But if it wasn't the Campfire Theory, and if it wasn't breastfeeding pups, how did a wolf end up living in one in three UK homes? Like Kurt, Greger holds no truck with early humans starting out with the express intention of creating something like a dog. 'Mild tolerance is the first step along this whole pathway,' he suggests.

Ecomorphs are different groups of the same species with a recent common ancestor, superficially the same, but pursuing different resource strategies. Take the killer whales off the Pacific Northwest. One pod hunts marine mammals; another pod hunts salmon. They use the same hunting grounds, they swim past one another all the time, but they just don't interact. You could say they have different cultures – 'like Sharks and Jets,' says Greger. In time, the two pods stop recognising each other as the same species. They stop breeding, swapping genes. Ultimately they diverge to a point where they couldn't have fertile offspring, even if they wanted to.

'Wolves are exactly the same,' says Greger. 'They are so plastic in their behaviour. They learn very quickly and they can take advantage of lots of different resources.' It is possible to imagine a wolf population that, rather than migrating with the caribou or hunting moose within its territory, begins to embed itself with hunter-gatherers, increasingly dependent on them for resources. Slowly, over time, these wolves become different from the others. Maybe they teach their pups that this arrangement is beneficial; maybe the humans teach their own babies the same. Gradually, a relationship forms. Ultimately, they realise that they can no longer live without each other.

'And this solves a very big problem,' says Greger. With the other theories, if a tamed wolf elopes with a wild wolf, you're straight back to square one. But if the socialised wolves have split from other wolves to the extent that they no longer desire to breed with other wolves, if you've turned off the gene-flow tap, then you have a much better way of explaining how different behaviour might embed.

How you might end up, one day, with a dog.

The next day, a Sunday, Kurt and I leave Vienna early and drive out to the Wolf Science Center, an hour outside the city. We race between fields of sunflowers and vines at quite alarming speeds. He tells me, with the increasingly warm summers, that the wine here is becoming extremely good.

The car park is full, and young parents wheel prams along the paths, past the enclosures. In the gift shop are stuffed wolf pups, alongside wolf mugs and wolf caps and snow globes with wolves inside and copies of Kurt's books. Kurt moves through the park with an easy familiarity, as though he is strolling through his garden. He points out the boar and the deer. Mouflon scale the wall of an old quarry face, moving upwards from ledge to ledge as though puppeted by string. But neither of us has come here for the herbivores.

We carry on. Kurt gestures expansively towards an

enclosure thick with vegetation. 'And this is where we have . . .' He pauses, checking himself. 'Not *we*. They are not my wolves any more.'

Kurt co-founded the Wolf Science Center in 2008, back before Austria had any wild wolves of its own. He would get to know each wolf, each individual personality. Some would snuggle up to you at night, while others would shit on your pillow. Kurt is in his early seventies and he does not have it in him to devote another fifteen years to raising the next generation.

At the end of 2020 Kaspar, the last of the founding wolves, passed away. The two penultimate members had died the year before, and the tributes left to them on the Center's blog are surprisingly moving. 'In the last few weeks and months, in which you have continued to deteriorate physically, you have become gentler in nature and also more open to us humans,' reads Kaspar's obituary. 'In the end we got to meet the wolf who had been hiding behind the working machine for years, the real Kaspar.'

'This is not my place any more,' says Kurt. 'Science is one thing . . .' He searches for the words, aware he is saying things that perhaps scientists should not say. 'But,' he concludes at last, 'there is a very strong mutual bond.' He whistles into the enclosure, as you might call a dog. 'Hello,' he says. 'Hello?' Nothing moves in the shrubbery. A visitor eyes him as though he is quite mad. 'They're probably hanging around the test house,' Kurt says. 'Waiting for something interesting to happen.'

The purpose of the Center was to raise wolves and dogs in identical environments: outdoors in large enclosures, in packs, bottle-fed from birth. Neither would be wild, but standardising the nurture would enable the researchers to focus on the nature of each animal, to see how the genetic differences between wolves and dogs manifest with everything else controlled for. Kurt describes the wolves as their partners in the research, although he seems to have less affection for the dogs. The work being done here is groundbreaking. There is nowhere else like it in the world.

The Center's ongoing experiments have uncovered small yet crucial changes in a dog's behaviour that have become genetically embedded over time. It is these changes that make it possible to share a house with them. 'Dogs have an inbuilt ability to realise what you want,' says Kurt as I follow him through the park. 'Maybe the wolf has this as well, but the wolf simply doesn't care.' A dog understands that its master's food is not for sharing, but a wolf will never accept this. To a wolf, the very concept of a master is anathema. A dog is a wolf that has not grown up, but that has remained in arrested development, never gaining independence. Give a dog a locked box containing food and it will look to its owner for help. Give the same box to a wolf and it will try to open it until the clock runs out, perhaps until the end of time. Point, and a dog will look where you are pointing; a wolf will look at your finger. A dog expects clear leadership and works best within a hierarchy. A wolf will only cooperate, at best, if it sees the roles as equal. Sometimes it likes to take the lead.

Kurt traces this cleft in their behaviour to the moment when we shifted from an egalitarian, hunter-gatherer society to a hierarchical, sedentary one. That is to say, it was people who changed first. He rattles briefly through the history of civilisation. 'Twelve thousand years ago, in Anatolia, the first megaliths were built. It's incredible that a hunter-gatherer society could have built these things, but there you go. When people came there they needed food, they needed accommodation, they needed sex. And people got into providing that. This was the first accumulation, the first time that some people stood above others. It probably wasn't easy. There were those who would cut off the heads of those who stood above them. We became hierarchical, patriarchal. We are still struggling with this today. Hierarchy is based on the control of resources. Ultimately, of course, it's about control over female reproduction. And with such a change of society, it's hard to imagine that this hierarchy wouldn't extend to how you treated your dogs.'

Dogs, then: the bestial consequences of our settled, hierarchical worldview. Every society, says Kurt, gets the dogs and the politicians that it deserves. I think of the huskies pulling sleds in Alaska, or of the Maremmano-Abruzzese defending flocks of sheep from wolves in Italy; or of how dogs on the fringes of cities are like weapons, while dogs in city centres fit neatly into handbags. It is this ability to adapt and morph, an ability inherited from their ancestors, that has enabled dogs to cement themselves so firmly into our lives.

We have reached the test centre, a nondescript building beyond a locked gate in the middle of the park. Kurt introduces me to Marianne Heberlein, head of the Center's animal team. Kurt has brought me here because I would like to meet a wolf. Of course I would. The Center receives occasional emails from people keen to meet wolves and who claim a special connection to them, describing how, when they stare into a wolf's eyes, they can understand its mind. A two-hour 'Wolf Visit Deluxe' costs 1,650 euros, although cheaper options are available. 'I would guess these people don't wash their hands for three weeks after touching one,' Kurt says. Not unlike the wilderness, or the Native American that it was once conflated with, the wolf has been reinvented in some circles as a romanticised symbol of our inability to comprehend the fine balance of the world. It is the noble savage, the spirit animal to have. You need only take a walk around the gift shop; or trawl the internet for posters of howling wolves silhouetted by a full moon in primeval, ice-bound forest: *Throw me to the wolves and I will return leading the pack*, says one. Or: *The tiger and the lion may be more powerful, but the wolf doesn't perform in the circus.*

I am to meet a wolf called Wamblee, loosely named for the Lakota word for eagle. Marianne leads me to his enclosure, where he lies stretched out in the shade. A wolf! After all these months of tracking Slavc I am in front of one at last, and that he is lying behind bars scarcely diminishes the moment. He rises to his feet at our approach. He stretches, yogic, his forelegs out and his back a low slope, and then he comes towards us, head hung low, moving through the enclosure in a fluid, loping trot. Once his coat was black, but now, at ten years old, it is far more salt than pepper. He is a small wolf, which is not to say that he is small. The tip of his right ear flops forward, doglike. He stares out through the wire mesh at us with bright, nicotine eyes. A wolf!

Outside, Marianne runs through the safety procedures. I sign a disclaimer. She asks me if I am planning on bringing anything inside the cage.

'Just my notebook,' I say.

'Probably best not,' she says.

Wamblee's pack had comprised Geronimo and Yukon, but a month ago they lost Yukon to a brain tumour. When she died, they howled for days. Now it's just the two old boys left, and Geronimo has been separated off into another enclosure for our meeting. Marianne and her colleague (there must always be two, just in case) enter within the perimeter, shutting and locking a first gate before opening a second that allows them into Wamblee's territory proper. Slowly, Marianne approaches the wolf and says some words to him. Then she pats him on the neck and palms him a little treat. It seems that he is in a decent mood, and so she asks Kurt and I to step inside.

To be invited across this threshold feels transgressive, almost shamanic. It also feels deeply counter-intuitive. I have spent the past two years reading about wolves, the last few months on Slavc's trail, and still I can't shake the feeling that I'm about to get torn limb from limb. No wonder the wolf's return makes people jumpy – its reputation far precedes the facts. There have been studies done on people upon entering wolf enclosures that show their heart rate drops and their heart-rate variability increases, which is to say, they become relaxed. I do not feel relaxed.

I am to stand with my hands down by my sides. Wamblee, I am told, has a particular phobia of human legs and so I must keep them, along with the rest of me, completely still. He roams between the four of us. He is a huge animal, well up to my hips, as long as I am tall. He is moulting with the late-spring heat, his greying fur coming off of him in clumps, and through his ragged fur I can make out the shape of him, surprisingly slim. He trots languidly around the cage, nosing Marianne, nosing Kurt. Alongside my fear, in no way at odds with it, is that urgent, all-too-human feeling of wanting to be liked.

The Latin nomenclature for the dog is *Canis lupus familiaris* – the familiar wolf. Watching Wamblee (without holding eye contact, as I have been instructed) is to recall every dog that I have ever seen. I feel I have some loose grasp of his feelings in that dropped head and dropped tail. It is familiar, yes, but there is something other – an eerie, unnameable wildness, a glint in the eye, this failure to conform to society's bounds that have been set out for the dog, and under the contract of which we have allowed it inside our homes. It is somewhat like seeing madness.

I have long thought that we need a word for the inverse of anthropomorphism – not projecting human characteristics onto animals, but that we are a little more like animals than we care to admit. Genetically we may be far more akin to apes, but in wolves we see aspects of ourselves that we find in no other animal. Watch a chimpanzee in a zoo and you'll recognise yourself, but observe wolves for long enough and you'll see elements of what you aspire to be. 'Chimps are Machiavellian critters,' Kurt said. 'I don't trust them. But wolves are very nice animals.'

Like wolves, we prey on every large mammal we share a home with. There are few species on Earth that hunt prey larger than themselves, because doing so requires working as a team, with all the organisation, social structures and division of labour that necessitates. Wolves fall into this rare category, as do we. Like wolves, it is our communal bonds, developed through pack living, that have made us so successful. There is no animal closer to us in its social organisation. Humans have developed the cognitive tools to be able to cooperate. We are able to respond flexibly to different social and ecological settings. We develop different cultures. And because of this, we have been able to occupy almost every habitat on Earth.

We admire wolves' family bonding, their loyalty, their

selflessness, the way they raise their young. They seem to care. Almost no male animal is so committed to enhancing the survival of the females and their offspring all year round, bringing food, raising the young, protecting the pups and the mother from attack. And human fathers, it is worth noting, walk out on their families far more often than wolves do. Wolves remind us of the best versions of ourselves. We get the dogs we deserve, perhaps, but none of us deserve the wolves.

Wamblee is still moving between Kurt, Marianne and her colleague, the three humans that he knows. And then suddenly, on one of his laps, he stops beside me and heaves his body into mine, his head pushed right up against my flank. I am shocked by the heft of him, the massive bulk. I can smell his hot, meaty breath. I feel blessed and shocked all at once. It is a dog, but of course, it *isn't*. By many metrics there are far wilder animals than this. But I am hanging out with a *wolf*.

Marianne seems pleased by how it's going. I am very pleased. She asks me if I'd like to try something. Yes, I say; I am feeling bolder now. She stands off from our group and palms another treat. Wamblee knows this game. I am to hold my hand low and offer the back of it, like you might with an unknown dog. Wamblee is to come and nose my hand, and then go to Marianne for his treat. And he does, moving between us, again and again. His moist nose on my hot hand. Kurt stands there stiffly, a parent watching their child at graduation, not quite able to let go.

There is one more game to play. Would I like to shake hands, asks Marianne. Once again there are rules to follow. I am not to hold his paw. I am not to push back against his paw, but neither should I let it drop. I am to hold my hand out in front of me and let Wamblee do the rest.

The wolf approaches and stops in front of me. I chance a look into his eyes. It is as though his presence carries physical weight. I cannot shake the sense that he is operating on some other, higher plain. And as I watch, he raises one foreleg to the height of my breast and lets it flop down on my outstretched palm. It is incredibly heavy. Enormous. An outsized, hairy paw in my small and naked one. His hot breath on my body. The claws are like sharpened cashew nuts.

We stand there together, shaking hands, reaffirming a contract made between us 20,000 years ago. Making promises that we are still not sure if we can keep.

And then he lets his paw fall, and he trots away from me once more.

I say goodbye to Kurt that afternoon. He must return to his house in the country and he drops me in Vienna on the way. I check into a hostel and spend the evening wandering the streets. Without the weight of my rucksack I feel light enough to fly. I go for a dip in the Danube, right in the centre of town, and dry off on the bank in the warm, late sun. It is easy to fall back into the rhythms of a city, its many preoccupations, all the things there are to do. But I am excited to get back on Slavc's trail. I walk to the station early the next morning. It is several hours on an air-conditioned train to cross the country, and from Spittal-Millstättersee I catch a bus back to Rennweg, and from there I hitch a ride with a farmer on an ancient tractor to the bottom of the road that leads up to Lena and Werner's place.

I head west up the Pölla Tal valley. After days in the city I am happy to be back here, back to walking pace. I follow a path that climbs and twists, and when I reach the mountain hut at Lanisch I cut south from the main path, climbing steeply now. It is hot and I take my shirt off and bend into it, and when I step into the cool of the pine woods my sweat dries and chills me in an instant.

The rock that makes these mountains is different now, granite in place of the limestone, that archetypal Alpine landscape, and it lends an altogether different, harsher character to these peaks. When Slavc came through it was 17 January and the snow was six metres deep. In similar crossings he got bogged down and turned back, but not this time. I'm not sure I'll get through, even now. There is still plenty of snow, although nothing like there should be, whatever 'should' means these days. As I come out above the treeline I can see the Sonnblick Observatory, perched up on its peak. Built in 1886, it has the longest and most reliable datasets for any mountain observatory in the world. This summer the snow will be gone entirely by 6 July, thirty-eight days earlier than the previous record.

The ground is wet with runnels of melt. As I continue upwards on the scree the patches of snow become one unbroken field until I am collapsing through it up to my knees, up to my waist, over and over, my bag hauling me down. Gnarled, angular shrubs push through the snow. The glare of the sun, the sweat in my eyes, shorts and snow and baking skin. I feel animal, and terribly good to be up here.

I have in my bag a book that is far too heavy, Carl Safina's *Beyond Words: What Animals Think and Feel*. There is a chapter that I read on the train coming back here, 'Two Ends of the Same Leash', in which Safina suggests that *Homo sapiens* is a chimpanzee that, like the wolf in the Campfire Theory, has domesticated itself. Just look at us. We are less aggressive, in particular our males. We are smaller and weaker, our musculature less developed, like the domestic variants of other wild animals. We keep playing into adulthood. As a dog is a wolf that has not grown up, so we are still juveniles. And that is not such a bad thing if we are all to live together.

We can romanticise the wild all we like, but it is certainly far less dangerous, and far less demanding, to live in a domesticated state. It is also a successful strategy for global domination – of the ten most populous mammals on Earth, only three (bats, rats and opossums) are wild. And yet domestication comes with its trade-offs. Safina quotes archaeologist Colin Groves: 'Humans have undergone a reduction in environmental awareness in parallel to domestic species and for exactly the same reason.' Farm animals are far easier to work with, because they're docile; domestication brings with it a 'decline of environmental appreciation'. Is it our nature, Safina asks, to be alienated from the wild? To watch wild animals only through bars? Is this the reason for our inability to understand our planet to the point of being unable to look after it? For our little temperature-controlled rooms? For our dogs?

Maybe this is why the wolf stirs something in us. Because we are still somewhat aware of the pact that we made when we took the bite out of the apple. And because seeing a wild animal moving through our domesticated space, keyed to some other rhythm, causes something long since buried to tremble deep within us. Maybe the sheep feel it in the same way when they cast an eye up to the peaks and the wild mouflon of their past. Out here, in Slavc's footsteps, I feel a little more on that threshold. Taking a step through the door of the cage and into another world. The wolf shows us what we were, and what we lost. It is Buck, Jack London's Californian house-dog in *The Call of the Wild*, who rediscovers himself in the boundless North. It is the werewolf. Is that why we have reserved for wolves such an acute and special hatred?

'Either you love your brother or you hate your brother,' Kurt had said to me. 'There is nothing in between.'

I make the ridge, 2,709 metres. Everywhere, serrated peaks, softened by distance and snow. I breathe it in, this clean, hard air. The sky is on the verge of summer. I am chilled and sunburnt and filthy and alive. The wind is blowing hard. This is the highest point that Slavc reached on his walk. It was 2.40 in the morning. The moon on the snow, too bright for stars. Did he ever look back, just for a moment, and admire the view?

I gaze out the way that I have come. My prints across the frozen ground, circling a frozen lake. The scree and the pine woods and the Pölla Tal, tracking the shape of the road that leads back as far as Rennweg. Everything I've walked, everything I've seen, reduced to landscape. And then Slavc was off again, a shadow sliding across the mountain's southern face, slipping downwards in the direction of the Mölltal valley.

There is less snow on this face. I descend a few hundred metres until the place feels less urgent. I build a big fire and sleep early, the crackle of yesterday's rain in the wood. The stars are bullets in the dark. The moon waited over the mountains and when I woke before dawn she was on the other side of the world, a deep desert yellow. The stars turned, and I slept on.

7

A wolf has been born, destined to burst in upon the herd of seducers and deceivers of the people.
Adolf Hitler, *Völkischer Beobachter*, 1922

In 1934 Rudolph Schenkel began his work with wolves in the Basel Zoological Garden in Switzerland. Published at the end of the Second World War, his *Expressions Studies on Wolves* posited for the first time the theory of the 'alpha' wolf, the idea that a pack of wolves is dominated by the strongest, fittest male, with his subordinates in constant struggle to depose him. At any one time Schenkel's study group comprised up to ten unrelated wolves, drawn from different zoos, held in an enclosure measuring ten metres by twenty. Their offspring could not disperse, so instead they were forced to compete. It is difficult to imagine a less natural situation, yet Schenkel's work became the key text for understanding pack structures in the wild.

In *Animals in the Third Reich*, author Boria Sax suggests that Schenkel's ideas were influenced by fascist theory and the Nazis' rise to power across the border. Schenkel describes the alpha's subordinates as another 'race' of wolves, as loaded a word as you could get in the 1930s. Maintaining leadership 'require[d] constant self-assertion', with the alphas dominating and subduing 'the weakest members of society', abusing them until they ceased to be 'a social partner'. It was a dog-eat-dog world that chimed with the politics of the day, and in many ways still does.

Following another three-quarters of a century of painstaking fieldwork on this shyest of creatures, we now know that a pack is, essentially, a family. It is not a group of weaker, needy individuals ruled over by an alpha, as motivational speakers and some of the more toxic corners of the internet would still have you believe. Yet while wolf science has since shrugged off Schenkel's ideas, the alpha has persisted as a metaphor because it chimes with how people think the world works. If wolves can be shown to operate like this, then we can legitimise our own behaviour as just part of the natural order. But such beliefs can have disastrous consequences.

On 17 June 2012, at eleven on a Sunday morning, a thirty-year-old female zookeeper entered a wolf enclosure in Kolmården Zoo in southern Sweden. The emergency services arrived soon after, but the ongoing attack was so ferocious that they could only watch until the eight wolves were finished with her. She received 200 puncture wounds to the chest, some of which penetrated her lungs. Her limbs were torn off, her throat ripped out. Kurt Kotrschal, called as an expert witness for the trial, described it as 'a hatred attack'. The zoo's handling methods were informed by the work of Swedish scientist Erik Zimen, in turn premised on Schenkel's long since discredited research. Zimen maintained that the way to handle wolves was to be the most alpha of them all. The courtroom was shown videos of the zookeepers at Kolmården kicking the wolves to subjugate them.

'The zoo director was a macho,' Kurt told me. 'He said you had to be the boss. But this is dangerous because sooner or later they will turn against you. Any sensible wolf knows it can kill you in a second.' The director was jailed; the zoo was fined. 'None of which made this young lady alive again,' says Kurt, 'but I hope others have learnt from it.'

In the early twentieth century Max von Stephanitz, a retired German cavalry captain, set out to re-create the 'primeval Germanic dog'. He wanted to breed the perfect animal, one that combined strength, intelligence, ability and a capacity to work, and the result he named *Schäferhund* – the German shepherd. He claimed that his creation was a direct descendant of the wolf (it wasn't), while lesser, impure breeds were tainted with jackal blood (they weren't). Worse still were the mongrels, which he described as 'products of free-love on the most modern and broad-minded scale'. This obsession with 'creatures of pure blood' extended to people, and in his book on the German shepherd, which stretches to more than 600 pages, he expounded that 'the Law forbidding intermarriage between members of highly cultured peoples with women of a lower race is therefore thoroughly sound and appropriate'. Such eugenicist thinking clearly foreshadowed the Nazi project, and it is little wonder then that German shepherds – embodying the supposed Germanic values that were fetishised by the Nazis – became highly sought after during the Third Reich. They were used in the death camps and on the battlefield. Hitler kept them, and named one Wulf; they were given cyanide capsules in the bunker the day that he and Eva Braun committed suicide.

In the mid-1930s Germany became the first nation in modern times to place the wolf under protection. It is a difficult truth that Nazi environmental policies were impressive, even for today. Hitler greatly admired wolves. It pleased him that 'Adolf' was a compound from the Old High German *Athalwolf* – 'noble wolf' – and 'Wolf' was a nickname that he used for himself from the 1920s onwards. Wagner's children knew Hitler as Uncle Wolf. He referred to the Hitler Youth as his 'wolf cubs', and he would go about whistling the theme from Disney's *Three Little Pigs*: 'Who's afraid of the big bad wolf, the big bad wolf, the big bad wolf?'

Hitler saw the war as an opportunity to turn back the clock on 'thousands of years of human domestication', to 'see once more in the eyes of a pitiless youth the gleam of pride and independence of the beast of prey'. The wolf was everything we were not. Man's bestial spirit had been sublimated by the Enlightenment, and Hitler intended for it to be unleashed at whatever cost. The SS he called his 'pack of wolves'. As late as 1945, as the Soviets neared Berlin, Goebbels launched Radio Werewolf. Each broadcast began with a wolf howling and urged every German to fight to the death and kill collaborators. Its motto was 'Conquer or die'.

Today, an equivalent line of thinking runs that our original passions have been repressed not by modernity but by wokeness and feminism and the state's intrusion into our lives. Lealtà Azione (Loyalty Action) is a neo-fascist contingent with chapters across northern Italy, and with a focus on 'building new men' to uphold the nation's values – its logo is a howling wolf's head alongside a sword emblazoned 'Italia'. From Turkey to Holland to the United States, far-right groups are channelling the wolf. For the nostalgia that is fascism's fuel, it is the animal that takes us back to a time when men were men, a pre-modern age of gods. In the alpha's iron rule, in the pack's cold aggression, in their bravery and courage, in their loyalty and obedience, in their traditional family values (they are monogamous; they are devoted parents), wolves are presented as embodying the Platonic values of the far right. The rest of us are the sheeple, docile and domesticated, and flocking towards our fate.

Rome's founding myth has the twins Romulus and Remus abandoned to the wilderness, saved by a she-wolf who suckled them until a shepherd took them in. The Capitoline Wolf is a bronze depicting the moment, kept on Capitoline Hill in Rome. At best guess it is fifth-century BC, Etruscan, with the twins added about a thousand years later. The she-wolf's mantle is thick but the rest of her is scrawny. Eight full teats hang from her chest and the twins kneel beneath her, mouths upturned, hands spread like supplicants. Mussolini covered the city with this image. It went on the Palazzo Fiat and in the Piazza Augusto Imperatore, it was placed on schools and covered markets.

If, for Hitler, the wolf was all bloodlust and aggression, then Mussolini's wolf was a more complex figure. Wild yet Roman, maternal yet fierce, she was fascism's embodiment. During the tenth year of his reign Il Duce sent out copies of the *Lupa Capitolina* to cities around the world with any tangential connection to the Republic. They went to Japan and Chile. Romania has significantly more than Italy.

The one in Eden Park, in Cincinnati, was gifted for the Sons of Italy national convention, and in recognition of the city's namesake, Cincinnatus, in whom Mussolini saw a kindred spirit. In its current form (it was replaced by a larger model two years after the convention) it has stood there since 1931. Kids clamber on its back for photos. If we're toppling statues you'd think these wolves would be right up there, and indeed, in 2022 someone took an angle grinder to the wolf's hocks, leaving just four paws on the plinth like forgotten gloves, and Romulus and Remus suckling on air. Whether stolen for scrap or to stamp out fascism is unclear. A replacement is currently under construction.

In 1870 the Kingdom of Italy had annexed Rome and

the Papal States and unified the peninsula, making Rome its capital. Two years later it installed a living wolf in a cage on Capitoline Hill. Harking back to the Roman Empire's founding myth, she was to be the vital, fleshy symbol of the power of the state over the Church, secular and earthy. When Mussolini came to power in 1921, he embraced this wolf, replaced every time one died in the intervening years, as part of his narrative of forging a direct line from the former Roman Empire to his nascent fascist regime. He added a new cage, with an eagle, for good measure.

In reality, the wolf was a lost and utterly unbalanced animal, her instincts perverted to neuroses as she withered under her captives' endless gaze. It is impossible to imagine a less lupine environment, or how an animal could be more divorced from its nature. The cage was bare, about the size of a prison cell, or roughly one hundred millionth of the territory of a wolf pack. There was a phrase in Rome that was common at the time – *Me pari la lupa der Campidojo*, 'You look like the she-wolf of the Campidoglio'. You would say it of someone who was anxious, someone who couldn't sit still. As a symbol of how the individual is dismantled under fascism it takes some beating. When the 1920s iteration passed away, one newspaper reported that she had died of a broken heart.

Mussolini was executed in 1945, but Rome's wolves limped on until the seventies. Male wolves would be brought in to mate with the *lupa*, to ensure the lineage. Much as with the ravens at the Tower, an empty cage was said to spell bad luck for Rome. One time she escaped. Once a theft was foiled. For three years in the fifties the cage stood empty but then she was reinstated, along with a second wolf, presumably for company. But by the seventies it was obvious that both fascism and the poor wolves had long ago lost their power, although in the end they were removed less for their latent fascist symbolism and more because an increasingly indebted city could no longer afford the dog food. Besides, a programme had launched in the Apennines the year before to try to save the wild wolf, and it was beginning to look a bit weird.

The cage is still there, on Via del Teatro di Marcello. There is nothing but a few rusting iron bars to indicate that, until just fifty years ago, this was the home to Rome's wolves. It stands empty now, a testament to sadness. An emblem, for the few who know of it, of a century of wolves' lives that were once again pushed into human service, conscripted to embody something they were not.

The season has hurtled on since I was last down in the valleys. The cherries are still tart but getting sweeter by the day. The meadows are awash with dandelions. Since coming down from the ridge beneath Sonnblick Slavc seems to have had it with the mountains. For the next few weeks he followed the network of valleys that striate western Austria, their filigree of rivers, railways and roads. The wolf, like me, like the water, all taking the easiest path through the landscape. The wilderness it is not. Slavc cut back east until he reached the outskirts of Gmünd and from there took the main valley south. Spittal an der Drau sits on the western shore of Millstättersee, the second-largest lake in Carinthia, a thin, deep slice of water curving along the valley's northern side, echoing the sky. It is lake weather, and everyone is splashing around on the beaches, eating ice creams, messing about in boats.

The Drava runs south of here, its valley forging a swathe across southern Austria. Slavc took a lesser valley, where the Möll flows into it, and I follow him upstream. He slinked through the foothills, first on the north side, then the south, keeping his distance from the little towns and their pink- and yellow-plastered churches that appear every few kilometres. He moved quickly, and then he holed up for a day and a night in the woods outside of Flattach, presumably with something he had killed.

I pass Flattach, still following the river. I stop in grand *Gasthofe* where I am typically the only customer and order suppers of *Käsespätzle* – egg noodles drenched in cheese and butter and topped with fresh herbs and fried onions – washed down with flagons of lager. It is excellent walking food. Stepping back outside in the last of the light, I squeeze into one of the small wooden huts that dot the fields and meant for the drying of hay, and I lie there in my sleeping bag, breathing in the earthy smells, listening to the scuffling of mice. The bells of cows clang through the night and leach into my dreams. The mornings are heavy, muggy and overcast. I walk on.

In mountain country, you grow up a climber or a digger. The locals here were famous once for tunnelling, like moles. There was demand for their skills in mines throughout the world. You can see how, with mountains looming up on every side, that you might want to dig your way out. There is a strange, portentous aspect here, quite unlike the other valleys I have walked through. Pine and spruce blanket the steep hills up to the peaks, and when the wind blows, their pollen blooms in great yellow clouds above the canopy, yet throughout the evergreen whole swathes of spruce are brown. It runs in great streaks to the valley floor, as far off as I can see. It is like the valley has been left out in the rain and gone to rust.

Storm Vaia hit southern Europe at the end of 2018. Fourteen million trees came down. The devastation was worst in northern Italy, but it fell this far inland. One researcher described the impact as 'a shock comparable to a human loss'. And yet worse was still to come. With so much fallen timber the population of the spruce bark beetle exploded, and from there they migrated to the living trees whose defences had been compromised by the increasingly hot, dry summers. A longer, warmer season is enabling the beetle to produce two generations a year, and across the Alps whole forests are imperilled. As the woods die the hillsides are destabilising, and landslips and flash floods are bringing the mountains tumbling down. As I walk I see rockfalls spread out across the valley floor like tidal waves frozen in time. In June towns to the east of here will be hit with floods and mudslides after a month's rain falls in four hours. From where I stand, I am watching an explosion in slow motion. What will be left, I think, when the dust settles?

Yet it is not the first time these forests have been lost. One morning in the hills I come upon a small chapel, plastered white. Its roof is wood-shingled and darkened several shades by the morning's early mist. The ceiling of the sky is low and close. Through the gaps of collapsed trees I can look down on the narrow stream that is hurrying through the gully, but the peaks are lost to cloud. I stop to rest, slough off my pack. It is a month and a half since Easter but there are still offerings of plastic daffodils and plastic rabbits. The walls are hung with cheap paintings of pastoral scenes: baby Jesus petting a lamb, baby Jesus releasing a dove. I can hear nothing but birdsong and the stream.

This is the Wolfskapelle. Story has it that this entire forest was burnt to the ground to drive the wolf from the Mölltal, more than a century ago. The chapel was built in 1905, lest anyone forget. A sign urges me to stop, light a candle, think a good thought. Every year on Pentecost Sunday a handful of locals make a pilgrimage up here to give thanks, bearing a three-metre-high cross. 'It is always said that we have forgotten how to live with the wolf,' said Josef Obweger, president of the Carinthian Association of Mountain Pasture Farmers, when he addressed the penitents this year. 'But this chapel proves the opposite. We have never lived with wolves.'

And yet, for all of this devotion, the wolves are back. Following a short piece about the pilgrimage that ran online in the local paper, someone commented below-the-line: 'I don't want to offend anyone, but I think a gun would be superior to prayer.'

Stumbling on the Wolfskapelle, I remember another roadside shrine that I passed some weeks before on the other side of Carinthia. I had crossed the Drava river and picked up the main road north to Klagenfurt. Truckers passed, leaning on their horns. Outside the village of Lambichl I came upon a few dozen electric candles at the roadside, and plastic flowers dulled by the weather. Among them were various framed images of a man who looked for all the world like someone playing Tony Blair in a Hollywood biopic, better tanned and better chiselled. A gleaming smile, a white suit or half-open shirt. *Forever in our hearts*, it said, in German, on a large poster where he was dressed in traditional Carinthian garb, backdropped by traditional Carinthian mountains. *This land is so empty, so empty without you. Thank you, Jörg.*

This was Jörg Haider, twice governor of Carinthia, and for many years chairman of the far-right Freedom Party of Austria (FPÖ). He died here in the early hours of 11 October 2008 when he lost control of his VW Phaeton. He was travelling at 142 kph and the alcohol in his blood was at nearly four times the legal limit.

Haider had become the leader of the FPÖ's youth

movement in 1970, at twenty, and rose rapidly through its ranks. By 1986 he was party chairman, and in 1989 he was elected as Carinthia's governor. Once a stronghold of Nazi support, Carinthia has a long and grubby relationship with the far right, and as Haider gained more of a mandate over the FPÖ's ideologies he dragged it ever further into the mud. In 1993 the FPÖ proposed a referendum on 'Austria First', its twelve-point, radically anti-immigrant bill. While the bill fell far short of passing, it spoke to the direction of travel in the national mood. In 1999's general election the FPÖ took 27 per cent of the vote, up from 5 per cent in 1986. They were the second-largest party in Austrian politics.

After protracted talks, the FPÖ negotiated a coalition with the Austrian People's Party (ÖVP), which had placed third in the election. This should have made Haider chancellor of Austria, but he had an unfortunate habit of praising elements of the Third Reich, expressing admiration at their 'proper labour policies' and how SS veterans were 'decent men of character', before grudgingly, ambivalently apologising. He was Islamophobic, anti-Semitic, a nativist, a showman. The EU sanctioned Austria for having broken the *cordon sanitaire*, the promise made in the wake of the Second World War to never again give the keys to a bunch of extremists. Haider, his position impossible, stepped aside. It was as high as he would ever rise.

Yet the top job is only one measure of a politician's reach. His funeral in the streets of Klagenfurt had all the pomp of deceased royalty. And he created a discourse that hauled everything to the right, not only in Austria, but across Europe. It was the first time that a right-wing populist party had been part of a European national government since the war, and it marked a watershed. Ruth Wodak, an Austrian linguist, speaks of the Haiderisation of Europe, of how the ground he broke legitimised a far-right discourse that has since been mainstreamed across the continent. In 2017, the next time that the FPÖ went into coalition, elected on the back of 2015's migration crisis (and a year after wolves successfully bred in Austria for the first time since the nineteenth century), the EU scarcely batted an eyelid.

Before Farage, before Le Pen, before Berlusconi even, it was Haider who wrote the populist playbook. A playbook devised in these few valleys in this corner of the Alps, and where its force today is as strong as it ever was.

I am headed for Stall, a small town of around 2,000 people in the Mölltal, because Stall has a wolf problem. Before this year there had not been wolves here for a very long time. Perhaps some of the old-timers remembered their grandfathers speaking about them, but even then it was hard to know what to believe. Slavc had wandered through town a decade ago, on 23 January 2012, but no one had noticed that. And a farmer down the valley had shot a wolf in 2014 because he thought, he said, it was a fox. But this year the wolf came and it stayed. The word *Stall* translates from the German as 'stable', a suitably pastoral name for a place that is now trying to bolt the door long after the horse has been disembowelled and eaten.

From the riverbank I see the thin spire of its church up on the hill, needling at the cloud. I leave the path and cross the main road and climb up into town. The place spreads out; there is no shortage of space. Two-, three- and four-storey houses, timber clad, with red and white geraniums tumbling from their window boxes, and steep roofs that foretell the winter snows. There is a bank, a *Gasthof*, a hairdresser's, a couple of poorly stocked stores trying to make a living in the shadow of the new supermarket. The border with the surrounding countryside is vague. There are sheep fenced just off the central square, and quad bikes zip along the high street with collies riding pillion. It doesn't take long to find the council offices.

I am here to meet Stall's mayor, Peter Ebner, of the left-leaning Social Democratic Party of Austria (SPÖ). Peter is a big man with a white beard and white hair. He is currently under investigation by the public prosecutor for the misuse of municipal funds and his resignation has been speculated on for months, but he is jolly and at ease when we meet. He seizes my hand and ushers me in. A few weary pot plants droop in a fug of smoke. I take a seat and we are joined by Michael Kerschbaumer, a local farmer in his forties, his hair spiked with gel, a crucifix and an eagle on chains around his neck. Peter's secretary serves us coffee and, as we talk, Michael works his way methodically through a pack of Marlboro Lights.

'We don't have a single person here who is for the wolf,' Peter begins. 'Not one, in the whole of the Mölltal. If you have to live with the wolf, then you cannot be pro-wolf.'

'It's unifying!' Michael agrees. 'There is a lot that farmers won't talk about, but they all agree on this.'

It had all begun in April. A farmer's wife had spotted two wolves near her house, one of which looked pregnant. She told a hunter, and the hunter told Ebner, and by the time that the mayor had convened a meeting, four days later, fourteen farm animals and two deer had been killed. While such surplus killing is rare in the wild, it is not so uncommon with livestock that have little by way of natural defences. Two hundred and fifty people showed up to that first meeting. The Chamber of Agriculture came, the Farmers' Association, the hunters, the *Almchef*, who speaks on behalf of the association of Alpine farmers. But because of the wolf's protected status, there was little they could do.

'And so I dared to say, "Then we'll shoot him,"' says Peter. 'We don't need it here and we just don't want it.' He grins. 'All hell broke loose! WWF came, and there were phone calls from Vienna, and there were all these letters asking me what kind of person am I? But that didn't bother me. I have a paper shredder.'

The town launched a petition that set out its demands for a 'wolf-free zone'. 'It is completely out of the question to think for a second that livestock protection is possible on the majority of our Alpine pastures,' it read. 'The question arises whether, with tens of thousands of wolves in Europe, it seems more important to have an additional thirty animals in Carinthia or to save Alpine farming from extinction.' It called for wolf hunting to be allowed at any time. It wanted wolf migration routes diverted using 'high-frequency acoustic deterrence'. It demanded negotiations with the federal government and the EU to downgrade the wolf's protected status. 'Within this wolf-free zone,' it concluded, 'every wolf should be removed without further ado.' It was signed by 'The Last Alpine Farmers That You Will Otherwise Have' and it gathered more than 8,000 signatures.

'It is unimaginable,' says Peter. 'Our great-grandfathers exterminated the wolf a hundred years ago because it was taking their food. And now we can't do anything!'

In fact, it is still possible to shoot a wolf. Article 16 of the EU Habitats Directive allows for the killing of a protected species under specific circumstances. It must be shown that the animal is putting people or property at risk, or is threatening public interest. There must be no viable alternative, and the killing must not jeopardise the species' conservation status. By the end of April, after the required two deterrence attempts, Stall was able to secure a derogation from Klagenfurt that it had a 'problem wolf' and that, if it came within ten kilometres of the town, then it was fair game to be shot.

Yet the system is undoubtedly unwieldy. A derogation

can take weeks to secure, during which time the wolf is not inclined to stop killing sheep, or to stick around waiting to be executed. Even then, when it does arrive, the permit lasts for only a fixed period of time. A wolf is not an easy animal to kill, and hunters today lack experience with this unfamiliar animal. Often it is the wrong wolf that gets shot. If the hunters do succeed, there are the inevitable public backlash and online death threats to contend with. By the time Stall's derogation order expired on 11 May, their wolf was still at large.

It is a short distance from having a problem with a wolf to having a problem with the EU. Recent wolf culls carried out in Spain and Austria were ruled unlawful by the European Court of Justice, and farmers across Europe are inclined to vote for politicians who say that they are going to go to Brussels and do something about it. They cast a jealous eye to countries that are not hampered by its bureaucracy. In Switzerland a cull in late 2023 wiped out fifty wolves, including two entire packs, before an appeal by environmental groups was upheld by the courts. Norway regularly culls up to half of its wolf population. The UK was once required to explore the reintroduction of extirpated species, wolves included, under the terms of the Habitats Directive, but since Brexit it is free to determine its own rules.

'In Vienna, they say, "Just let the wolf in,"' says Michael, an FPÖ voter. 'The FPÖ are doing the most to stop it. They're not doing enough, but they are trying.'

The FPÖ, Haider's old party, dismisses any livestock

protection measures. Guardian dogs are 'aggressive', shepherds 'don't work' and fences 'are not an option for our country', all according to the provincial party chairman of FPÖ Carinthia. His name is Erwin Angerer, like a *Mr Men* character. When we meet in his offices up the valley in Mühldorf, he explains to me that the wolf's status 'will have to change'. I put it to him that a change in EU law will not come about because one corner of Austria wishes it so, but he tells me there is no other way. 'The next thing that will happen is that they will attack people up in the mountains,' he says, despite abundant evidence to the contrary.

It is an issue worth campaigning on. Just 3 per cent of Carinthians are farmers, yet a recent survey commissioned by FPÖ Carinthia found that almost 50 per cent of respondents — regardless of where they live, their gender, or their level of education — want to see large carnivores removed from the state. For the time being, encouraged by politicians who tell them there is no point in protecting their animals, the farmers continue sending their livestock to the mountains for the summers, into what one NGO described to me as 'a state-sanctioned slaughterhouse'. To embrace the role of underdog, at the mercy of an elite, is a typical populist manoeuvre. It serves to dramatise the situation, creating further crises for the very people who are most in need of a solution. 'I would shoot a wolf if I saw one,' Michael says, and before judging this, it is worth considering what that means putting on the line. If convicted, the maximum sentence is three years in prison and a fine of 30,000 euros. And yet he sees no other option. Such people are the collateral when politics becomes about inflaming anger, rather than improving people's lives.

'Save the Alps', a pan-Austrian group formed in 2022, lobbies for similar demands to the Stall petition: wolf-free grazing zones and the prevention of pack formation. It embodies traditional Austrian values, its logo a snowy mountain in red and white, its gatherings opening with patriotic anthems such as 'Loyalty to the Land of Tyrol', performed by men and women in lederhosen. A large event in Lienz in the autumn of 2022 gathered farmers from across East Tyrol and Upper Carinthia for a day of impassioned speeches and poetry against the wolf. It was live-streamed on the YouTube channel of RTV Regionalfernsehen, a broadcaster sceptical about many aspects of coronavirus, and which cooperates with the far-right channel AUF1.

'Save the Alps' draws heavily on the idea of *Heimat*, a word that translates loosely as 'homeland' and invokes a patriotism and romanticism for traditional values and identity. The Alps are in thrall to their own myth, a myth perhaps best articulated in Johanna Spyri's *Heidi*. The region marketed as 'Heidiland' is three hundred or so kilometres to the west, into Switzerland, but the self-conscious identity is just as much here, in the wooden balconies and geraniums, the snowy summits and mountain air and therapeutic mineral spas. *Heidi* tells the story of a girl raised on the *Alm*, on a diet of bread and goat's milk, by a benevolent grandfather who is at one with the mountain. But it is the Alps that are the main character, the embodiment of all that is true and pure, and in explicit contrast to the city life below. When Heidi's friend from Frankfurt comes to visit, she renounces her wheelchair and walks thanks to the divine intervention of the mountain air. It is one of the best-selling books ever written. Crucially, there is not a single wolf.

In 2019 the FPÖ haemorrhaged support in the wake of a corruption scandal, and the coalition government collapsed. But three years on, and to the background of a fresh wave of immigration, it has turned things around. Voters don't bear grudges for long, it seems, or only against those less fortunate than themselves. Their new chairman, Herbert Kickl, ticks every box going. He has opposed both Russian sanctions and welcoming Ukrainian refugees. He does not think Islam has a place in Europe, nor asylum seekers in Austria, and he questions Austria's participation in the European Court of Human Rights. He attended rallies against the Covid-19 vaccine, promoting quack alternatives, and framed the government's response to the pandemic as an elite takeover of the people and their bodies. He describes the EU as a threat to national sovereignty. Such populism is popular, among both the old and young. And nowhere is the FPÖ doing better than in Stall, where in the recent state elections it returned 53.8 per cent of the vote, giving this small town the strongest support for the far right in the entire country. In the wake of the vote, Peter Ebner (SPÖ) wrote to his community to admonish them for their choices.

Yet there are other existential threats facing Stall, besides the wolf. As well as running his farm, Michael Kerschbaumer works in the wood mill on the edge of town, managed by the municipality and employing roughly 160 people. But 1.5 million cubic metres of forest will be damaged by the spruce bark beetle in 2022 in Carinthia alone. Infested wood is practically worthless to the timber market which underpins so much in these valleys. If these woods go, then Stall's viability goes with it.

Peter doesn't see the spruce bark beetle plague as a problem of climate change, but rather as one of too many trees. The pastures weren't grazed, the trees came back, and the beetle has got the upper hand. Within three years, Peter says, half of the trees around here will be gone, and the so-called experts are telling them that they don't know what to do. They are replanting, but in drought conditions the southern-facing saplings do not take. The forest was the inheritance for Stall's children, but now their wealth is being ravaged before their eyes. What is there, then, to keep them here? When the young people leave, communities collapse. Schools close, Airbnbs thrive. The gender split in those under thirty is now 60:40 male to female, and Carinthia's population is projected to decline by 12 per cent during the second half of the century. It is in such embattled places, those most vulnerable to change and most keen to resist it, that the far right finds good traction.

'Farmers work their whole lives and get a pension of a few hundred euros,' Peter says. 'And then foreigners come and get eight or nine hundred euros a month and a phone and an apartment. It makes people angry.'

'The other parties say it's okay to let foreigners in,' says Michael. 'No one knows when to say it's enough.' At the peak of the refugee crisis, 5,900 asylum seekers lived in Carinthia, around 1 per cent of the state's population. In 2024 that number is down to 2,893. But their spectre is enough to ensure that, nationally, the FPÖ is leading in the polls.

'At my job, if I say something wrong, I might get hurt by the foreigners who work there,' Michael continues. 'Not killed, but hurt.'

'They're not all the same,' says Peter. 'But a few of them are aggressive.'

'Do you have lots of foreigners moving here?' I ask.

'No,' says Peter, shaking his head. 'Not much. They like to live in the cities where they know they can be in peace. Here it's a bit more complicated.'

This combination of desperation and populism is fertile ground for conspiracy, and none is more prevalent than the belief that the wolf did not make it here of its own accord. 'The wolf did not fall from the sky in Carinthia,' a WWF (World Wide Fund for Nature) spokesperson was recently forced to say. 'We have been warning of this development for years.' Yet plenty of people believe that this is exactly what did happen. It is hard to credit that an animal, a dumb beast, without preparation or compass or any credible volition, could navigate its way across the country for several thousand kilometres and suddenly appear where there have not been wolves for centuries. It is much easier to believe that it fell off the back of a lorry.

Slavc's journey, I am informed frequently by farmers, is a story for fairies. It is just too convenient, too neat a way to bridge Europe's separate wolf populations. Far simpler to believe in humans playing God. Slavc's GPS map was fabricated, I'm told, the collar driven to Italy. Peter says that a car crashed in Tyrol and wolves escaped from its trailer. The Stall petition included a demand to control the transport of wolves through Carinthia to prevent them from being illegally released. It does not help, when people spot these animals, that they are sometimes wearing collars, making human intervention undeniable. Whenever I questioned why scientists might feel the need to be smuggling large carnivores across Europe, the answer was always the same: money. Someone, somewhere, somehow, was getting rich off this.

The first pack in Austria formed in the scrubland of a military training base, and rapidly the story spread that the army – and by extension the government, the establishment – was caring for them. Rumour has it there are farms in Bulgaria and Romania where wolves are bred for export, the implication being that home-grown wolves might be acceptable, but that these are migrants, refugees.

Most incredibly, in Italy I am told that wolves are deployed by parachute. 'Well, in that case,' I ask, 'how did they take the parachute off?' 'They thought of that,' came the ready reply. 'The parachute cords were made from pig intestines, and when they landed the wolves ate their way out.'

All of this puts me in an odd position. It becomes very hard to explain what the hell I am doing here to people who don't believe that Slavc even made the journey in the first place. It gives me flickers of self-doubt. They look at me kindly, as though I have told them I am following a ley line. To be in thrall to the scientific data just makes me one of the sheep. And we all know what happens to sheep these days.

'No one dares tell the truth about the wolf because they're scared,' says Peter, leaning forward in his chair. 'It's the same with saying that the vaccine isn't doing people any good.' For the wolf is not the only scientific fabrication to have plagued Stall recently. This town has the lowest take-up of the Covid vaccine in the whole of Austria, at 36 per cent.

'What's wrong with the vaccine?' I ask.

'I nearly died!' Peter splutters. 'I couldn't walk! They did so many tests. In the end the doctor said that maybe a tick bit me. I didn't have a tick. And then the doctor said, "I can't tell you what's really happening." I said, "Doctor, you don't have to tell me."'

'Is that why people here didn't get the vaccine?'

'I have never had anything in my life. And suddenly, after the vaccination, I nearly died. The people said,

"Yes, if the mayor, if that *buffalo* gets sick, then we don't want it."'

For a long time the EU has been the true wolf of this piece, thanks to the money it funnels into conservation projects and the protection that it affords large carnivores. But now, perhaps sensing the way the wind is blowing, even the European Commission (the EU's executive body) appears to have turned on its own laws. Things have got personal. In September 2022, in Lower Saxony, a wolf attacked and killed Dolly, Ursula von der Leyen's thirty-year-old, and apparently favourite, pony. (She had no electric fence protecting her.) The president of the European Commission is a passionate equestrian. Strategically, this was a terribly poor move on the wolf's part. 'The whole family is horribly distressed by the news,' von der Leyen told the press. Citing 'numerous reports of wolf attacks on animals' and an entirely unsubstantiated 'increased risk to local people', she requested an in-depth analysis into the wolf's status in Europe. On the basis of that analysis, published a year later, the European Commission has proposed downgrading the wolf's level of protection.

European elections were on the horizon in 2024. With populist parties polling well across the continent, von der Leyen's centre-right European People's Party (EPP) was keen to chase the agricultural vote. Only 2 per cent of European voters work in farming, but their voice is loud and they symbolise a much wider discontent about the green transition. A series of agrarian protests were soon to sweep Europe, with farmers demonstrating against legal mandates to curb nitrogen emissions, reduce water use and ban the use of certain pesticides. The lives of farmers have always been hard, but right now things feel particularly acute. New demands, clumsily implemented, are enough to push people over the edge. Roads were blocked by tractors in kilometre-long tailbacks; the police were sprayed with slurry.

The wolf is one more part of this story, another thing seen as legally imposed by the EU, with scant regard for those who must endure its policies. As Hubert Potočnik told me many months ago, it is not difficult to mobilise people against something with teeth. A 2022 German study found that wolf attacks led to far-right gains of between one and two percentage points in subsequent municipal elections. Plenty of right-wing parties across Europe have gambled that aligning themselves with the farmers' cause is a potential route to power. In Germany the AfD (Alternative for Germany) has backed farmers protesting against a government scheme to cut diesel subsidies for tractors. In Holland the Farmer–Citizen Movement, a populist party formed in 2019, became the biggest bloc in the Dutch Senate in the 2023 provincial elections.

Beginning in the dark corners of the internet, the story being spun is that farmers constitute a nation's soul, a soul that is now imperilled by an agenda to bankrupt farmers and grab their land in order to house refugees and starve populations into submission. I have seen the many hardships facing farmers throughout my journey, and I understand their very real anger. But as a far right of political parties and internet pundits like Russell Brand and Tucker Carlson piggyback on their concerns, reality is obscured. The zone is flooded with shit. There are good reasons to protest billionaires buying up swathes of farmland, or how agriculture has been mismanaged by the EU. But, as during the pandemic, genuine issues are being conflated with a dangerous narrative of a takeover by a shadowy global elite that intends to rewire society and replace white Europeans with refugees.

Journalist George Monbiot has written extensively on this. Viewing farmers in such a way, he suggests, is not dissimilar to the Nazi vision expressed in the slogan of 'Blood and soil', locating those who work the land as the true people of the earth, and threatened by these alien invaders. Farmers on these protests have displayed flags and insignia that recall Europe's fascist past. Monbiot quotes from Robert Paxton's book *French Peasant Fascism* that 'it was in the countryside that both Mussolini and Hitler won their first mass following, and it was angry farmers who provided their first mass constituency'.

This is the power and the danger implicit in reductive narratives, in scapegoating. Whichever way you look at it, what it means to be from places such as this is under threat. Predators, dying forests, shifting demographics, farms closing – I understand why change is terrifying. Yet rather than unpick the complex reasons – wage stagnation, neoliberalism, rapacious agribusiness, climate change, war – the populist claims it is those who support the wolf, like those who support the migrant, who are threatening to destroy the natural order. As with the migrant, the wolf is portrayed as a challenge to sovereignty. It is a symbol of the city come to tear the heart out of country life, of that which is patriotic and true. The populist promises that such changes can be stopped. And even if they can't, as Haider demonstrated, the weaponised impotence of losing can be the most powerful win of all.

'The wolf has no place with us,' Peter fumes. 'Every single one should be shot down. And of course our government should contact Brussels and tell them we must do that. The wolf can be in Russia, it can be anywhere, the French can have it, I don't give a damn. But we in our small country don't need it.'

'Perhaps you need your own pilgrimage,' I say, thinking back to the Wolfskapelle.

'We don't need a pilgrimage,' says Peter. 'We need to be able to shoot it. And anyone who says otherwise is shitting in their pants.'

Italy, Summer

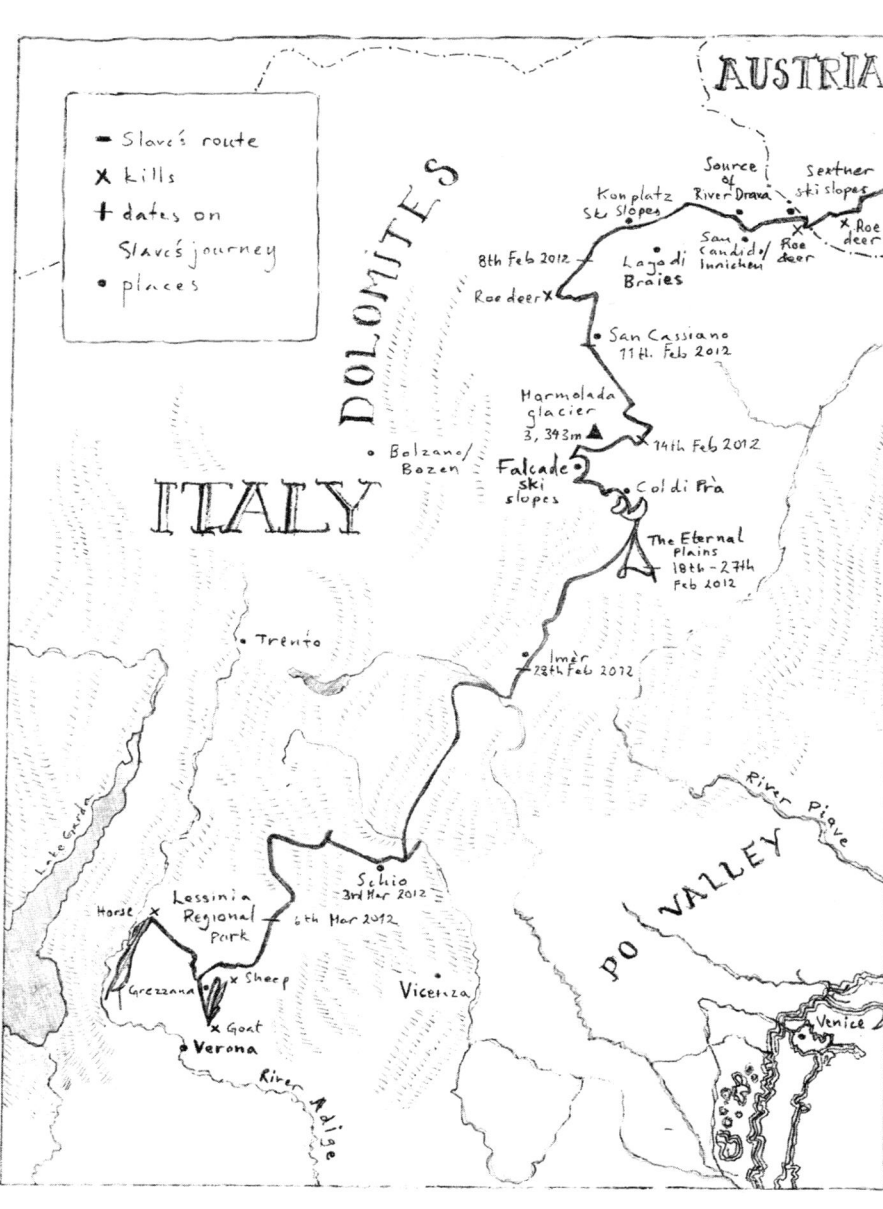

8

The wolf and the lamb will feed together. The lion will eat hay like a cow. But the snakes will eat dust. In those days no one will be hurt or destroyed on my holy mountain.

Isaiah 65:25

Early morning at a tobacconist's in Italy. The doors are flung open and I am at a table on the pavement with my cappuccino and brioche. There is a chill to the air and the street is in shade, but it will be hot, again.

A bird, flying high, catches the sun upon its belly. My rucksack slouches beside me at the table, my mute but amiable travelling companion. I had woken early in the woods and come down the narrow path to be in town in time for breakfast. Dogs are barking, roosters crowing. There is a thick mist down the valley, no view below but cloud, so that to be above it, in these clear mountains, feels the most wondrous privilege. There are two men at the bar, studying the paper laid between them as though searching for its secret. The one standing is tall, stirring his coffee, the chink of spoon on porcelain. The other shorter, larger, seated, smoothing the lines on his forehead with a quick finger and thumb. A grimace slips across his face. The coffee machine steams. Italian pop on the radio. The barman potters in his Sisyphean task of keeping his counter on the right side of chaos.

I take the paper when they leave and go to sit back down with it. It is 5 July. Staring up from the front page is a composite of headshots. Some of them are in climbing helmets; some are backed by glaciers. All of them grinning, all utterly unaware.

I have enough Italian to get the gist. 'MARMOLADA AVALANCHE,' says the headline. 'DEATH TOLL RISES TO NINE.'

Two weeks earlier. It takes me three days to walk from Stall to Italy, through the large town of Lienz and down valleys to the border. The frontier, once again, is inconsequential, marked by a soupy stream dribbling from a mound of gravel and bisecting my own path via a culvert. And yet, however insignificant, however abstract the notion, I am thrilled to be in Italy. The wolf and I have come a long way now, and it is something to look at a map and to know that you have gone the whole way on legs. Coming towards me is an old man leading a small dog on a tight leash, and he is dressed in a tie-dyed, psychedelic vest bearing the image of a wolf's head. Some kind of omen. To the south, the mountains are building.

It was 4 February 2012 when Slavc stepped into Italy. It was cold still, and the nights were still long, but occasionally on the air he may have caught a scent of spring. He could not know it then, but he had covered a large part of his journey. In a few more weeks he would find what he was searching for. In a few more weeks he would be home.

I stop in San Candido, also called Innichen, the first town inside of Italy, for a coffee. I find a café and sit down, all ready with my Italian which I had taken lessons in online throughout the pandemic, only to find that everyone is still speaking German. I am a bit deflated. It is still strudel for breakfast. It occurs to me, sitting here, how loose these borders really are. I think back to Stefan and the other Slovenes I met in Carinthia. And South Tyrol, where I am now, which was handed back to Italy after the Second World War but remains defiantly more Austrian than anything. You notice such things when you walk. That countries do not contain separate, impregnable identities, but that language and culture and disease and windblown seeds and wolves and weather bleed from one into another.

Later, I fill my water bottles where the Drava is being born, the same river that I had crossed and that Slavc swam, then a half-kilometre wide, those many weeks ago near Klagenfurt on the far side of Austria. So it's an Italian river really, bubbling from the hillside like a miracle and bustling down through the trees, channelled through a hollowed log to make a spout for drinking. I sit for a while in the shade. I wonder if Slavc drank here too – there are fixes a kilometre or two off to both the east and west. I wonder if he knew it as the same river, by whatever internal compass he may have.

I leave the valley and turn south and start to climb. The Dolomites rear up on the horizon, beckoning. Slavc's path tracked both low and high as he made his way south through these mountains, but I decide it would be a sort of madness to follow him down some main road along a valley when a beautiful path lies immediately above. I think I can bend my rules a little. I've been down in the valleys for weeks now and I am desperate for the mountains.

That night I pitch my tent in a field of flowers, just out of sight of the road. On 5 February Slavc entered the Sextner ski area and killed a roe deer beneath the chairlifts. He stayed for two nights, feasting, before moving on again. The families looking down from the ski lifts at the dismembered animal, blood and viscera smeared across the snow.

In the foothills of the mountains there are little chapels and crumbling hotels, both built on a passing trade that no longer exists. One of these, the Bagni di Braies Nuova, had dozens of rooms, dozens of thermal baths. An information board out front has a sepia photo from its heyday, several horses hitched to traps outside, and it tells of famous Alpinists who planned their summer ascents from its dining rooms. A lone cleaner stands outside the place now, smoking, a single car in the overgrown parking lot. A tiny, crappy playground, as though children in times past only had the need for one single swing between them.

I keep climbing up through woods, up to the basin of the Lago di Braies. There is a large car park here and this, suddenly, is where all the people are, whole coachloads and families out rowing on the water. It is a shock, after so much time alone. Lago di Braies is having its moment as an Instagram destination and you can rent the boathouse for a private shoot for 150 euros. The waters turquoise, the ridge of the Croda del Beco more than a kilometre above, imperfectly mirrored on its lightly ruffled surface. It is an hour to walk to the lake's far end and there I take a path of white scree bright as snow, leaving the crowds and the water behind and climbing in a long series of slow switchbacks towards the crest above. The calls of eagles echo off the mountain walls.

I am always amazed at the individual character of different mountains, this interplay between the weather and the world. I have never been anywhere that looks anything like this, the peaks needling to points and etched with startling geometries, furrowed and sharpened and worn as though a wild ocean has been frozen in time. Lago di Braies is a puddle of swimming-pool blue, far below. For days it has been sunny but now it seems as though it will crack. From up here, with a view like this, you can get a handle on how weather works. There are vast amounts of it rolling in as though the whole sky is in motion, the clouds bunching into furious columns and thunder muttering off to the north. As the clouds darken, the serrated ridgelines above me catch the sun, standing out in such stark relief against the sky that they appear two-dimensional. My path hugs the base of the *Forno*, the Furnace, and then turns for the saddle, weaving between great blocks of stone that have tumbled from the peaks however many millennia ago. I stop to pull on a waterproof. I am a couple of hundred metres below the pass. The sky has grown so black that it is purple.

After all this time I still think I can outrun the rain. Then a sudden clap of thunder rends the sky and the world becomes a monotone and the hail begins to fall. I am well above the treeline now and there is nowhere left to shelter. I decide that I am best off getting over the ridge and down the other side. I scurry upwards, bent beneath my pack, the hail rattling off of it. Lightning cracks on the next ridge, far closer than I would like, the air trembling with static. I am panicky, exhilarated. I make the saddle, 2,389 metres, and slither down the other side as fast as I can go, towards a mountain refuge where the land starts to plateau. I am soaked, but by the time I make the hut the sun is already out again, the storm hurtling off to the south. I peg my clothes to the washing line and sit on the patio outside, watching the peaks dissolving in and out of cloud, the shifting banks of grey and blue. There is a bar, and the man behind it grins at the state of me. The wine is a euro a glass.

But my God, the Dolomites are beautiful. For days and days it is like this. Off the main trails I see no one but marmots, bounding clumsily across the meadows like tiny, chubby deer, shrieking when they see me and diving underground. I have a heady sense of freedom, of pitching a tent where I feel like it and of waking up in the morning to the next day laid out before me. When the mists blow in, in the thin, high wind, it is not dissimilar to Wales. Sheep and the bells of sheep. But then the mists clear and violent peaks rise around me on every side as though I am walking through the centre of a crown. Water pipits gust along in small flocks. All the tiny mountain flowers, the yellows and pinks and whites and purples, clinging on to nothing.

I spend nights in wood-clad huts built a century ago, sleeping on mattresses in the rafters. Some are staffed but most are not, a modest sanctuary marked on the map, with no requirement but to leave it as you found it. There is rarely anyone else. The beams are a maze of woodworm, marked by soot and teenage graffiti. Their kitchens smoke-blackened, the smell of half-combusted wood, their pantries full of half-used packets of pasta, hardened cakes of soap, mysterious bottles that might be the dregs of home-made grappa or might be fuel for a stove. After dark I sit and write at large tables pocked with burns and knife marks, and when I step outside to piss beneath a hurricane of stars, the flickering candle at the little window is the single pocket of humanity in this vast, mountainous world.

Every evening the wind builds around dusk. The mountain herbs, mint and rosemary and marjoram, shiver out their scents. The wind grows until it is raging and at night my dreams are wild and muddled. One night I dream of a strange man outside my house, and I run around locking doors and windows while everyone I live with meets me with that terrifying indifference that people have in dreams. In the morning I wake and descend the ladder to find a filthy wraith of a man standing in the hut's kitchen, grasping a scythe. A grubby stub of a cigarette is wedged between his lips like an errant tooth, an ancient, almost empty rucksack sagging off his back. A ring in his ear, a grey streak in his beard. His face is sour, long since unused to making any effort because he's not expecting anyone else to see it. I wonder about my own face.

His dog waits beyond the open door. It has the matted look of an animal that lives entirely out of doors. The man gives me the merest wave of greeting, as though stopping a fly from settling, and takes his leave. When I leave an hour later, after coffee and porridge, he is nowhere to be seen. The whole night has been so confused that I wonder if I imagined him. But as I begin my climb down towards San Cassiano I can see a shepherd and his animals far below me. From this height the flocking sheep look like maggots on a wound.

He is in no way surprised or even particularly interested to see me again, but we stop to pass the time of day because we are the only two people for some distance. He offers me a cup of water from his canteen, and as we stand there, both looking out across the view, he takes a pouch of tobacco from his shirt pocket and crafts a cigarette. Sometimes when I meet these shepherds they are Italian, like now; other times they are migrants, Eritrean or Gambian or Moroccan, doing what they used to do back home. When I explain my project, he looks at me as though nothing would surprise him any more.

'The wolf is very smart,' he says. He slides the nail of one thumb across his cheek the way that Italians do, smart enough to cut. *Furbo* is the word he uses, 'sly' or 'cunning', a grudging respect for the wolf's deviant system of morality. It is a mark of respect in a country that has been known to have little patience for getting things done via the proper channels. 'I first saw a wolf in 2014. In 2017, two. Now they are everywhere. I have nothing against this wolf. But it is very, very hard. He scares me. I must look after my loves.' He pulls the spare threads of tobacco from the end of the cigarette and drops them back into the packet. He finds his lighter and inhales reflectively. 'They told me I must shoot the wolf,' he says. 'I am a man of peace!'

From the Medesc Pass I can see the town of San Cassiano, a kilometre below me, framed in the valley bottom and soaked in the early evening sun. I surf down the scree, keeping myself propped upright with a stick. Cutting first one way, then back the other, carefully edging downwards, at last reaching the treeline where scrubby pines spread out across the landscape. With every hundred metres of descent, the wild strawberries get sweeter. Dead trunks wrinkled and riven with age look no different from the rock I have descended.

By the time I reach San Cassiano my knees are aching and I'm ravenous. Out-of-season ski resorts, like beach hotels in winter, always seem like strange, architectural errors that no one quite realised until they built them. There are great hotels of plate glass and wood cladding, their varnished balconies stuffed with geraniums. The hotels are not empty – the Dolomites are currently pushing summer hiking as a second season – but the town could comfortably accommodate several thousand more people. I walk along the main street, peering into outdoorsy shops, overwhelmed by the quantity of restaurants.

I sit down outside a pizzeria and order. There is a well-dressed, middle-aged couple at the next table, and seeing my rucksack they ask me what I'm up to. When I tell them, the woman answers with one of the most remarkable stories of animal dispersal that I have ever heard.

When she was little, she says, her daughter kept two tortoises. One they named Tortellini, the other Tortalloni. They made for lovely pets. Her daughter liked to play with them, and when her friends came round they would take these tortoises out of their hutch and let them roam about their little garden. Tortellini never went far, but Tortalloni had a different streak. Often they would pick her up heading out the gate, or in the neighbour's yard across the street. Then one day they couldn't find her anywhere. Tortellini was left alone. And that was the end of that.

'Eight *years* later we were on holiday, not far from here,' she says. 'About thirty kilometres from home. And Antonio was driving, and at the top of a pass he braked for something crossing the road.'

She must already have suspected when she got out of the car. You don't get tortoises in this part of Italy. Besides, she says, the shell pattern on a tortoise is as unique as a fingerprint. I cannot believe what I am hearing. It was Tortalloni. They put her in a box and took her back home.

The woman sighs. 'But she never was the same after,' she says. 'She had become wild in her time away. It looked as though something had tried to eat her. She bullied Tortellini terribly.'

That night I walk down to the river and find a small copse where I can conceal my tent by the water's edge. By the time I have it up it is dark. I crawl in, shattered, and lie there, listening to a thudding bassline from some bar up the valley. I am half asleep, but cannot sleep. At one in the morning on 11 February, Slavc was just a couple of hundred metres from here. It would have been the peak of the ski season, and if the nightlife is keeping me up in the off-season then it must have been incomprehensible for him. How must he have reckoned with these baffling distortions of his world? Drifting in this liminal state, I feel as close to my wolf as I ever have.

The next day I leave San Cassiano and wander upriver along the Rü Tort, cool beneath the trees that line its banks. This is the Alps as playground: overpriced cappuccinos; artisanal salamis strung up like bunting; walkers fitted out in wicking sportswear, their hiking poles clicking like the appendages of insects. Hundreds of cyclists, uniformly pumping; the golf courses kept watered and lush while the rest of the land gasps around them. I follow the valleys from San Cassiano to Corvara, Corvara to Arabba, ski towns all of them. By the time I leave

Arabba the sun is already low. The path climbs straight up through the forests once again, cutting back and forth across the groomed and grassy lawns of the pistes that scribe swathes down through the trees. Cows graze on the slopes. Rows of snow cannons are lined up in batteries, taking aim at climate change.

I climb on to the pass. I am bathed in sunlight, topless, content, but where I crest Passo Padon, at 2,370 metres, and cross the watershed, everything changes in an instant. I step onto the shaded face and into a fierce wind that dries my sweat and chills me in a moment. Wind can make me anxious, and I trot on down the other side, suddenly worried about where to sleep. And there, on the opposite mountainside, is the Marmolada glacier, and ripped down the side of it, the large, grey mess of its new wound.

I find a dilapidated hut to sleep in, the sort of place, back when these mountains were alive with farming, that would have been used for the storage of hay. Many of its planks are missing and the wind rushes through unimpeded – it serves little more than the animal need of having a roof over my head, although frankly if it rained I would be soaked. I put some dinner together and eat it in my sleeping bag, my back propped against one wall. Through the broken slats I can see the glacier, its wicked, ice-blue scar.

On 3 July, three days ago, as I was somewhere around San Cassiano, a section of the Marmolada glacier collapsed. The serac was eighty metres across, twenty-five metres high, a block of flats. It was a sunny afternoon, a Sunday, and there were plenty of people on the trail to the peak, the highest in the Dolomites. A torrent of ice and water, mud and rock, swept away everything in its path. It finished just shy of Lago di Fedaia, more than a kilometre away. Eleven people, nine Italians and two Czechs, died; a further eight were injured.

Marmolada – known as 'The Marble Top' – is named for its perpetually white surface. Now it looks as though it has been sliced in cross-section, exposing the bare, dull rock beneath, rock which will not have seen the light for several thousand years. All day long a helicopter has been flying transects across the sky, still searching for survivors. I feel voyeuristic, sitting there in my sleeping bag, but it is impossible not to gawp at something that so entirely dominates the view. Worldwide, glaciers are increasingly vulnerable, but the Marmolada was not thought to be among them. Yet the day before the collapse it had been 10.7°C at the summit. The Alpine snow season decreased by thirty-eight days between 1960 and 2017. Later there will be a public inquest which will find that the disaster was 'unpredictable', which is to say, it wasn't anyone's fault. I have spent the past twenty years profoundly concerned about climate change. I have marched and protested and written and parented with it forever on my mind. But looking out on this gash on the mountainside, made just seventy-two hours ago, is the closest I have come to witnessing climate breakdown in the present. The drama of it has never struck me harder. I can see what we stand to lose, what we have already lost. I am horrified.

Italy is particularly vulnerable to climate change. The Mediterranean is warming faster than other seas, while the country's latitude, on the border of two climatic zones, means that Sicily is now seeing a more tropical, African climate, while northern Italy is having weather that Sicily had fifty years ago. There is the fascination, after a tragedy, of the oblivious selfie taken moments before. Sometimes I think of us all like that, smiling for the camera. It takes the actual death of people who had actual lives, who were loved, to be able to understand, in a moment of clarity, that the whole view is in a death spiral. People caught up in the machinations of the planet as it shifts to a warmer state.

During the First World War twelve kilometres of tunnels were carved out of the Marmolada's ice, the glacier riddled with caverns used as dormitories, kitchens, infirmaries, radio rooms, a chapel. Since then it has lost 85 per cent of its volume. It has, at tops, two decades left. All across the Alps, as the glaciers retreat, relics of war are emerging, diaries and postcards and animal bones sucked clean of marrow. The occasional corpse, still in uniform. Some things die slower than others, but if you know how to look right, you can see their final moments.

We have lost 70 per cent of the global glaciated surface in a century. To the west, where glaciers mark the border between Switzerland and Italy, they are slithering around so much that it is hard to know where one country ends and another begins. Even keeping to the goals of the 2015 Paris Agreement, half of the world's glaciers will be gone by 2100. Currently we are on track to lose more than two-thirds. There are ski resorts in the Alps that are now spending huge sums to swaddle their glaciers each summer, dragging millions of square metres of white fabric over the ice in an attempt to slow their melt and wring a few more seasons out of them. And yet one day, not long from now, out-of-season ski resorts are all that we will have left.

I lie down for the night, deeply uneasy. The helicopters will be back out in the morning. If glaciers are the memories of winters past, then there is an awful lot that we are now certain to forget.

I have left behind the high Alps with their classic peaks of snow and granite, their pale-brown cows. I have left behind the spruce, replaced by juniper and pines that smell resinous and hot, their roots snaking over dusty, burnished stone like runnels of petrified water. This feels more like the Mediterranean now. A different camber to the topography, a more familiar flora, a climate and a way that the light falls on the pale, calcareous rock that Slavc would have recognised in his bones.

Gone is the German now, replaced by my muddled and butchered Italian. Gone are the noodles and the schnitzel. It was Valentine's Day when Slavc came by the small town of Caviola. Still the houses are Alpine, several storeys, their peaked roofs at acute angles for the snow, their wooden balconies carved with wooden hearts and festooned with the ubiquitous geraniums, but we are both very much in Italy. Slavc cut south, down to the hamlet of Garés and then over the Palalada ridge. After much decision I decide to follow him, on what is marked on the map as a *percorso pericoloso*. The path is stick-thin, precipitous, hugging the mountain's side and snaking over one dry gully after another. I shuffle along it, giddy with height, and having a wonderful time when I forget to be scared. Up here, for the first time in a very long time, I see a beech tree, more comfortable in this more forgiving climate. By now they have lost their giddy sheen of spring and are weary with the heat. It is like seeing an old friend, and I wonder how it must have been for Slavc, seeing these trees that he grew up with, a sense that he was coming, at last, to something approximating home.

For the first time during his journey, after two months on the road, he lost momentum here, becoming becalmed in the troughs of these peaks. On 18 February he killed a deer, and then he roamed about a section of the map marked as the *Piani Eterni* – the Eternal Plains. There were plenty of red deer and chamois here, plenty of woods. It was far from anywhere. Perhaps, for the first time since leaving home, he considered staying. Maybe the beech trees had struck a chord. Or maybe he was simply dispirited and exhausted, unable to continue in the unforgiving snow. Unusually for him he rested for a long time at high altitude, and then he returned to feed on what remained of his kill. Then he killed again. And then, after the best part of ten days wandering in these mountains, he was off south-west once more.

The sunshine screams, and on the breeze the pines and herbs. I cannot possibly carry enough water. From the Col di Prà the ascent is almost two kilometres to the Altipiano delle Pale di San Martino. The path climbs up through the Vallone del Miel – the Valley of Honey, with expansive views back over the wooded valleys below. The salt runs in my eyes and my shirt is plastered to my back. Every creek marked on the map is dry. I am completely desiccated. I emerge above the treeline in an amphitheatre thick with grass. There are butterflies everywhere, lacquered black with large white spots, and bright wildflowers in their millions, and no shade anywhere. I must find something to drink.

I am drenched in the relentless sun. From here the path begins to climb in earnest, cutting up through a field of boulders fallen from the cliffs above as though the world is still in the process of being born. The rock takes on an incredible presence in this heat. The bluff above me is sheer and leonine, weeping colour. And I notice that one patch of the cliff is shaded darker. I climb up the boulders to reach it. There is water falling from the sky. It is a miracle that I cannot understand. It is cascading down in droplets, and looking up into it tumbling down is like driving through snow at night. I stand there, holding out my mug beneath it, listening to the drip on its enamel, the water delicious on my bare skin. It takes more than an hour to fill my bottle, mug after mug, from this wall of rain. The beauty of the moment does not take away from the basic fact that things are desperately, achingly dry.

I reach the high plateau, slick with sweat. The place is lunar, the path marked with cairns that rise above the surrounding rubble. Apart from the little flowers, the pink snowbells and blue gentians and pale-yellow poppies, everything is a dusty grey or brown. The lake marked on my map has shrivelled to just a few centimetres deep and I lie in it, warm as a bath. A clutch of chamois watch me from an outcrop, unmoved but untrusting. There is one small glacier, roasting in the sunshine, and I scuttle quickly beneath it. All afternoon I cross this place. I have never seen anything like it. Peaks in jagged, wild formations scour the horizon on every side. There is a blush of moon in an otherwise utterly blue sky.

All afternoon I have had glimpses of a mountain refuge across the moonscape, and now its west-facing windows are iridescent with the setting sun. Clouds are forming below and gusting up the valley. All through the Dolomites I have seen crosses set on impossible promontories, silhouetted against the sky, although they seem more testament to those who hauled them up there than to God. The mountain hut is the cross's modern equivalent, salvation and the impossibility of constructing something so far into the wilderness, in a place otherwise so godforsaken.

It is close to dark by the time I reach it. The Italian flag gusts in the evening wind. The temperature has dropped dramatically, but when I pull open the door of the hut the heat barrels out of it. The wood burner is blazing. Every table is taken. I haven't seen anyone all day because everyone is *here*. It is quite a shock. Lone and wiry hikers, climbing couples planning 5 a.m. departures for a summit, large groups of men with large glasses of lager, families that make me miss my own. The woman behind the bar finds me a place and brings me a bowl of stew and a jug of wine. There are good refuges and bad ones, and some feel full of warmth and stories, and this is one of those.

They are all talking at my table about the Marmolada glacier. All paths leading up to it have been closed, and there are politicians and climatologists saying that's how it should stay. In an increasingly litigious culture, local mayors are worried about who is responsible.

'They can go fuck themselves,' says a man across from me, in that profound way that Italians can say it. 'Whoever closed a mountain?' He is maybe in his fifties, head shaved, a single earring. He has a taut energy that fills the place, like a bird caught in a room. A guide, he knew two of those who died. 'The Austrians are saying we should only climb in spring. The Austrians know nothing.'

'They were Alpinists,' says a woman. She has the sinewy body and piercing eyes of a climber, of someone comfortable in conversation with their fear. 'It's not like the people who go up in flip-flops.'

'There are sacred mountains in the Himalayas,' another man says. 'Maybe there are places we should let alone.' I wonder if this is what it will take, a natural world that has become so volatile that we are awestruck by it once again.

Rolling a cigarette, the guide shoots him a look. Glaciers have always claimed lives. In 1802 the first roped party to climb the Marmolada lost one member, a priest, down a crevasse. He was never found. It was not closed then, and it has not closed since the beginning of time.

'Draghi said it won't happen again,' says the guide, standing to go outside for a smoke. 'What will he do to stop it? They have cooked our planet and everything is more dangerous. And now they will take our mountains away from us as well?'

'Up there you are alone with your own choices,' the climber says.

And I think: *just like we're all down here with ours.*

I leave the refuge early the next morning, and plunge down into the valley.

Slavc came through Imèr on the last day of February, still hunting for where his heart lay. A little more south, a little more south. Imèr from the Latin *imus*, the 'place at the lowest point'. It nestles between peaks on every side, baking in the sunlight. The cherries are bursting and the figs are nearly there. The apricots tanned and ripe, the walnuts coming on.

In 2011, when Slavc was still in Slovenia, 200 people gathered at a rally in Imèr that was described by the papers as a banquet of bear meat. You could have your bear grilled or you could have it stewed – a very Italian sort of protest. The hundred kilos of meat – about one-third of a bear, or four quarter-pounders each – had supposedly been brought in from Slovenia, although when the police came to break up the party, following a tip-off, there was a notable absence of import papers. (Despite Slovenia being subject to the Habitats Directive since joining the EU, controlled hunting has continued to be permitted in order to manage what is one of the highest bear densities in the world.)

The bear is one of Europe's trio of large carnivores. Since Teddy Roosevelt gave his name to the stuffed toy it has had the best PR, welcomed into every baby's crib (there's what happened to Goldilocks, of course, but Goldilocks was always hard to warm to), but of the three it is also the most unpredictable. Like the wolf, the bear was effectively extinct across the Alps by the end of the twentieth century, but its population in the local region of Trentino has been climbing since, and by 2011 had reached thirty-five. Livestock has been killed and beehives have been raided, the honey-frames discarded through the forest like the wrappings from a takeout. The bear banquet was organised by the populist right-wing Lega, the party which Matteo Salvini would take the helm of in 2013. They were already professionals at getting headlines and making all the right people angry.

There's a frisson, I suppose, in working your way through the grilled meat of a critically endangered animal, as though you really could be making a difference to the numbers. Bear flesh has something of the lion heart about it too, the sense of a hunter imbibing an animal's vitality and spirit. As with the wolf, to both hate the bear and to want to become one with it are in no way contradictory.

I ate bear once, in Alaska. I wasn't trying to imbibe its spirit, just trying to be polite. By common consensus bears taste of whatever they've been eating, which can be more or less anything. Catch them in berry season and they may be pleasantly zingy, but often they're a reminder of why we don't usually eat carnivores: intense, gritty and sour. But the cuisine in Imèr, for once, was not really the point. Maurizio Fugatti, Lega politician and bear-banquet diner, told the press in embattled tones that the lunch was intended to 'send a clear signal to citizens who have the right to reconquer their territory and freely circulate'. To save the locals, he carried on, they chose to eat the bears. 'We have made our point,' he concluded as, under the gaze of the *carabinieri*, they put the uncooked meat back in the freezers to await a more enlightened age.

Twelve years later and Maurizio Fugatti is president of Trentino, the region that encompasses much of the Dolomites, and they have still not eaten enough bears. The population in the region now rides at upwards of a hundred. Historically, brown bears would have been found all across Europe (and until the time of Jesus, or thereabouts, in Britain as well). Fugatti says the numbers are out of control, that they need to be reduced – culled or deported – by up to seventy. But you can take that figure, like your bear, with a pinch of salt. A 2003 paper estimated fifty to ninety bears in the Trentino region as only the 'threshold for a successful reintroduction'.

The two sides have cleaved to cultural ground that will be familiar by now, but there is a crucial difference between the wolf and the bear. Wolves are to travel as bears are to napping. Bears are solitary animals, they lumber about, and their dispersals are much shorter and much rarer. And so it was, at the turn of the millennium, that the EU felt that they needed a little help. Over the course of a decade they captured ten bears in Slovenia and brought them to Italy. As a conservation story it has been a great success. But there is one other crucial difference between wolves and bears as well. Because on 5 April 2023, sixty-five kilometres north-west of here, a bear known as JJ4 killed twenty-six-year-old Andrea Papi.

The story of JJ4's family is operatic in its tragedy, and this final act has once again split Italy on where it stands regarding wild animals. 'No surrender, no coexistence' is just one of the hashtags. Seen from one angle, it does appear a kind of madness to choose to reintroduce a large, unpredictable carnivore to the midst of an inhabited region, one popular with tourists and with hikers. Those worried for their safety can no longer be painted as hysterical. Papi's death has only entrenched the belief that these animals were eradicated for a reason, and that on the right side of extinction is where they should stay.

JJ4's mother, Jurka, was eight years old in 2001, 'a splendid ninety-kilogram specimen', when she was brought from Slovenia to the Dolomites. There she met Joze, who had been transported from Slovenia the year before. In time they had five cubs. JJ1 (Jurka Joze 1) was christened Bruno. In the summer of 2006 Bruno began to roam the Austrian/German border, and when he set foot in Bavaria he became the first bear to grace Germany in 170 years. Germany was hosting the World Cup, but the media still found time to be enthralled. The papers reported his every sighting, but after two weeks of Bruno taking chickens and the occasional sheep and outwitting those sent to track him, Bavaria's environment ministry gave the order for him to be shot. 'It's not that we don't welcome bears in Bavaria,' said an official, unwelcomingly. 'It's just that this one wasn't behaving properly.' Bruno had harmed no one, but he did seem eerily fearless. Footage showed him at midnight, lounging outside the local police station in Kochel, gorged on honey he had pilfered from a nearby resort and burping to himself.

A trio of hunters did not hang about. Bruno was shot at 4.50 on a Monday morning, outside the small town of Zell. Germany could only manage third place in the football and its only bear had been shot. The Italian government demanded expatriation of the body but the Bavarian government refused; the corpse lay on its land. Bruno ended his days stuffed in a museum in Munich, eating honey from a hive while small model bees swarm about him. 'I have to go and lecture developing-world countries about how they should save their elephants and tigers,' said Heike Finke, spokeswoman for Germany's

Wildlife Alliance. 'It's embarrassing.' Whether Bruno's corpse is displayed as an emblem of hope, or as a warning to others who might try to enter Germany outside the safe and legal routes, is not entirely clear.

Was Bruno's lack of fear learnt from his mother? Jurka raised her cubs alone. Unusually for a bear she was almost exclusively a carnivore, and was completely unfazed by people. It is likely she had been fed by someone and associated people with food. A fed bear, as they say, is a dead bear. Did she teach her cubs that there was no shame in helping yourself to a chicken? Her offspring were unusually bold, a family of pioneers. JJ2 became the first bear to enter Switzerland in a hundred years, before disappearing in 2005. JJ3 went to Switzerland, too, but also failed to fit in, and in spring 2008, after one too many raids on bins and beehives, he was also dispatched by hunters. His final misdemeanour was said to be swiping a cooling cake from a windowsill, the ultimate hobo crime. For a bear, not behaving as one should – not being *wild* enough – is a fast track to a death sentence. In 2012 JJ5 was deemed to be too close to human settlements and a decision was made to collar him. He died while under sedation.

There is something terribly clumsy about all this. The bears and the humans both blundering around, trying to work it out with each other. The family had been more or less gutted. Jurka herself had already been carted off to a bear park in the Black Forest, guilty of having wayward children and of not being sufficiently scared of people.

'She has put on quite a bit of weight,' reported the local paper, and there she is to this day, with her own blog. She has made multiple escape attempts. 'Her yearning for freedom is unbroken,' said Bernd Nonnenmacher, director of the park. 'That will never change.'

And so we come to JJ4, Jurka's last surviving offspring. It was a bright afternoon in April when Andrea Papi left his home in Caldes to go for his usual run in the woods up on Monte Peller. His girlfriend raised the alarm that evening when he did not show for dinner. His body was found in the forest, with deep gashes to his neck, his chest and arms. A bloodied branch found near the body suggested that he had made some attempt at defending himself, and DNA discovered on the branch implicated JJ4, just nine years younger than Papi. After a two-week bear hunt by forty rangers, she was lured into a tube trap with a pile of fruit and taken from her three cubs to a secure enclosure while the courts pondered her fate. Seven people have been attacked by bears in Italy in the past two decades, but until 2023 never fatally. Andrea Papi's death is the first fatal bear attack in Western Europe in modern times. (Eastern Europe is another story. Romania, which has more brown bears than any other country in Europe, has seen twenty-six fatalities over the past two decades.)

Unlike the rest of her troubled family, JJ4 had not left her birthplace of Trentino, and yet by the time of Papi's death she was already known to the authorities. In 2020 she had attacked two hikers on the same mountain, lacerating their legs. The administrative court had ordered that she be put down, but protests by animal-rights groups, and ultimately an intervention by Italy's then environment minister, granted her a reprieve. In August of that year she charged two foresters; two years later she charged a biker. Yet every request for the animal to be euthanised was blocked. Maybe the deaths of her three siblings had strengthened the resolve of those who believed she deserved protection, the last in the family line. By way of precaution, JJ4 was fitted with a tracking collar in order to keep tabs on her. By 2023 the batteries had run out.

In plenty of countries an animal that attacked, let alone killed, someone would immediately be put down. If it was a dog, there would be no question. Yet a week after Papi's death, a local administrative court issued a stay of execution on the death warrant that Fugatti had ordered, following a legal challenge from animal-rights groups. As the appeals have ground on, JJ4 has now dodged death four times. The current plan is for her to live out the rest of her days behind bars in a refuge in eastern Germany.

Anti-carnivore campaigners have seized on Papi's death. 'I would shoot her tomorrow morning if only I could,' swaggered Fugatti, calling for half of Trentino's bears to be killed immediately. 'Happy Easter!' wrote an activist in Italy when he WhatsApped me the first news report, just hours after the attack. Yet even Papi's mother has refused to hold the bear culpable, and disagreed with the court rulings to euthanise it. So where should we lay blame? Is it the fault of those who planned the bear's initial reintroduction, the architects of a conservation project that has become too successful for its own good? Or is it the fault of politicians who, rather than educating the public about coexisting with a transforming ecosystem, have instead politicised the problem? Or is it the fault of the animal-rights groups who are so persuaded that every life is sacrosanct that they refuse to countenance the death of an animal that has become so obvious a threat? 'A young man died because we couldn't put down that bear,' said Claudio Groff, coordinator of the Large Carnivores Division of Trentino. What is certain is that, where the wild no longer exists, it falls on us to pass judgement. In 2024 Fugatti successfully ordered the death of two more bears, M90 and KJ1, the first for approaching people and residential areas multiple times, the second for wounding a hiker. Both executions proved as controversial as ever.

It seems to me there must be an understanding that this is also what we speak of when we speak of rewilding. Certainly we should manage the risks as best we can, but rewilding means that the wild gets a hand back in the game, with an agency all of its own. As I saw in Alaska, those who have always coexisted with these animals know that this is not something to be taken lightly. 'The problem with large carnivores,' Hubert Potočnik had said to me in Slovenia, 'is that people either want to hug them or kill them. And neither is compatible for their survival in a human-dominated landscape.'

ITALY, SUMMER

I look at photos of JJ4, splashed across the tabloids. The words they use about her – 'brutal', 'a lust for killing' – suggest a calculated, malicious intent. I look into her eyes. You've killed a man, I think. But there is nothing there to see. I am just looking at a bear.

Part of its rebrand in recent years has been the widely put-about assertion that a wolf, or a healthy wolf at least, would never kill a human. At least for North America in the twentieth century this held water, and with most wolf science coming from the United States, such thinking was extrapolated globally. Yes, there was a catalogue of bites, nips, stalks and other threatening behaviour directed at hikers, bikers, field biologists and small children, but this was more or less glossed over by the dominant narrative. Even when all the evidence points to the contrary, there are those who will choose not to see it. *Grandma, what big eyes you have.*

Then, in 2005, twenty-two-year-old Kenton Carnegie was killed and partially eaten while on an evening stroll outside his mining camp in a remote part of Saskatchewan, Canada. Such was the cognitive dissonance a wolf attack presented that the death was at first blamed on a black bear, despite the fact that wolves had recently been seen feeding at the camp's open garbage dump, and despite wolf tracks in the snow around the body. So strongly held was the belief that wolves could not present a threat that a previous, exploratory attack on other members of the camp was not treated as the danger that it was. The coroner concluded that wolves were most likely responsible, but there were plenty who refused to believe it. 'What killed Kenton Carnegie?' asks Canadian biologist Valerius Geist. His answer: 'The myth that wolves do not attack people.'

Because they do. In 2010 Candice Berner, a teacher in the Alutiiq community of Chignik Lake, south-west Alaska, went for a jog after work and never came back. Four members of the community came across bloodied snow as they drove back to their village that evening, and they found her body dragged off downhill, away from the trail into the bush. DNA samples ascribed the kill to a local female wolf 'in excellent body condition' (suggesting this was not a kill made from a desperate hunger) and implicated several other members of the pack. It was the first time DNA evidence had been used to prove wolf involvement in a kill. 'Wolves are no more dangerous than they were prior to this incident,' concluded the report into Berner's death. 'People should not be unnecessarily fearful.' But try telling people that.

The academic authority here is John Linnell, lead author on two papers that document wolf attacks on humans from first records up to the present day. From Russia to India, Iran to Norway, 'there appears to be no doubt that wolves have on rare occasions attacked and killed people'. Using death records in parish registers, historian Jean-Marc Moriceau has identified 5,400 victims of wolf attacks in France between 1571 and 1920, after which time wolves were extirpated. He attributes these deaths primarily to the social conditions of the time – children herding sheep on the fringes of shrinking forests. In the Po basin, to the south of the Dolomites, there were 112 attacks in the 400 years preceding 1825. Of these, seventy-seven people died. And then, after 1825, nothing. The wolves, and the forests, were gone.

The majority of the attacks documented by Linnell were carried out by rabid animals. Rabies is a horrendous disease, incubating for weeks or even months before the onset of a fever, a prickling at the site of the original wound, and then a progression through a list of bizarre and terrible symptoms including hyperactivity, fear of water and aerophobia (a fear of draughts), before eventual cardiac arrest. Until Pasteur's work at the end of the nineteenth century, a severe bite from a rabid animal was invariably a death sentence. Despite effective modern treatments, rabies still kills 50,000 people a year.

Canids are the principal vector reservoir of rabies: foxes, jackals, dogs, wolves. Rabies derives from the Sanskrit word *rabhar* – 'to do violence'. Rabid wolves, notes Linnell's report, exhibit an 'exceptionally severe "furious" phase'. They will chase vehicles, clawing off tail lights and chewing the bodywork. 'In January an aggressive wolf was reported,' records a 2002 paper compiled by the Alaska Department of Fish and Game. 'When the . . . police arrived the wolf attacked the police car, flattening a tire and puncturing the bumper with its teeth.' They will destroy their own families. Biologist

Richard Chapman describes a crazed wolf that fought several other members of its pack. 'This wolf was shot when it approached the author,' writes Chapman, back when scientists were scientists. 'Within four weeks at least six other members of the pack were dead.'

But it is in reading about these attacks in relation to people that we can start to understand quite how horrifying they could be. *The Annals of Wales* recorded eighteen men being bitten by a rabid wolf at Kermerdin in 1166, 'who almost all perished immediately'. There are records of wolves biting up to forty people in a single sitting. To give just one European example: in 1756 a wolf runs into a village in Salernes, France, and attacks twelve people and a pig. Wounds range from a bite on the ankle to 'having all the face, head and neck torn off'. Over the coming months at least six of the survivors die. 'The circumstances of the two children's deaths are awful,' the parish priest wrote. 'Joseph Dauphin began to refuse eating and hate water, having occasional fits and trying to bite people . . . Marie Anne Boudou was more furious, she also hated water, she was locked alone in her room where she broke her head and body while falling from time to time, and in these excitements, died with no remedy.'

Both the initial, frenzied attack, and then the survivors' descent into insanity, would have weighed heavily on a community's collective mind. It is easy to imagine how such horrors were retold down the generations, and how a single incident like this could colour a whole culture's attitude towards an animal.

But it isn't always rabies. Healthy wolves are also known to kill. Sometimes it is what Linnell calls a 'provoked attack' – typically a shepherd defending their flock – and sometimes, just sometimes, it is just that kind of wolf. India has seen several waves of fatal wolf attacks in recent decades, predominantly on children, typically in villages that rub up against degraded habitat and where the wolves have become desperate for food. Since April 2024 nine children and an adult have been taken and killed from villages in the Bahraich district, on the border with Nepal. In Sweden, the Wolf of Gysinge attacked thirty-one people between December 1820 and March 1821. There were twelve deaths, all but one of them children. The wolf that was eventually killed had been a pet for several years before being returned to the wild, suggesting that wolves that have lost their fear of people present a far graver threat. This, argue the hunters, is why we should be allowed to shoot them.

The most famous big bad wolf of them all is the Beast of Gévaudan, which has acquired a mythic status and popular culture all of its own, and with a body count best estimated at 113 deaths and a further forty-nine wounded. Gévaudan was part of southern central France, in the region of the Massif Central. In 1764 an animal began attacking people. Some believed it was the bastard child of a bear and a wolf, others a hyena escaped from a fair, others a werewolf. It was said by those who glimpsed it and lived to tell the tale that it had red eyes, walked upright and smoked a pipe. The local bishop said it was sent by God to punish the heathens of Gévaudan. In the parish registers the deaths were recorded, simply, as '*Bête*'.

Captain Duhamel of the Clermont Prince Dragoons was enlisted to hunt it down. Noting the beast's predilection for women he put his men in dresses, but after seven months the wolf was still at large. Then, as now, there was a European press all too eager to sex up the details, and as the story spread the Beast became symbolic of the failures of France. Louis XV took it personally. He put a 6,000-livre bounty on its head. But it was not until the summer of 1767, after many more deaths, that a young farmer, Jean Chastel, finally killed it. It is now thought that the Beast was probably several wolves, possibly hybrids, but with Chastel's killing the case was considered closed and the problem appeared to go away.

Such historical reports are often dismissed. Chroniclers are considered to be hysterical and hyperbolic, the product of a less enlightened age. But the fact remains: if wolves pose no threat to people, why do so many stories tell us that they do? Such dissonance is perhaps the most dangerous element of all, for it is in the space where things don't make sense that conspiracies will thrive. In an age when scientific fact is politicised, there is just as much harm in presenting the wolf as harmless as there is in painting it as the hound of the Devil. So yes, wolves do, on occasion, kill people. So do bears, and cows, and wasps, and adders. Despite huge increases in the wolf population in Europe, there have been just six documented fatalities in the past century (Finland in 1932; Italy in 1956; Spain, first in 1957, and then another two deaths attributed to the same animal in 1974; and Central Russia in 2015).

The wolf hasn't changed, but we have. Once we lived side by side with wolves and sent our children out to tend the sheep, but our chances now of crossing paths with one are vanishingly small. What we do live side by side with is dogs. In 2016 there were forty-five fatal dog attacks in Europe (the most up-to-date figure for the continent). In 2023 there were sixteen fatal dog attacks in the UK alone, not to mention the approximately 15,000 sheep killed by dogs off the leash each year. Yes, there are an estimated ninety-two million dogs in Europe, compared with 21,500 wolves, but the point is not to debate whether wolves or dogs are the greater danger, but to interrogate why we so readily invite dogs into our homes and our kids' lives, while the return of the wolf touches something quite so elemental.

Despite everything that I have learnt over these past months, I still find it hard to comprehend the sheer outrage that the wolf's return provokes. It stirs something deep within us – a primal, collective fury as we backtrack on a battle that we had once thought to have won. Why is it that young children are more terrified of wild animals than of cars or strangers? Why do urban adults have dreams of being devoured? Such subconscious preoccupations may be an evolutionary hangover from our primate past, and yet in studies, babies do not appear to be innately afraid of bears or snakes. Instead we seem to have a capacity to acquire that fear, and to a much greater extent than to modern threats, to an electric socket, say, or a gun. Author Barbara Ehrenreich suggests in *Blood Rites* that while 'biology left us with a capacity for powerful physiological responses to predation, it is culture which continued to activate this capacity long after the actual threat had vanished or declined'. The fairytales, the conspiracy theories, the tabloid headlines – they all prod at something within our ancient brains. For those who wish to stoke that fear, we can prove highly receptive.

Ehrenreich argues that much of human behaviour – our lust for and fear of violence, our cooperation, our communication – evolved from living, for a large part of our history, as prey. While it is now hard to believe that animals played an integral role in shaping human destiny, she argues that this is our 'original trauma'. Our vanquishing of the beast is our most common mythic trope. Typically depicted as the individual hero conquering the gorgon, or the dragon, or the snake, it was in reality a collective struggle against the many carnivores that filled our lives. 'Compared to this victory,' Bruce Chatwin expands in *The Songlines*, 'the rest of our achievements may be seen as so many frills.' At last we became top predator. Nature became objectified, out there, no longer able to touch us. 'You could say we are a species on holiday,' Chatwin wrote. But that was 1987, and all holidays must come to an end.

When I walked to Istanbul, things felt stable. I was young, and I had little by way of responsibilities. Too young, and too naïve, in fact, to appreciate that my easy passage across the continent was a product of certain aspects of myself: my gender and my skin colour and my class. Climate change was a far-off threat that would probably be dealt with. Politics appeared to be bending towards justice.

For much of this walk, following Slavc, I have seen the wolf as a symbol of change. There are dramatic changes happening all across the Alps. Migration, depopulation, melting glaciers, dying forests. I have seen how people are scared of their lives changing, how they want it all to stop, and how politicians of a certain stripe continue to stoke those fears while promising that everything can stay the same.

But I realise now that I, too, am terrified of change. To see the Marmolada's scar on these hot, dry days is to understand that I also don't know how to make meaning in a world that feels increasingly outside of my control. There is nothing more capable of exposing the lie that we have liberated ourselves from nature than when it turns around and eats us. The return of the wolf is not going back to anything. We are all plunging forward into an uncharted world, and the only fantasy is that we can stop it.

9

I loi e le pegore no jè nè mai d'acordo – The wolf and the sheep have never gotten along.
                                                Lessinian proverb

I come down out of the Dolomites to the scorched cities of the plain.

In Asiago, thirty kilometres south-west of the end of the Dolomites, it is 37°C at half-past eight in the evening, and two hours later, outside the *gelateria*, the neon sign on the pharmacy across the street says 33°. I sit on a bench eating ice cream. Half a moon is hammered to the sky. In my tent, pitched out of sight among vines beside the road, I toss and scratch at mosquitoes, my sleeping bag unzipped to my waist. A steady thrum of crickets keep up their song all night. The next morning I peel myself from the tent, dazed and stupid with the heat, and carry on again.

It is too hot to climb and I keep to the roads. The tarmac hurls back heat. Pelotons of Lycra-clad cyclists zip past me in their own microclimates of breeze. I gorge myself on peaches from roadside stalls, the juice streaming from my chin. In Schio the bubbling public fountain is surrounded by geraniums, and dozing on a bench beside it I think of mountain streams, I think of swimming, I think words like *quench* and *slake*. The fountain trickles endlessly, the very idea of endless water. The ripples' shadows on the basin's tiles, like the memories of all the swimming pools of your youth. I fill my water bottle, soak my cap, plunge in my arms up to the elbows. A hundred metres out of town and I am sweating once again, as hot as I have ever been. All I want to do is keep on walking to the ocean and get in. All I want to do is sit in the shade, ordering spritz after spritz, which is what everyone else seems to be doing. But I am not where I am going, not yet. Mad wolves and Englishmen. At small train stations awash with heat someone gets off, someone gets on.

The Po, that great river eighty kilometres to the south of here – the river that Virgil called the 'king of rivers' – has sunk so low it has exposed ancient villages and the detritus of the Second World War. The paddy fields that supply Italy's risotto rices are dry, and much of the harvest has failed. In places you can walk from bank to bank. Veneto has declared a state of emergency, and four other regions also. The drought spans the continent. Hunger stones, the records of droughts in centuries past, are emerging from the exhausted water. *If you see me, weep* is carved into one that has been revealed on the Elbe.

I think: *this is the coolest year of the rest of your life.*

One night it rains. The smells of the burnt land are

unlocked from the earth and in the morning they rise up on the steam of the road, and then it is hot once more. Ahead of me the peaks of the Carega massif hove into view, punching up into the aching blue of the sky, above the thick and shimmering air.

It is the Carega that marks Lessinia's eastern rim. Lessinia, the place that Slavc and I have been bound for, these past months. It is the border that marks the end of this story. But it marks the beginning of another one, too. A story that is, if anything, yet more remarkable.

Slavc first set foot on Lessinia's plateau on 6 March 2012, at around eight o'clock in the evening. It was not yet quite dark, and it was not so cold as it had been. He had climbed steeply up through beech woods on a north-facing slope above the ski resort of Recoaro Mille, and then crossed the ridge that marked Lessinia's border beside the refuge at Montefalcone before descending the southern face of Monte Anzin. Where the land flattened out the forest ended and he swept across the open pastureland, quick and silver in the dusk, towards the small cluster of buildings at Caliari. It was brighter out of the woods, but the light was fading quickly. Some few stars pocked the deepening blue. He moved in the shadow of the Carega, its pale, serrated faces, its broken ridges, its pinnacles of rock. Not far off was the col called the Bocchetta Mosca sul Carega, which was once known, in Cimbrian, as *Bokatelja 'ume bolfe* – the Pass of the Wolf. The land, holding its breath, calling him back.

This place, he knew this place, so much like the place that he had left. He knew its trees, its beech and oak, and the way that their leaves gave beneath his feet, and how they smelt on the chill dusk air as their sap began to rise. He knew its rock that was much like limestone, its curve and polish, its outrageous shapes. He knew its gentleness, its naked, rounded hills, its peaks so much lower than the massifs he had come through. He knew how the wind came up off the plains in the evening as though the hills were breathing in and how, from further off than that, there came sometimes a scent of the sea. For months he had walked through spruce, through granite, through passes close to 3,000 metres high. For months it had all been so unknown. Now, all of a sudden, this feeling of home.

The barns at Caliari were illuminated. The cows were being milked; he could smell their slurry, their stagnant stench. He passed in shadow, a darker shape to the quickening dark, at a resolute trot that did not deviate or let up, and it was as though they inhabited two different churches, different creeds, two entirely different ways of being on this earth. He passed Caliari and came to a metalled road and crossed it, and then came to another. A car swept around the corner, its headlights washing over him, his eyes flaring an unearthly, incandescent red. He knew cars, and he stood sentinel on the verge as it slowed and stopped before him, its engine idling, a man's stunned face at the glass. The smell of diesel; the human smell. Then he roused himself from his stupor and trotted across the road before the car and carried on back into the night.

This was what his eyes were made for. In the daytime his eyesight is comparatively poor, but when it is dark he can see *everything*. As the night progressed he moved further south, through the patchwork of wood and pasture and village that characterised this place. He was drawn on a thread. He stopped to drink at a small stream engorged with snow melt, the Chiampo, and then he carried on again.

The farmhouse – what they call here in dialect the *malga* – was set by itself, high up, at the end of a chalk track that glowed a pale grey in the now starless night. It was built of the same rough, rose rock that these mountains were also built of, its roof lain with the same thick stone slabs. Embedded in the stone were the fossils of ancient bivalves and ammonites, back from when all this was ancient sea, when these peaks were hundreds of metres deep, before that sea receded and left behind the mountains formed of the creatures that once had lived beneath its waves. Still they are turning up fossils of fish from the highest mountain peaks. The smell of humans was distinct here but it was from a day ago, maybe two. But there was another smell as well. And then there was the sound.

The wolf stood before the dog and observed it as it might observe a landscape. The animal was going berserk, hurling itself to the length of its chain and being snapped back to earth. Its eyes roamed in its sockets, its drool fell in strings upon the ground. The wolf stood there, watching it, one forepaw raised and cocked. Back and forward the dog went, barking, barking. The wolf weighed the equation and found nothing to be lacking, and at length he turned his back and moved on, loping through clouds of his own breath.

For days he wandered, moving south, losing altitude. Lessinia, they say, is like a jellyfish. Its bell the high plateau, its tentacles the many spurs that fan out towards the plain. Between the spurs are the thin and wooded valleys, the *vaji*. Valleys unused to sun through the winter months, shaped by time and gouged by water, the wrinkles of the landscape. By the next night he was following one spur, down to the plain below. And it was near to Romagnano that he passed close to a hobby zoo, and in one of the enclosures were three wolves, a female and two males. Did he see them, hear them, sense them on the wind? It was perhaps the first time on his journey that he had crossed the path of another wolf. For four months – a good portion of his life, and an eternity for an animal that is located in the present – he had not seen his kind. He stayed in the area ten days. It was the longest that he had spent anywhere since leaving the territory of his pack. Yet they could not come to him from behind the bars. And at last he moved on again.

It was high above the town of Grezzana that Slavc killed his first domesticated animal. Picture him, the arrogance of his adolescence, and how he must have hated this weak prey. Its feeble terror, its inability to flee. Yet it had been many days since he had eaten. To kill it was like snapping twigs. A moment of true emotion in its dumb, mute life, before he dragged it to the ground. Picture him, as he stood over this ruined sheep, its innards pawed out onto the earth and steaming still, burning through the skein of frost that skinned the pasture. The only meat he had known was lean and gamey: roe and boar and fox. This was milky, full of fat. He ate his fill. He got a taste for it. Five nights later he killed two goats. For the first time in a hundred years in the central-eastern Alps, wolves and people were brought into intimate relationship.

By now he was down on the Veronese plain, a kilometre or two off Verona's suburbs, among great orchards of peach and cherry trees. A few pomegranates still clung to otherwise bare branches, bright orbs on another dull day. The planes taking off, the planes landing, the monotonous thrum of the ring road. This was not what he had intended. This no longer felt like home. His sudden taste for dumb animals had led him here and he turned tail back the way that he had come, his belly full and moving fast.

A day later and he was up against Lessinia's western rim, where the cliffs plummet 1,000 metres to the Adige valley's floor. He walked the high ground, looking for a way through. For months he had been pushing west and now, for the first time, he had come up against a barrier that he could not navigate. The Adige sweeps a wide, flat swathe across the landscape, a fertile corridor that runs north back towards the Alps, up towards Trento, Bolzano, Austria. The river from up here is a stripe of grey that meanders about the valley floor, through the bare fields and empty orchards and between towns roofed with terracotta. Today, the air was wet and brooding. The ground saturated, the snow gone. These higher hills were empty of the farm animals that go away in winter and do not come back until the sun returns. But at lower altitude, in Lessinia's upper villages, he found what he was looking for. One night outside of Fosse he found a lone horse in a field. She snorted, stamping, the fear rising off of her in gusts of scent. She was too big for him to take alone. He drove her off a cliff, her great legs galloping at the air, and for the next few nights he returned to the base of the rock to scavenge her broken body.

He continued to explore the low ground, looking for a way west. On 19 March, at 2.50 a.m., he was in the shrubbery of a large house on the outskirts of Sant'Ambrogio di Valpolicella. On 25 March, at 1.20 a.m., he was somewhere between a gravel pit and some tennis courts. Yet each time he kept returning to the high places of Lessinia. Each time, something kept on calling him back.

On 27 March, it says in the scientific notes, 'the wolf's moving behaviour changes'. He starts to 'exhibit territorial pattern'. In other words, he is home. What makes wolves stop is as mysterious as what makes them set out. The landscape was familiar. The Adige valley blocked his progress, so that the logic of forward motion that had pulled him gravitationally for months had been persuasively cut off. The killing was good.

But there was something else as well. Because on fence posts and young beech trees, from scat on the ground, he was picking up another's presence. A female, of breeding age. Had Slavc dared to hope, in all those months of travel, that there was another wolf out there? That his journey might not be in vain?

At night, on the wind, he heard her howl.

For a hundred years there had been no wolf packs in the whole arc of these Alps, not for thousands of square kilometres. Not in Italy or France, not in Switzerland or Austria. There was the occasional lone wanderer from the more wooded parts of Eastern Europe, an errant adolescent on a doomed search for other wolves, but even they had stopped coming, more or less, decades ago. But once this place had been unthinkable without them. I imagine the ancient beeches in these forests, trees that would have been used as scratching posts by wolves in centuries past, turning to meet them now. *Where were you?* And the mountains, too, of course, which think far slower even than the trees.

You can find their names on the old maps, slumbering in the archives: Valle Lupina, Valle Luvaria, in ora Prete Lupis, la cascata del Lupo. There are 245 place names derived from the wolf in Trentino alone, the region north of here. They are found not only in the mountains, but also on the plains. There is the Via del Lovo – the 'wolf road'; and in Peschiera, near to Lake Garda, In Ora Fosse Lovàre – 'beside the pit for trapping wolves'. There are close to 1,500 families in Italy with the surname Lovato, and many live hereabouts. Slavc passed close by the mouth of the Fumane Cave in Valpolicella, a place once inhabited by both early modern humans and Neanderthals, and which contains the oldest rock art in Italy, red ochre paintings of half-human, half-animal forms. Bone fragments of wolves found in the cave show clear signs of butchering, probably for furs, some 35,000 to 40,000 years ago. Our history here has been entwined with wolves for a long time. Such dates call into question whether it is the wolf or the sheep that can lay best claim to this place.

But by the Middle Ages Italy was, as they say, developing. The trees were logged, the wild prey fled, and the wolves turned their attention to the ever-expanding livestock market. In 1303 in Mantova, you could get paid three lire for a live wolf, thirty soldi for a dead one. Vicenza built a wall around its city to try to save its sheep. In 1370 in Udine, the city ordered a blacksmith to construct 400 traps for the wolves that were 'devour[ing] children in an abominable manner'. By 1397 you could get five lire for a live wolf in Verona. In many regions hunting game such as deer and chamois was the prerogative of the nobility, but anyone was allowed to shoot a wolf. There was no such thing as a closed season. Even with that sort of attention, there remained enough wolves that eighty a year were still being shot in Friuli into the seventeenth century.

It is complicated, anywhere, to document a 'last wolf'. There are far more stories than facts. A lot of people like to lay claim to the last, whereas of course the true last wolves would have lived out the remainder of their days far from humankind, profoundly lonely and afraid. The last wolf in Lessinia is said to have been shot around 1860, according to the old-timers in Giazza. There is a stone, in a field, to commemorate the event. And a fairly common consensus has the last wolf of the Italian Alps being shot about 160 kilometres north-east of Lessinia, about fifteen kilometres from where Slavc crossed into Italy, at a place known as Malga Campobon:

> 'Mr Mina Antonio, who, with hard work and courageous boldness, on the evening of May 24th, 1929, at precisely 21:00, in the Campu Gon locality, managed alone to shoot and kill a furious Wolf who spread terror there in a flock of Sheep that were scattered in those surroundings. At the same moment he managed to save a sheep that the ferocious and furious animal had bitten.'

This note, written by Antonio, was attached to a photograph. In it, the wolf is sprawled on her side, a rictus of a grin. She is pale, and the first thing you notice is how small she seems. Her mouth is open and her tongue is lolling, her ears pricked, her eyes narrow but open. Three men sit behind her, each of them holding a rifle, two with hats and all in suits, and all of them staring directly at the camera. *What?* it seems as if they're saying. *What would you have done?*

I drop my bag in the small mountain town of Velo Veronese, at a pizzeria on the square. There is a hotel with four rooms above the restaurant, and I will stay here for some weeks. The market is on – peaches and artichokes and the hard local cheeses. Velo's church is imposing, built of the same rose limestone as the farmhouses. The town's buildings cluster about it in a teardrop. It sits on a small, round hill looking out over Lessinia's lowlands and up to the higher land to the north.

Lessinia is hemmed in by deep valleys on three sides and by the Veronese plain to the south. Its cluster of mountains and its high plateau stand as a land unto itself, 10,000 hectares of land between Verona and the Little Dolomites, a grazed and wooded bit of the low Alps that never quite makes 2,000 metres. There is not the drama of the high peaks here, but neither is there the dull monotony of the plains, where the white towns steam and reek like carcasses in the unflinching summer heat. The limestone smoothed out by millennia of weather, the gentle pastures and the shaded forests of chestnut and of beech.

For a thousand years now, since the migrants came down out of Bavaria and logged the forests and replaced the predators with sheep, this has been a land that moves to the rhythm of people and their animals. It has not changed much since, not really. The meaning of these places is found in their constancy, in season following season from one year, from one generation, to the next. It is what makes it possible to live alongside land. By any measure there are more impressive mountains, but the longer that I spend here, the more it gets beneath my skin. Not many people, even in Italy, have ever heard of Lessinia. Or they hadn't, until Slavc arrived.

Velo's pizzeria is run by Manuela and Massimo, and after months in a tent it is particularly luxurious. They run it with Massimo's parents, and with their daughter, who toddles about behind the bar. Every evening, once the kitchen is closed, they sit together for dinner, and some nights they invite me to join them. Massimo is a hunter, and he takes great pleasure in showing me hunting magazines and talking about the wolf. He has videos on his phone of wolves, and he tells me about the time a group of farmers dumped a grotesquely slaughtered cow in the main square so that all the world could see what a barbarian this noble wolf really was. One evening Manuela has a spare ticket for the opera, and we drive with her mother out of the hills and down into Verona for *risotto all'amarone* and a three-hour performance of *Aida* in the Roman amphitheatre. The moon rises fat above us, and Verdi's music rolls around the ancient walls, his tragedy of duty and nationalism and love.

I intend to spend the summer in Lessinia. My walk is over, and Slavc's as well, but another story began when he arrived here. As every biologist I have spoken to has told me, Slavc's journey might have been extraordinary, but more astonishing still is how rapidly the wolf has repopulated these lands, as though it has never been away. It is not only the biologists who have been taken by surprise. A transient wolf is one thing, but it is when wolves stay and set up house that they change the lives of those around them. Lessinia is the crucible to understand all this. The repercussions of Slavc's journey continue to unfold, altering on ecosystems and politics and the lives and dreams of those who live here.

Several days after I arrive I go for dinner with Luca Signori. We meet in the car park of a pizzeria on the edge of Bosco Chiesanuova, the prettiest and most touristy of Lessinia's small handful of towns. Looking away from town it is all stars and meadows in the dark. Luca has sandy hair, a boyish face, the dark-green fleece and combat trousers of people who are most at ease outside. He has a broad scar in a puckered line across his bald patch. His truck is emblazoned with the insignia of Lessinia Regional Park: a stone farmhouse, low pasture, high pasture, snow, blue sky, all in strips of bold colour, like stained glass. Luca has worked in Lessinia since he was a young man, a few decades ago now. First for the *Corpo Forestale* and then, when everything got reshuffled, for CUFAA (*Comando unità forestali, ambientali e agroalimentari*). There is nowhere in the world that he would rather be.

We go inside. Dave Brubeck's 'Take Five' is playing in the background. The place is full of Austrian and German hikers, their camper vans parked outside. We are seated in a corner and I order the Monte Lessinia, a pizza of early ceps from the woods and a smoked, local ricotta, and a carafe of young red wine.

'The first time I heard people speaking about wolves, it was a friend of mine,' says Luca, as we wait for our food. 'A hunter, at Sant'Anna d'Alfaedo – 2010? He called me to ask if there were wolves in Lessinia. "You must have seen dogs," I said. "There are no wolves here."' Luca shrugs theatrically. He can laugh at himself now. But you must understand how unlikely a wolf was, like seeing the Beast of Bodmin. There were a handful of wolves in the Apennines, far to the south on the other side of the plains, and there were some off to the west, on the border with France, also several hundred kilometres away. That was it. 'My friend kept on insisting,' Luca says. 'I didn't think anything more of it. I believed that bears would come back here before wolves did. And then, for a good bit of time, I heard nothing.'

The following summer a farmer stopped Luca and asked him the same thing. It's impossible, Luca told him. He had worked in the forces for long enough that he put a premium on hard evidence, not stories. Besides, he was out in the woods every day of his life. Since he was a boy he had dreamt of seeing wolves. If anyone should know, it should be him. But the farmer shook his head. 'I know what dogs look like,' he said.

The end of 2011, just after dawn. In northern Slovenia, several hundred kilometres away, Slavc was pacing the perimeter fence of Ljubljana airport, and Luca was driving the high road that climbed past the mountain refuge at Branchetto in northern Lessinia. There were some few stars still out in a frozen sky – the Shepherd's Star, Orion – the land grey with the snow. 'I remember it like it was yesterday,' he says. 'Right beside the road there was this body, but it wasn't a carcass any more. It was only the ribs. Practically only the spinal cord. The only way I knew it was a goat was because they kept goats at Branchetto. Otherwise . . .' He puts down his cutlery. 'I had never in my life seen an animal like that. We just couldn't imagine what could have done that to a goat.'

The spine belonged to a pregnant female. Another goat vanished the same night. Two weeks later the predator came and killed again. This time both goats were strangled, bite marks on the neck, one only fifty metres from Branchetto. Only Carmelo, the billy, survived, and he began living on the roof of the woodshed. The man who ran Branchetto had young children, and now only one goat, and he wanted to get to the bottom of what was going on. The next night he kept watch from a high window.

Just after one in the morning what looked to be a dog stepped out of the night. And yet the man knew dogs, and this one moved in some eerie, otherworldly manner. When it picked up a human scent on its kills, it turned tail and slunk back into the darkness. The whole time his own dogs kept mysteriously silent. It had to be a dog. But the word that had come to his mind unbidden, before any other, was *wolf*.

Luca had heard enough by now that he borrowed

some camera traps. They set one up behind Branchetto, and another on the goat carcass that was some distance from the refuge. The winter lay thick and hard upon the land. The days burnt briefly between long, dark nights. And in late January they got their first picture. The image is grainy, black-and-white. The animal is off to the side of the frame, head lowered, its muzzle almost to the ground. It is spotlit, and behind it the snow fades into black, as though it is onstage. The tip of its tail is black. Seen in the camera's infrared, its eyes are flaring whiter than the snow.

How can you believe in something that does not exist? Besides, said Luca's colleague, the picture looked wrong. The animal was too small. The tail was too long. Sometimes they came across dogs on walkabout when they were out in the forest. If an owner had a job in Verona, they might leave their dog off the leash during the week. Yes, it had to be a dog. Four days later the camera trap took another image; a month later, another. Luca emailed them to Luigi Boitani, Italy's pre-eminent wolf expert, and about to become a very busy man.

Quite possibly a wolf, came the reply.

Luca was beginning to believe in fairytales. Then in April they found shit in the snow. It was so full of hair it looked more like roadkill. It did not take long for the genetic analysis to come back from the lab. Luca stood holding the printout, and there it was, in black and white. A wolf, it said. Young. A female. *Canis lupus italicus.*

Wolves had come back to Lessinia.

A female. Who was she? Where had she come from? Wolves of both sexes disperse, and there is little to choose between them in how far they can travel. That she was of the subspecies *italicus* confirmed she was descended from those hundred or so Apennine wolves of the Abruzzo that had survived the wolf's extermination, but it was very unlikely that she had come directly here from there. Between those mountains and Lessinia lie several hundred kilometres of open plain, one of the most intensively farmed and industrialised areas of Europe. Probably she was descended from one of those wolves that had pioneered the Western Alps from the Apennines in the early 1990s, aided by new environmental protections. And had then forged a path east for several hundred kilometres through the chain of the Alps, through empty land, to come by herself to Lessinia.

Whether the Italian wolf warrants its own subspecies is still contested, but having been separated from any other wolf population for centuries it is smaller than the European grey, about the size of a good German shepherd, with slight variations in the skull shape and unique genetic markers. They have a beautiful tawny colouring blended in with their grey, and black bands across their back, the tips of their tail and their ears, as though they have been brushed with ink. But the most important question was not where she had come from, but whether she would choose to stay.

During that fevered winter, as we know, another wolf

tale had been brewing. When the first hunter asked Luca about wolves in Lessinia, Slavc was learning to hunt sticks in the south-west of Slovenia. Casting a straight line across the Adriatic, he was 240 kilometres away. By the time Luca was stopped by a farmer at Bocca di Selva, the pup had been collared. And by the time Luca found the goat at Branchetto, Slavc was on the move. Word had got about within the European wolf community about this new female in the Italian Alps, and members of the Slovenian team began joking, as Slavc carried on ploughing west, that that was where he was headed. The Italians had sent over pictures of their wolf while Slavc was still many months and kilometres away. A Tinder of two, with a very wide catchment. But the months went by, winter became spring, and it was beginning to look less like a joke.

Slavc entered Lessinia on 6 March 2012. Neither team could believe it. In the park they got hold of an antenna that would let them track his collar. Unlike their female, who might grace a camera trap if they were lucky, this one they could get a fix on. For several weeks they watched as he roamed the perimeter. During work hours they found any excuse to go and check a point; at weekends they went back out from sunrise until dusk. They became, it is fair to say, obsessed. These were men who grew up with a child's love for nature which they were never required to grow out of, and now two wolves had turned up on their patch.

'How did your family cope?' I ask Luca.

He laughs. 'I've always been a bit solitary,' he says. 'For me, it's quite normal. It's the most beautiful thing in the world. So, you know, my family was quite used to it.'

But this male always gave them the slip. They trekked across Lessinia in the wake of a mythical animal. They would go to check on the carnage that he left and find nothing but blood and bones. He was always gone, always one step ahead, a farcical game of cops and robbers, and they were left there empty-handed once again, with nothing but a deep and grudging respect for his intelligence. By then he had become quite effective at hunting on his own. There was the horse in Sant'Anna that he coaxed off a cliff. They put camera traps on his kills, but then he never went back to them.

'There are wolves that will pass quite happily in front of a camera trap,' says Luca. 'And then, there are the other wolves.' Perhaps having been trapped in his youth had made Slavc acutely aware of the smallest sign of human interference.

Then, on 12 April, they got a fix at Castel Gaibana, high on the crest that defines the north-east of the park. On its southern face it looks out over the defunct ski lifts at San Giorgio; to the east it falls away to the wooded Valle di Revolto. They had had a heavy snowfall days before, thirty centimetres. That was typical of Lessinia – you thought it was spring, and then you found yourself slogging up a mountain, up to your knees. The light was sharp and clear and the hills had never looked more beautiful. The male had passed by just hours ago.

The men picked up his track, climbing the ridge. They were familiar prints by now. Far larger than the fox, with a longer gait. This one was a big wolf and his tracks were bigger yet, different from the slighter prints of the female. A wolf's tracks are not so different from a dog's, but a wolf will place its hind feet directly where its front feet fall, while the dog will straddle them on either side. It is this that gives the wolf its remarkable profile, so that if you watch one running from head on, it is like a knife slicing the air. If one wolf follows another they walk in step, with the leader breaking trail, so it can be impossible from their prints to discern their number. Besides, while a dog's tracks skitter about, the chaotic meanderings of a child, the wolf's line is straight and true and keen, an arrow shot from a bow. A wolf can maintain a bearing for miles, like those psychogeographers who hold an undeviating path across a city by scaling garden fences and crawling through people's windows. One ranger told me about a wolf's trail he picked up that did not once swerve until it reached the kill site that it was aiming for, *six kilometres away*. As though it were guided by something *else*.

'So we were following this track,' says Luca. 'And then we saw this other track, meeting it.'

It was coming in from the opposite direction, equally single-minded, their female. And there before them, recorded in the snow, was the moment of their meeting. Picture them. These two wolves, tails raised, sniffing, revolving in slow orbit. Neither would have seen another wolf for months. Each could have been forgiven for thinking that they were the only wolf left in the world. And then it all rushed back in a flood – the other's smell, another being, their own kind. The culmination of two separate journeys that each had staked their life upon. There was nothing else like them for several thousand square kilometres. A needle in a haystack does not come close. Did they have some notion of the odds? They must have; in some way, they must have.

Their tracks fell into step together. The two wolves climbed higher and higher on the ridge, one following the other. One of the men took a photo. It shows a single line of prints that split into two, before returning to one, over and over, a double helix. As though the wolves couldn't quite contain themselves. 'Their track went first uphill, and then it went down the other side,' Luca says. 'And the track was beautiful. Because when they went downhill you could see where they were playing. The tracks were all messed up where they were rolling and playing, tumbling over each other.' The manifestation of their happiness, carved into the snowpack, there for all to see until the thaw.

'How did you feel?' I ask.

'Ah,' says Luca, searching for the words. He spreads his hands out expansively, as though trying to encompass the magnitude of his emotion. His eyes glisten. '*Bello.*'

The waitress comes back. Luca orders the tiramisù.

I have the apple-and-walnut tart. The restaurant has emptied out, and it is just the two of us left talking.

That spring Slavc and his partner, by now christened Juliet by a local journalist for her proximity to Verona, were scarcely out of the papers, the power couple of Veneto: 'THE WOLF CONTINUES HIS HOLIDAYS IN VAL SQUARANTO'; 'WOLF ACQUITTED – TWO SHEEPDOGS RESPONSIBLE FOR THE CHAMOIS MASSACRE'; 'SLAVC FEELS AT HOME AND GOES SHEEP-HUNTING'; 'THE TWO WOLVES OF LESSINIA HAVE DECIDED TO STAY.' The coverage was measured, broadly positive. Slavc and Juliet were settling in okay.

But then, in August, two hunters came across a dead female wolf at the crossroads outside the village of Fosse. A photograph shows her weak, emaciated body, tongue flopping from her mouth. The autopsy found in her stomach a half-digested bait package laced with pesticide. Had Juliet taken her baptism to heart? It also showed thick marks around her neck, consistent with her having been tied up. There was trauma to her chest, sternum and neck. Probably she had been killed elsewhere and dumped, but it was hard to determine anything for sure. Probably she had suffered a great deal. You didn't need to be an expert to see that this was an Italian wolf, but the team conducting the autopsy noticed what seemed to be important differences between Juliet and the wolf on the slab. She appeared smaller, older, in poor health, and the characteristic black markings on her tail and on her forelegs looked different to those grainy images from the camera trap. They waited for a more detailed genetic profile. When it came back, they were able to confirm that this wolf was not Juliet. There was, incredibly, a third wolf in Lessinia. Or there had been.

Like Juliet, this was another female wolf whose genetics suggested that she had also made a vast journey across the western Alpine arc from somewhere on the French/Italian border. Could she have followed Juliet's scent markers across that great distance? It was a reminder that to make such a journey is one thing, to be successful is another. Several months after wolves returned to north-east Italy, this female that was never named became the first one to be murdered. She was sent to the incinerator. 'They should have put her in a museum,' Luca says.

It hadn't taken Luca long to realise that there was not much point in chasing the wolves across the mountains if he wanted to observe them. They had been in Lessinia a matter of months and were already more at home than he was after a lifetime. He needed to learn their behaviour, and wait for them to come to him. He needed to become an expert.

The first time he saw the couple together was in early May. A wolf had been spotted several times at the watering holes near Parparo, and that morning Slavc's collar showed that he was back there again, in the woods below the ponds. 'I knew the place,' says Luca. 'They could not go east to Giazza because there are the rocks and overhangs. If they went south in the woods, sure, we would lose them. But if they left by the west or the north, we might see them in the meadows. I called up my colleague and said: "Let's do a stakeout."'

Luca arrived in the mid-afternoon; his colleague came down an hour later. They stationed themselves above the mule track that leads down to Giazza. Roe deer grazed the meadows and Luca wondered why they seemed so peaceful if there were wolves nearby, but that first summer everyone was still getting the hang of this new arrangement. 'It was like when I am waiting for poachers,' Luca says. 'You know that it's going to happen, and you can't sit still. You go crazy.' Yet by half-past eight it was nearly dark and once more they had seen nothing. Another wasted day, another wild wolf chase. Luca began packing his cameras away. The men started talking. Luca took one final look through the binoculars before they left, and that was when they saw them.

'Juliet was walking behind. It was dusk. The light wasn't the best. But *Madonna*. That moment was beautiful.'

He dabs at his mouth with his napkin. 'I got excited in a way that I have never experienced,' he says. 'My whole body was trembling. I felt stoned. I was so emotional I had to lie down.' He puts a finger to the scar on his scalp. 'I had a head operation,' he says. 'Strong emotions are not good for me. I have to lie down to relax. But that time the emotions were too powerful.'

We order grappas and espressos. Luca gets his phone out. He swipes through images. Luca has taken up photography since the wolves arrived. The local paper described him as trading his pistol for a camera at weekends, 'as if a Verona player, after matches or training, spent his free time at the Bentegodi Stadium to keep his muscles toned'. He shows me a female wolf that he came across in the forest two years back, one of Slavc and Juliet's daughters. She is sun-dappled, mid-lope. Her eyes gaze into the lens and her belly is swollen with pups. Her fur is yellow, orange, brown, and he counts out the black stripes of her markings for me, markings like her mother's.

Then he pulls up a video. It is a wall of green, a hillside pasture. It is spring and the birds are singing. Three wolves are moving across the frame, climbing on a diagonal to the slope. The shot zooms in. Two are smaller, one is larger, moving slightly apart. Luca points at it. 'Slavc,' he says.

He has no collar now. It detached at the end of his first summer here, as they are designed to do. They had followed its signal to one of the thin valleys that snake north to south through Lessinia, and just when they thought they were nearly on top of him they found the collar in the leaf litter, given the slip once more. In the shot, two cows are standing in the topmost corner of the frame, apparently untroubled by the wolves' presence. One of the two smaller wolves stops, straddling a tussock of grass. Her tail is erect, as though being yanked up by a string. When she moves on, Slavc ambles over, sniffs, and cocks his leg. Then he moves on. His mouth hangs agape. His ears are pricked. And then he halts and turns his head, and for a moment he seems to stare directly into the camera. As though he *knows* he is being watched. His muzzle catches the sunlight and burns white. The camera shifts, as though shying from the intensity of the moment. And then he lowers his head and trots on. He catches up with the other two wolves, and together they climb to the brow of the hill.

Then they are gone.

It is 3.30 a.m. and I am violating the terms of the rental car, driving off-road on the gravel tracks of upper Lessinia, climbing through the grasslands below Monte Tomba. My headlights bounce around in the darkness. A hare, all eyes, bounds across the road and lollops up the verge. Over to the east, across the valley, another set of headlights snakes along the contours of the hills. We meet at the spot that he had sent last night, a dropped pin on the map. We get out, shake hands, whisper '*buongiorno*', huffing with the cold.

Gaetano Pimazzoni carries his tripod across his back, yoke-wise, and I follow him away from the cars and down slopes that are wet with dew. He has dark and wispy facial hair, his face wrapped in a scarf against the chill. The moon is full and he is walking fast. For twenty minutes we move in silence. Off to the east a rim of paler light arcs along the ridgeline of the mountains. A slow wind stirs, sucked up by the hills from off the plains, and it carries on it the scent of water and of peaches and the dry heat of the day that is yet to come.

We pass the squat shapes of the *malghe*, still held in the earth's shadow. There are a hundred or so of these thick, stone farmhouses spread out across Lessinia. They are the land's sentinels, the ruins of the future. The wind flows unimpeded across the swells of this naked land, grazed down to the quick. Venus blazes in the west.

'Here,' Gaetano whispers, at last.

We are in the middle of a meadow. He pulls a mat from his pack and sits down on it and I sit down beside him. He hands me a camouflage blanket and I wrap myself in it like a shawl. He sets his camera on the tripod and mounts an enormous lens, draped with more camouflage. And then he settles down into an otherworldly state.

Several times a week Gaetano drives from Verona to be here in time for sunup. We sit cross-legged, side by side. He scans the hillsides with his lens. We are staring into darkness, but the shape of the hills is becoming evident as the black pales towards blue, the Primaneve refuge and the spike of its telecommunications tower at the summit. There is the ponderous presence of cows nearby.

You look for long enough and everything begins to lose all depth. You look for long enough and you start to forget why you are there. I shift and brush against the warmth of Gaetano's knee, but that is all the warmth there is. My fingers seize. My legs ache. My nose drips. I need to piss. Occasionally from the nearby *malga* there is a burst of noise and light, sirens and a cacophony of sound. This wolf deterrent, much like the rest of them, has next to no effect. In other places they blast AC/DC, and the wolves get on with their killing to a background of hard rock.

Time passes. I try to access a meditative state but it is like praying beside a monk. Gaetano has spoken about the art of waiting, about how it is a beautiful thing, and I try to think about that instead of coffee. Gradually, the light diffuses through the sky. It flares on the clouds' edges, while the clouds themselves retain the dawn's dull grey. The temperature drops one more degree. It is in this moment, when the land is at its freshest, that anything seems possible.

The clouds in the west are pinking now, and in the east I can see where the sun will be appearing, a thick yellow bruising the horizon. The peak of a mountain to the west is bathed suddenly in light and crows are rushing places. As the day brightens, Gaetano points out to me a featureless mountainside of grass. I shrug, not understanding. He takes a photo and zooms in on his camera's screen to show me. It is the body of a cow. '*Morto?*' He nods. '*Ieri?*'

He shakes his head. 'Two or three days ago,' he mouths.

If I summon all of my attention, I can distinguish its mark from the other shadows, and as the quarter-hours pass, it hoves into view. I understand that we are staking out a crime scene. Gaetano hopes that the wolves will be back for their next meal. There is a flicker of movement, and a falcon flies right at us before banking at the last moment and darting off across the hills.

And now the sun. It bursts over the horizon like an epiphany, and with it my mood lifts. Gaetano warms his gloved hands in the light. The land changes rapidly. Hollows that ten minutes before I could almost convince myself were wolf now lose their menace. The cows are on the move, another day of grazing. In the binoculars, in the low light, each of their heads is haloed with flies. The air is so still I can hear them chewing. They pass their fallen comrade, eerily unconcerned.

And then! There is something moving on the ridge above the corpse, picked out against the brightening sky. I raise my binoculars. It is not a cow; it is smaller, grey. A bolt of adrenaline surges through my body, the sort of feeling that for a moment makes you almost wish it wasn't true in case the very feeling of it is more than your body could contain. My tiredness evaporates. I grab at Gaetano's knee and urgently hiss, 'There!'

'*Capriolo*,' Gaetano says. Roe deer.

And so it is. She raises her head and I can see her more clearly now. Her little white bum. I remove my hand from Gaetano's knee. But my heart is racing. And for the next half-hour I am alert again, glassing the slopes backward and forward, backward and forward. I am convinced that the wolf is about to enter into this drama. I am convinced that we are being observed, in our makeshift blind, wrapped in brown-and-green blankets in the middle of a hill. I no longer feel the cold.

He does not come.

But now I understand, I think. I understand what brings Gaetano out here, dawn after dawn, in all seasons and all weathers, ever since the wolves first came here, a decade ago. It is *that* feeling, of plunging into another animal's world. I have known it very few times. Twice when I crossed paths with bears in Alaska. And once in Namibia, a very long time ago, when a springbok walked into our camp at dawn, and we lay there in our sleeping bags on our camp beds watching it move, and the man – a local Himba man – lying on the bed beside me hissed, 'That is the wildest animal that you will ever fucking see.'

I had that feeling now. Not even for a wolf. Just for the possibility of one.

We must go soon. By eight o'clock the sun is high and the mountain peaks are aflame. Gaetano has a job to get to. He begins to pack his things. I massage the blood back into my legs and stagger to my feet.

'No wolves. *Niente.*' He shrugs. All part of the job. Next time – *la prossima volta*. 'It can be hard,' he says with a smile, 'to stay awake at work.'

The wolves are out there. Watching the kill site perhaps, and watching us, waiting for us to leave. And there is something else that is easy to forget in the disappointment. That I have woken up at 3 a.m. and come and obligingly sat for hours in the dark, and in the cold, so that a wolf could look at *me*.

The full moon still hangs in a pure blue sky as we walk back to the cars.

10

A Wolf, passing by, saw some Shepherds in a hut eating a haunch of mutton for their dinner. Approaching them, he said, 'What a clamour you would raise if I were to do as you are doing!'
Aesop, 'The Wolf and the Shepherds'

In 1220 the future Saint Francis of Assisi was living in Gubbio, in the Apennines. He was recently back from the Fifth Crusade. Gubbio was impressive even then, a Roman amphitheatre and a new cathedral, the whole town encircled by thick walls. Francesco would have been pleased to be back home, but there was a war in Gubbio as well.

A recently arrived wolf had begun by eating sheep but had quickly got a taste for shepherds. By the time Francesco came on the scene, the situation was so bad that no one could go outside the walls, because even if they went armed, 'as if going to battle', they were certain to be devoured. A painting by the Sienese artist Sassetta, done a couple of centuries after the fact, shows the countryside littered with body parts. Gubbio was under siege.

Francesco walked out to confront it. He was already renowned for his ability to speak with birds and fish, and this pagan talent did not seem to count against him. As Francesco approached the den, the wolf charged him. Francesco stood his ground and drew the sign of the cross in the air. He commanded it, in the name of Christ, to do no harm. The wolf stopped running, clapped his mouth shut, and curled up at Francesco's feet.

'Thou hast done much evil in this land,' Francesco told him. 'Thou dost merit the gallows as a thief and a most iniquitous murderer. All men cry out against thee, the dogs pursue thee, and all this city is thine enemy. But I will make peace between them and thee, O Brother Wolf. To the end that thou mayest no more offend them, and that they may forgive thee all thy past offences, and that neither men nor dogs may pursue thee any more.'

It is written that the wolf made a sign that he agreed. In Sassetta's painting he is raising his right foreleg to Francesco, like a dog taught to shake hands. For their part in the peace deal, the citizens of Gubbio agreed to feed the wolf if he turned up at their door. This was domestication as religious experience, divine and instantaneous. The wolf became like a fat stray cat. Two years later, when he died of old age, Gubbio 'mourned his loss greatly'. When Francesco died, four years after that, he was canonised by Pope Gregory IX and became the patron saint of Italy.

Yet without Saint Francis mediating, both wolves and men quickly forgot their respective sides of the bargain.

Across Italy the wolf kept eating sheep and shepherds, and men and dogs found themselves unable to forgive. The next few centuries unravelled as we know. By the 1960s wolves in Italy had been so effectively and systematically eradicated that there were fewer than a hundred left, clinging on in two isolated populations in the southern Apennines, not far from Francis's old stomping grounds.

Yet perceptions towards the natural world were changing. For the radicalism that defined the era, nature was one more persecuted minority. WWF opened its first offices in Switzerland in 1961. The first Earth Day was in 1970. In the United States the Endangered Species Act was signed into law in late 1973, and the wolf was added to the list a year later; the Bern Convention did the same for wolves in Europe in 1979. In the same year, Pope John Paul II declared Saint Francis the patron saint of ecology. Farley Mowat's *Never Cry Wolf* (1963) sold several million copies, despite one reviewer claiming it to be roughly as factual as 'Little Red Riding Hood'. In both Canada and Russia the book galvanised protest against the state-sponsored culling of wolves.

In 1970 WWF and the Abruzzo National Park, home to some of Italy's last wolves, launched *Operazione San Francesco*. It aimed for the same reconciliation that the saint had achieved in Gubbio: a peace between human and wolf. People, and presumably wolves as well, were to be asked to forgive past crimes. Wolves aren't known for bearing grudges, but when it came to us, things were more complicated. The team sat with shepherds, listening to their concerns. They worked with priests and mayors and schoolchildren, supplanting fiction with fact. Students from across Italy came to the new visitor centre to listen to the wolves howling at night. The head of the Abruzzo Park was photographed playing with a rescue wolf named Ezekiel.

It was dazzlingly effective. Hunting was banned in the park, as was poisoned bait. In 1973 a three-year Italy-wide truce was issued by the Minister for Agriculture and Forestry, and in 1976 it became permanent. By the end of the 1970s the wolf population in Italy had doubled. By the 1990s it had doubled again, aided by new European legislation. Juliet, and her journey, and her legacy, were only possible because of the decisions taken by a few brave individuals, on both sides, who were able to forget past horrors.

Today Italy is experiencing an explosion in wolf numbers that is dramatic even for Europe. The best population estimate – 3,307 – is higher than that of any other European country. This land was an empty stage waiting on its protagonist – hollows that could be dens, saplings that could be marking posts, deer that could be prey. All life is pregnant with a desire to thrive. The world has a remarkable capacity for renewal. No one imagined it possible that within a decade of Slavc and Juliet's arrival wolves could have stitched themselves back into the fabric of the area so completely. Lessinia has four packs now, two wholly within the park and two more at its edges. In the eastern Italian Alps, fanning out from here, there are at least a hundred wolves in a dozen or so packs, and they are expanding year-on-year. Some of the couple's descendants have dispersed back to Slovenia, where they have formed packs of their own.

In 2020, in Lessinia alone, wolves killed 173 farm animals. In 2021, another 234. Meanwhile, at least 300 wolves are killed illegally in Italy each year. In May 2023 nine were poisoned in the Abruzzo. In Tuscany, a wolf's head was left suspended at a roundabout, along with a note signed 'Little Red Riding Hood'. They have been found skinned, suspended from road signs and motorway flyovers, some kind of warning to other wolves or to those who support them. The peace that Saint Francis and the wolf of Gubbio brokered remains as precarious as ever.

Later that month I move my bag from the pizzeria in Velo to Emma and Giacomo's place in a hamlet outside of Cerro Veronese. It was Emma who had taught me Italian online during the pandemic and by coincidence they have just relocated to Lessinia, part of a wave of young people moving to the countryside as rural villages empty out, as rents in the cities keep on climbing and a new culture and better internet make it more possible to work from home. They are wonderful people and they love their new life here. We take their dog on long walks through the forests and tend to their vegetable patch, which is exhausted from the heat. Their house is tiny and ancient and cool, the interior all wood, and from my bed up in the rafters I can reach out and touch the thick pink stone of the roof. Most of the year their village is all but empty, but come the summer the Veronese arrive to open up their summerhouses, fleeing the heat of the plain below. They are mostly old, and they spend their days chatting in deckchairs in the shade of vines, waiting until the hour comes when they can pour an aperitif.

The farmhouse known as Malga Folignano di Cima is an hour north of their place. It is high up and fringed by deep valleys – by the Vajo delle Ortighe to the north and west, the Vajo del Buso to the south. I drive up there one afternoon, bringing Giacomo with me to translate, because despite my best efforts to learn Italian before I arrived I had not reckoned on the dialects. To the east the land plateaus before it rises gently to the highest parts of Lessinia. Birdsong snags on the air and the mountain flowers tremble. Maybe it is cooler up here, but it is hard to say for sure. Off to the south is the Po Valley, washed in haze, with a thin stripe of ruffled cloud running both ways above it as far as the eye can see, like breakers on the shore.

The farmhouse is squat and made of stone, the roof great square slabs of it with narrower slabs covering each join so that it looks not unlike the keyboard of a piano. I have been invited up here by Modesto Gugole, a farmer whose family has owned this *malga* for generations. Modesto is in his eighties but he looks decades off that. He is dressed in green overalls and a beige fisherman's hat, thick grey sideburns poking out beneath. We sit together at his table. There is little ostentation to the room, a hollowed lump of stone. There is a wood-fired range and a marble sink and glass-fronted cupboards stuffed with pasta and polenta and decorated with photos of his grandkids. A crude wooden ladder leads to the sleeping quarters in the roof. Carved into the soot-blackened stone of the lintel is the year of its construction: 1867. He pours us coffee with a little grappa, a little sugar.

'My life is an inherited thing from my parents and my grandparents,' Modesto says in a slow rasp. 'They always did this work. Lessinia developed when there were no wolves here. My grandparents destroyed them. Lessinia became very populated thanks to our work. There were so many animals up here.'

Sometimes the old-timers will come back up here, for old times' sake, and they will ask what happened to everyone. The *malghe*, the farmhouses, would have thronged back then with animals and people. You can still see the stone-built sties that would have housed the pigs. There would have been horses, donkeys, sheep. They made cheeses up here, and every two days the donkeys would carry the truckles down to the towns to sell.

Some of the *malghe* are guesthouses now, feeding tourists, not cows. No one makes cheese in the mountains any more, and every other day a lorry comes to take their milk away. Most farmers are too busy making hay or holding down another job to spend their summers up here, and they rarely have anyone to help them, so is it really any wonder that the wolves come?

Yet Modesto ensures that Malga Folignano di Cima is occupied all summer long. He has two hired hands who live up here for the season, and every morning he drives up from his house in Campofontana before dawn with his two middle-aged sons, and they do not leave until after the evening milking. Modesto has been up every morning at four since he was a boy and often he can still outstrip the others in his capacity for work. They have lost five or six cows to wolves in the last ten years, but compared to others who he knows, they have been lucky.

'The situation with the wolf is serious,' he says. 'I love my cows. A farm not far from us was attacked two weeks ago. They ate everything. The owner told me: "One more attack and I'm giving up."'

Modesto has a herd of 160 cows. There are ninety up here for the summer, while the rest are down at Campofontana. The annual rhythm of the mountains is dictated by the transhumance – bringing the grazing animals up to the Alpine pastures for the summer to grow fat on the fresh grass, taking them back down to the valleys before the first of the winter snows. It is a domesticated migration that echoes the former mass movements of wild herbivores, and it is what mountain people throughout the world have always done, the days of ascent and descent celebrated in the villages they pass through. Many farmers still live this way, but most now use trucks to ferry their animals back and forth. Modesto is the last cow farmer in Lessinia to undertake the journey on foot. For him, tradition still has a value that modernity cannot match. He invites us to join him in the autumn.

'In 2011 our politicians brought a wolf to Lessinia for money and for votes,' Modesto says. 'This was a part of Italy that had nothing. But they did not understand what a disaster it would be.' He presses a finger into the table. 'I have argued with the politicians for the past ten years and they say to me, "It's true, we did it for the money. But we didn't think what would happen afterwards."'

A grey kitten walks into the kitchen and forces its small head against my ankle.

'They live in the city,' he continues. 'They know nothing of us. They don't care anything if our farms are closed. It's completely another mentality. They do one job, but they don't agree with my job, although they don't know what I do? Go to hell! I don't want them to lose their job, even if I don't know what they do. But they eat my cheese and drink my milk. They are outside of reality.'

'Do you feel like the wolves are more important than you?'

He nods. 'Bravo.'

The kitten climbs my leg and begins needling at my thigh. I scoop it to the floor and it goes to hunch over a saucer of milk, as though it has made a kill.

Modesto is clear that the wolf is not the only problem they are suffering. Their milk is organic, which commands a better price, but still the market is underpaying while the price of everything else – electricity, diesel, feed – goes up by the week. The weather is the worst he has ever seen it, dry as a bone and roasting, even at this altitude. It burns the grass so that the cows won't eat it. But nothing compares to the wolf.

'This is the biggest change we have ever had,' he says. 'I don't know what to tell you, but it will finish in disaster. It's usually a hard life to work with the cow, but with the wolf it is too much. The politicians have to understand that either the wolf stays here or us.'

He stands and says he must be getting on. Modesto does not like to sit around. I follow him outside and from there into the sheds. The cowbells clang and echo, the lowing of the cattle filling the building where they are gathered at one end, heads bowed in the antiseptic light. The ancient generator throbs outside. Modesto has donned a white apron and is now down in a concrete pit in the middle of the barn, along with the two young men who help him. One of them swings the gate open and the first eight cows enter the stalls. They shovel feed into the trough and while the cows are occupied they disinfect their teats with a blue liquid, wipe them clean, and get the milk flowing with a few deft pulls. Then they clamp the pumps onto the udders. Giacomo and I stand there watching, calling to the men above the mechanical, rhythmic slurping. The cows wait patiently, chewing. And once the milking has finished, a few minutes later, they let the cows out of the stalls with a quick slap on the rump to hurry them outside. Then they hose down the shit and do it all again, for ninety cows. Tomorrow morning they will do it once more, three hours each time, and they will do it each morning and evening until the summer ends. An icon of San Francesco blessing the dumb animals, dangling on a wire by the feed hopper, is the only concession in the whole place to aesthetics.

Later, outside, when they are done, I find one of the young men collapsed in a chair in the last of the warmth. He is holding his phone like he's been shot in the stomach, staring at it as if they were his innards he was scrying. Hassan Tahiri is twenty-seven. He has a big smile and wrecked teeth. We speak in Italian, both of us enthusiastic amateurs. I tell him he looks tired. He tells me that he is up every morning at three-thirty to round up the cows for the morning milking, and that he does not get to bed until after dark. Summer is just one endless day, punctuated by moments of snatched sleep.

'Modesto really likes to work!' he grins.

I ask him where he is from. Morocco, he says, same as the other man. 'You're far from home,' I say, and then feel foolish to have said it.

'Morocco is a beautiful country,' Hassan says. 'But without money, an impossible country.'

As a boy he had done similar work with animals, up in the hills outside Marrakech, alongside his mother and his father and the rest of his family. The soft dawn air and the cries of his brothers; the steaming milk and his aching wrists. Sometimes it seems to him as though he has not travelled far at all. Moroccan cows, Italian cows – they are really much the same. And then at other times it seems that he has come to the very other end of the earth.

'I feel good here in Lessinia,' he says. 'It is not racist here. But if you are a foreigner, you feel the distance.' The Italians called him *'migrante economico'*, as though that were an insult. As though Italians only wanted their grapes and their strawberries and their tobacco and their tomatoes picked – all jobs that he had done in the first years that he was here – or their chickens and their turkeys slaughtered, by people fleeing war zones. 'What was he running from?' Italians would ask him. Well, nothing, although the ongoing drought and the crop failures at home, the failure of the tomato harvest, the wheat harvest, the olive harvest, meant that he never thought about moving back. Here he could dream of his own car, his own workshop, his own business, although his few snatched hours of sleep each night were not so conducive to dreams. He had been in Italy for seven years and this was his first summer in these hills.

As a child Hassan had dreamt of Europe and of the life that he might have there. They all did. And when he was twenty he left his village and his parents and his seven brothers and his sister's grave and he took a plane from Casablanca to Istanbul. He had spent some weeks there on the Asian side before he had met a Moroccan who told him that he could get him into Greece. His fee was 800 euros. They were on a bus for eight hours and it dropped them at a beach not far from Izmir. They were Syrians and Moroccans, plenty of kids. It was March and the weather was abysmal. The sea churning and heaving; the wind slicing across the sand. There were two boats, both of them entirely unsuitable for the number of people that they were. There was a woman beside him shepherding four small children and she asked for his help to get them on board. The only other choice was not to go.

Waves slopped into the boat. Spray soaked them through. There were not enough life jackets, there wasn't even space to sit. For the most part they stood in silence, eyes on the sky, awaiting their reckoning. The men bailed as the water swilled about their legs. They were in sight of Greece when the other boat went down. They could see that it was foundering, rolling in the waves in a way that was unnatural, taking too long to right. Then it flipped and went, astonishingly quickly. Someone made a phone call but there was nothing they could do. Their pilot turned their boat for Turkey. Six of them died of the cold on the way back. Three children. The only thing to do was not to think about it. The only thing to do was try again.

The next time Hassan made it to Lesvos. They stuck him in Moria, which at that time was Europe's largest refugee camp. It housed twice as many people as it was built for and at night he slept fitfully in a shipping container, dripping sweat and slapping at mosquitoes as children howled in the dark. He left one night on a ferry, clinging to the bottom of a truck. There is something about a person clinging to the base of a lorry that encapsulates everything about the cruel logic of free trade and hard borders. From Athens he took a bus to Thessaloníki, and from there he set out north, on foot, in the direction of Macedonia. He had the clothes that he wore and a blanket. He followed the roads, walking the verge. Walking at night, hiding from cars. The road signs were in Cyrillic, but when he could charge it he had a map on his phone. He had already worn through his shoes.

People were very kind to him and the police were very bad. Twice in Serbia they arrested him. The first time they sent him back to Macedonia; the second time they beat him and let him keep on walking. 'Here it is,' they said, 'welcome,' they said, 'if you want Europe so bad.' Back home he had dreamt of Europe, but he had not dreamt of this.

He reached Belgrade, then on into Hungary. The Hungarian police made the Serbs look like angels. Then from Hungary into Austria. Walking, walking, day after day after day. He had heard good things about Austria, and in Innsbruck he applied for asylum. For three days he was held in the police station without water or food, he said. From there they transferred him to another refugee camp, which is where he heard that his application had been refused. He fled to Germany, but he had been told you could wait there for years without papers, and so from Germany he turned south. He had a cousin near Verona. He came here. It had taken him eight months.

'I only want a good life,' he says. 'I'm not escaping from anything.'

Modesto is by no means the only farmer in Lessinia making use of this new influx of labour. West of here, a few kilometres outside the small town of Erbezzo, is a migrant reception centre, and several of its residents have gone on to find work on the *malghe*. A former NATO command centre, it was requisitioned in 2017 by the prefecture as a CAS – *Centro di Accoglienza Straordinaria* – an emergency reception centre for migrants. As with many other centres across Italy, and with similar places across Europe, what had been intended as temporary shelter in exceptional circumstances has turned into long-term, often chronically unsuitable, housing. In 2019 the Migrant Observatory of Verona tried to have it shut down, citing its 'isolation' and 'segregation'.

Typically refugees are transferred here directly from Lampedusa, and some end up staying for years. Twenty euros a day are spent on each individual, including their stipend. Following cuts implemented when Matteo Salvini was deputy prime minister in 2019, there are now no language classes, no psychologist, no nurse, nothing to do. I have been to visit, and although I have worked on refugee projects in both England and Greece, I have never seen anywhere so unlikely. A compound of beige buildings stuck out on a promontory, surrounded by slack barbed wire and scraps of woodland. In winter it can become cut off entirely. A few years ago eight members tried to flee during a snowstorm and were picked up on their way into Verona. In 2018 a thirty-nine-year-old Nigerian man, Eso Matthew, died of a heart attack here. It took the ambulance more than forty-five minutes to arrive.

Reception centres are meant to be located in inhabited places to enable integration, but the nearby hamlet of Vaccamozzi, with its seven inhabitants, pushes that definition to its limit. It is the most isolated centre in the whole of Veneto. 'As long as they're in there, I don't worry,' one of Vaccamozzi's inhabitants told the local paper when it first opened. 'But the idea that they go around, especially at night, scares me.' At a packed meeting in August 2017, held for local residents, Erbezzo's mayor, Lucio Campedelli, spoke of having to 'suffer the presence of strangers' and of how Italy's response to the refugee crisis now amounted to 'support for the invasion'. 'Anyone who thinks we will be able to integrate these people is living on the moon,' echoed Raffaello Campostrini, mayor of nearby Sant'Anna d'Alfaedo. Mauro Gaspari, deputy mayor of San Martino Buon Albergo, pointed out that, because fewer than 4 per cent of migrants to Italy were granted asylum in 2016, 'it is clear that we are not dealing with refugees'. He called on the local mayors to be heroes.

I have wolves on the brain, of course. But as I read these statements from those who were supposed to be the moral compass of these mountain towns, it is easy to draw comparisons. Wolves and migrants have always been here. Lessinia was largely colonised by Bavarians a thousand years ago, and the remnants of the Cimbri language, still spoken in a few pockets such as Giazza, recall that migrant past. The Cimbri were woodcutters, and the wolves would have receded along with the forests until all the memories were felled. The sorts of things that I was reading — that the Lessinians were there first, before the wolves, before the migrants — stretched the facts to breaking point. The Lessinians were migrants, and Lessinia meant wolves. But people believed it, that was what was important. As much as they believed that they had no need of either.

I ask Hassan if he has seen wolves.

'Of course.'

'Did you have wolves in Morocco?'

He isn't sure, but they had foxes. They would come in the night and kill a newborn lamb or newborn kid, and they killed chickens by the dozen, and his family had no love for them. He had not thought about wolves much until he came up here, but he has seen them four or five times since. A presence in the dusk. One time he was driving this track before dawn and there was one crossing the road, its eyes held in the headlights for long moments, eerie and artificial. They say the wolves came from the east. And he has no love for them, either. But in how they move through the shadows, and in how they carve a living in this land, taking what they feel that they are due, and in how these men speak about them, in all that, they stir something in him. He cannot put his finger on what, exactly. But he is moved.

*

One evening while I am finishing dinner with Emma and Giacomo I get a message from Paolo Parricelli, Lessinia's park warden. It is a message I have been waiting for since I first met him some weeks before. 'Tomorrow morning I will go to inspect a cattle predation nearby Sant'Anna d'Alfaedo,' it says. Would I like to join him? The next day he collects me early from the car park in Fosse and we wind up into the hills, in convoy with the vet. We park on a gravel track beside a battered pickup and a woman and a man get out and all of us shake hands.

Crickets scatter before us. It is nine-thirty, and already it is blisteringly hot. The couple whose cow it was leads us through tall grasses to the place. The woman is in a singlet and jeans and boots, her skin dark from a long summer of sun. The man carries a rope coiled over his shoulder and is dressed as though he has just quit a cross-country run, in cap and tiny shorts and vest with grey hair tumbling from the neckline, old plimsolls and hiked-up socks. His limbs twitch with thin sinews of muscle and his eyes are red and tired.

We smell the stench of it before we see it, the sweet, damp death smell, rising on the new day's heat. The cow is collapsed at the base of a rose bush. Its head lies cocked at an awkward angle and a fly wanders over the orb of its eye but apart from those slight aberrations it seems to be resting only. I walk around the shrub to look from the other end. The hindquarters, from the thurl down to the hock, are almost entirely gone, as though the cow has been sliced in cross-section by a dull blade, leaving only ragged flesh and a ruin of innards and blood and shit that is heaving and pulsing with maggots, so that it appears the creature's anima is still throbbing within it. I gag and hold an arm across my face.

'Ceradini saw the female wolf, and he said that she is twice the size of a dog and that she also has pups,' the man says. 'Yesterday this cow was missing, and my heart ached for worrying. She has never been missing.'

The vet is in wellies and an old band T-shirt, a surgical mask kept halfway up her arm like a vestigial fin. She snaps on gloves and takes a scalpel from her back pocket and draws the blade the length of the cow's neck. She peels back the thick layers of skin and fat to expose the animal's trachea, the creamy pink of fat and flesh of a recently healthy cow. Flies swarm about her as she works.

'There were five chamois at Claudio's,' the woman says, watching the vet slicing away. 'Peacefully eating in the meadow. Why don't the wolves hunt them?'

'Too much effort.'

'They run too fast.' It is one of those husband-and-wife routines, rehearsed many times and played out for our benefit. 'But tell me, how is the wolf natural if it only fills its belly with what we put out to pasture?'

'Here's the haematoma,' the vet says, pointing at a thick and diffuse clot of blood that she has exposed beneath the skin. 'She was alive when she was taken. This is not post-mortem consumption.'

'They ate her alive?' asks the farmer.

The vet nods. 'Some attacked directly from the belly, others from the neck.'

A neck bite rules out a killing by a dog: a dog would never take down a cow like this. But, frankly, look at her. There is a thirty-metre swathe of flattened and bloody grass that stops at the corpse, as though a bulldozer has been driven across the land. The haunches have been eaten off her while she was still alive and thrashing. These people have seen a lot of death, but no one finds it easy to look on this dispassionately. The pain she would have gone through is incalculable. Her organs exposed to the cold night air. How many wolves would there have been? How long would it have taken her to die?

'Poor girl,' says the man. 'She was sweet like bread, this one.'

'She wasn't healthy at first,' the woman says. 'She couldn't digest milk. I looked after her. She was like a baby girl.'

'Women are better with beasts,' the man says. 'That's the truth of it.'

'I cried when I saw her dead,' says the woman. 'You can't see certain things.'

The vet stands. She wipes the sweat from her brow with a forearm. Three days dead, she estimates. A farmer might check on their herd once a week, and a kill can pass unnoticed for days. It is so easy to get confused in the fog in these mountains, and when a heifer gets separated and turns up in a different herd they say that the wolf can smell its difference. Its vulnerability, its confusion. That wolves prey on the ones that are lost.

When the vet has finished her work, the man takes a penknife from the pocket of his little shorts and slices the belt from the animal's neck and removes the large domed bell. It clangs once and falls silent. He bends and attaches the rope he carries to the animal's forelegs, and then together the couple heave the animal back to the track. Later it will be picked up by a waste-disposal unit. This is policy. Leaving the carcasses upsets the tourists, but it also means the wolves must kill again.

Back at the cars, the vet takes the paperwork from the passenger seat and leans on the bonnet to write. She fills out the basics of her autopsy and confirms 'wolf' in the notes. A wolf kill will entitle them to compensation, although the bureaucracy can take months.

'Is this the fifth?' the vet asks.

'The sixth this summer,' the woman says. 'Let's touch iron there are no more.'

The man puts his hands together in prayer and rocks them back and forth, the theatrical gesture of a wronged footballer. 'It's a fucking brothel,' he says. 'It isn't worth it any more.'

'We must be able to shoot them,' says the woman. 'I've nothing against wolves, but they don't belong here.' I have so consistently heard this – that while people don't have a problem with wolves, in theory, that this is not their place – that I wonder where exactly is left for them.

'Someone said in Asiago there is a set-up you can get that shoots the wolf with rubber bullets if it turns up,' says the man.

'No, it doesn't work like that,' the vet says. 'Where somewhere has a lot of predations, they can set up a system that warns the farmer on his phone when the wolf comes. The farmer calls the guards and they come with rubber bullets the next day. It is not a machine shooting the bullets.'

The man shrugs. 'Well, what do I know?' he says.

'Some people brush tar on the backs of the cows and say that protects them,' says the woman.

'We've tried everything,' says the man. 'Everything has failed. At San Bortolo they built a fence one hundred and seventy centimetres high and the wolf jumped it and ate their goats.' He removes his cap and examines the inside of it, runs a hand through his greying hair.

'You should come up yourselves and scare the wolves a little,' Paolo says. 'Make some noise. Show yourself around.'

The man shakes his head. 'I'm not in bed all day. I was up at two o'clock this morning.'

'It needn't be often. Maybe it won't help, but you could try.'

'I'm sorry, Paolo, I'm not coming. I work fifteen hours a day. If I also work nights? You go crazy. It makes no sense to me.'

'It is for the politicians to decide if they want us,' says the woman. 'They should put on guards at night.'

Two hikers pass in fluorescent, wicking outfits, mirrored shades and hiking poles, their tiny dog anxious and yapping at the carnage of the body of the cow that is now lying on the verge. '*Buongiorno*,' one of them says breezily as these different worlds collide.

The farmer inclines his head. '*Salve*,' he says, gravely.

'There is nothing I can do,' Paolo says again. Lacking a wolf or a politician to absorb their anger, he is the closest to a representative they have. 'Speak with Valdegamberi.'

'And Valdegamberi will say speak to Veneto,' says the woman. 'And Veneto will say speak to Roma. And Roma will say speak to Brussels. And they will keep on passing the buck. I have heard it all before. But whose land is this?'

The vet slides the documents across the bonnet of the pickup.

'Well,' the man says as he signs. 'It will be fate, as long as they give me my five thousand euros.'

'I don't want five thousand euros,' says the woman. 'I want my cows back.'

The next day I am up early at Podestaria, in Lessinia's northern uplands. Beside its *malga* and refuge stands an ancient church, dedicated to Saint Bartholomew. Today, 25 August, is his saint's day, and traditionally it marks the time when the flocks leave the mountain pastures for the valleys. A congregation of farmers sit in the pews, straw hats held in their laps. Above the altar, two pieces of beaten copper depict Christ: *Grata Perenne Memoria Della Sua Prima Vista Pastorale.* The double meaning of 'pastoral' has never been clearer to me than now. This flock of men, seeking guidance, to in turn protect their flocks.

Back outside, the prayers done with, it is time to start the drinking. It is a quarter-past nine in the morning. On one side of a pickup is a large poster of a wolf looking dapper in black tie, dressed for dinner, with a red line slashed through its muzzle. 'The mountains will never be yours,' it reads. Many of the farmers are wearing white T-shirts emblazoned with *Io sto con gli allevatori* – 'I stand with the breeders.' There is thunder in the hills away to the south, over towards Monte Tomba.

The annual gathering at Podestaria has been going for forty years. There is a ceremonial crowning of the *bacani*, the farmers of the year, and it is a moment for the breeders to come together and show off their animals. But this year there are no animals. Next month at the Fiera del Bestiame di Erbezzo – 115 years old, and the most important fair in Lessinia's agricultural calendar – it will be the same, the cows and calves and sheep replaced with cardboard silhouettes to demonstrate what a future without farming here would look like. It is only cataclysmic events, such as wars and pandemics, that have stopped them gathering before. Today there is another. A few days ago a white flag was raised on the pastures in symbolic surrender. *Demonstration out of desperation* said the small placard in Italian beneath it and, beneath that, the old saying for good luck, *in bocca al lupo*, – 'In the mouth of the wolf'. It is not unlike 'Break a leg', conferring luck by wishing its opposite, and was used originally among hunters. The traditional comeback is *Crepi lupo* – 'Kill the wolf!'

By mid-morning a lot of the farmers have a few beers inside them and the polenta won't be ready for another hour at least. The atmosphere has become a little tense. Stefano Valdegamberi, a local politician on the regional council of Veneto and a member of the far-right, populist Lega, gets up on the flatbed that is the stage. A recent investigation by the Organized Crime and Corruption Reporting Project claimed that he was on the Kremlin's payroll, promoting pro-Moscow views within the EU, although he denies this. He has been an observer at several Russian parliamentary elections, where he has been 'struck by the transparency of everything'. Whatever he is, he is very popular up here. He hails from a farm in Lessinia; he is one of them. His Facebook timeline, alongside Russian propaganda and reflections on Cimbrian (the local, ancient language, which he is fluent in), has occasional photos of him with his sheep. When a wolf was illegally shot here in 2018, the animal-rights group Lega Anti Vivisezione (LAV) condemned the killing with a statement on Facebook beneath a photo of the dead animal. 'The next photo will be one of the LAV!' Valdegamberi commented, a death threat that he shrugged off by saying that he often used 'irony or paradoxes to encourage reflection'.

Many farmers believe that he is the only one who wants to do anything to help them. In 2021 Valdegamberi proposed a law 'for the containment of the wolf where it causes serious damage to breeding'. His proposal was condemned by environmental groups, which claimed that 'the wolf question in Lessinia cannot be resolved with legislative culling acts solicited by social tension and with propaganda purposes'. When we sit down together for a coffee some days later in his home town of Badia Calavena, Valdegamberi tells me that what upset him was not the predictable reaction of the 'ideologists' to his proposal — by which he means the bunny-huggers — but the reaction of the politicians and the agricultural unions. He describes Coldiretti, Italy's largest agricultural union, as worse than an enemy. 'If they want to do something, they can move government and policy,' he says. 'But they want to be environmentalists even more than the environmentalists.' This is the ground that Valdegamberi covers in his speech that morning at Podestaria, so that by the time he sits down and Alex Vantini, the president of Coldiretti Verona, climbs up onto the trailer, the crowd is feeling boisterous.

'I won't hide from you how hard it is to be here, and to be president, in a year and during a situation like this,' Vantini begins, sounding as though hiding is exactly what he would like to be doing. 'Not only because of the issues with the animals, but also because of the increase in raw materials, and the drought. We already heard about the gap between the world of politics and farmers. I represent you, and I want the farmers behind me. Whoever wants to, come up onstage with me.'

No one moves. Vantini looks around. 'Why don't you come down here?' a man shouts.

'We're not for coexistence,' Vantini says, beginning to go off-script. 'I'm upset that politicians, even on this stage, are blaming the unions. We have said that we are in favour of management.'

'*Cos'hai* fatto?!' the man shouts back – 'but what have you *done*?!' He elbows his way to the front of the crowd. He has on mirrored shades pushed back on his short, spiked hair, a tattoo of flames snaking up one thick arm.

Vantini makes a circle with his thumb and first finger and moves his hand back and forth to accentuate his speech, as though measuring a beat. 'Why do you applaud someone who made a proposal that didn't go ahead?' he says, referring to Valdegamberi's speech.

'At least he's done something!'

'When the law is on the table, we will respond favourably. That's the process. We don't make laws.'

But everyone here is pretty sick by now of process. Process has not saved their cows. 'Go study the law!' the man cries, right in front of the stage now. 'I know it off by heart!'

Several others pitch in. Vantini looks well out of his depth. They stand before him, all of them yelling. I can't understand everything they're saying, but what's clear is that the wolf has concentrated the entirety of their frustration and their fear, like the sun through a magnifying glass. The adrenaline rushes through me as I watch them square up to each other. And then Vantini cuts it short and goes and sits down, looking flustered and shocked.

The man with the flames up his arm is Enrico Beltramini. After things have calmed down I introduce myself, and he invites me to his house for beer and meat. I go round a few days later, to a small village not far from Velo. I sit at the table in his smart, modern kitchen while Enrico sharpens a knife until it gleams and slices three steaks from a loin. He was a shepherd in Lessinia for ten years until one of his guardian dogs attacked a tourist's dog and bit its paw off. These days he is a butcher.

'Like the wolf!' his girlfriend laughs, looking up from her phone.

'The wolf is very interesting,' Enrico says over his shoulder from the stove. 'He is a thinker. A perfect soldier. I hate him so *much*. But I respect him. Because he is a great animal. The king. He is not good or bad. The wolf does what the wolf does. Simple.' Enrico is someone else who, I suspect, despite his hatred for the wolf, would not mind being resurrected as one.

He drops the steaks into a smoking pan and serves them up still bloody, seconds later. He sits down across from me. On the other arm, the one without the flames, there is a tattoo of a pair of crossed handguns, with *Beltramini Clan* inked out around it in a looping, elaborate script.

'They tell me that if a wolf sees me, it runs away.' He wags his finger. 'No. The wolf is scared of nothing. The wolf isn't interested in you. Everyone is underestimating him. He is the apex predator of the food chain. We shouldn't be surprised if he eats someone this year.' When I tell him that there are people campaigning to reintroduce the wolf to Scotland, he laughs as though the whole world has gone insane. 'There's a reason why we killed them,' Enrico says. 'It's all written down in the stories.'

Like every former wolf territory, Lessinia has its share of wolf stories that have long outlived its wolves. Poor Maddalena of Camposilvano, eaten in 1655, the right side of her body devoured while she was out doing her laundry (it is said the wolf will not touch the left side because that is where the heart beats). Or the man from Gaspari who would howl from the hilltops to scare his neighbours, but one day howled so realistically that he summoned an actual wolf. It pursued him all the way to the stables, and although the man survived, his hair turned white and he stammered for evermore.

After we have devoured our meat Enrico scrolls through images on his phone that he has gathered, a harrowing album of the war.

'Look at this one. The lungs are out. You can't save that. Look here. And here. This is at a bus stop where the kids wait to go to school. See that? First it pulls off the skin, and then it eats it. Like an orange! First thing he eats the liver, then all the soft parts, and then it eats the meat.' He taps his temple. 'The wolf is a thinker,' he says again.

He stops on a picture of a wolf here in Lessinia. 'Look,' he says. 'That wolf one hundred per cent has dog in it. Too many wolves are becoming hybrids. It messes up the genetics. Now there are no more Italian wolves. We're losing the race. We're losing the true Italian wolf.'

Italy will hold elections next month, after Draghi's government fell in July. The Fratelli d'Italia – the Brothers of Italy – a party with neo-fascist roots, is looking as though it could win. Will it make any difference to their problems?

'The wolf is a problem of the mountains,' Enrico says. 'In the mountains there are very few votes; in the city there are a lot. If you say we can kill the wolf, you won't get more votes. The only politician is Valdegamberi. *Forte*, Valdegamberi. He's interested in traditions, the ways of life of Lessinia. Very good. Very intelligent. Only he is interested in Lessinia because he is from here. Once they leave for Rome, they don't care.'

Short of an all-out genocide, a change in the law to permit the killing of wolves would probably not achieve much in places like this. As I've mentioned, shooting wolves can perversely increase both predations and wolf numbers by destabilising packs and making them dependent on animals that are easier to hunt. Besides, those that get shot are often the inexperienced youngsters that might otherwise have gone on to disperse, so it can make little overall impact. And yet I do find myself wondering whether, if it isn't going to endanger local populations or the wolf's conservation status, at this point making it easier to shoot wolves might not be the simplest solution. The feeling of impotence that farmers have is far more damaging than anything the wolves are doing. Downgrading the wolf's protection level to that of, say, a jackal or a chamois, would make it easier to manage hybrids and problem wolves, and those encroaching on suburban areas. But more importantly, it would shatter the illusion that the wolf is a sacred animal, a totem of the urban elite. It is quite evident to those living in the countryside that the wolf is doing fantastically well, and to be unable to do anything about it – to be unable to look after one's land and animals and livelihood – only serves to enflame division. Conservationists argue that downgrading the wolf would set a dangerous precedent, but without some sort of concession to the way the farmers are experiencing this, I do wonder what will happen next.

'Sooner or later this facade will fall,' Enrico says, fixing my eye. 'There is a breaking point. I don't know if it will be tomorrow or in ten years, but sooner or later it will happen. Because the wolf is too much. It's too heavy. It's too heavy on everything.'

11

'The grassland is a big life, but it's thinner than people's eyelids. If you rupture its grassy surface, you blind it, and dust storms are more lethal than the white-hair blizzards. If the grassland dies, so will the cows and sheep and horses, as well as the wolves and the people, all the little lives.'

Jiang Rong, *Wolf Totem*

Mattia Cacciatori lay in his bed, listening to the rain hammering on the caravan's roof. Such sounds were not so cosy when you knew that you must be up and out in it at first light. When you knew that the sheep would be standing around in it, sleepless, trying to keep pointlessly dry as best they could, sodden, and the young lambs drenched and freezing.

He cannot sleep when the sheep cannot. You feel it in yourself when they're not right. Sometimes he dreams about them. During the night he will dream that there has been a birth, or that one of the ewes has aborted, and when he wakes he will find that it is so. Sofia used to tease him. They would leave the flock with a friend and go to Val Camonica to visit her mother for lunch and all day long he would be restless, unable to shut up about his sheep. He told her there would come a time when she wouldn't be able to go a whole day without thinking about the flock, and she'd laugh when he said that; 'Fuck off,' she'd say, 'you probably, not me.' You might catch her being sentimental about people, now that her wandering days were done with, but she wouldn't be going soft over sheep. And then, just last week, three lambs died of the heat and Sofia could not stop crying. She cried for a long time. There is a feeling that he gets, in the throat, when he knows something is not right with them. It's a mental illness, he sometimes jokes, but the good kind. It is not unlike being in love.

Sofia lies asleep beside him. The broken mattress sags and they pooled together in its middle. He leans into her warmth and lays his hand upon her gently swollen belly. His son in there, or his daughter – too early to say. Today is Sofia's birthday, but apart from that it will be a day much like every other. She will be thirty-five. Mattia is thirty-three.

But perhaps, at last, the drought has broken. It rained like this yesterday morning, too. Three years ago – a year ago, even – he could not spend those hours out in the rain like he did yesterday. He'd curse the weather. You can't even read when it's raining. But it's different now. He'll jump around, he'll dance, he'll sing, he won't keep one eye on the clock. Every season that passes he becomes more of a shepherd. Not bad for a city boy from Verona.

The sheep, of course, need rain, although not this much all at once, not so that they won't eat and so that the wet grass bloats their bellies. But something is better than nothing. It had not rained in months. The pond was dry, the grass paper-thin, what they call *coltellini*, little knives. The flock had to eat eight-hour days to fill their bellies with this shit, a full-time office job. Every summer there are problems with water, but never has it been this bad. All across Europe it is bad, but nowhere is as bad as Lessinia. The water drains from it like a sieve. Every day he must drive down to San Giorgio and fill the 500-litre water tank and haul it back. Water has been a problem for a lot of people for a long time, Mattia thinks. For poor people. For desert people. But now there is a time coming when we must all learn to survive.

Somehow he sleeps again. In his dream he is back in the deserts in Bolivia. He is sitting with friends and they are sharing a meal, and in every direction the barren land rolls on to distant peaks and the sky so blue it induced vertigo. Perhaps the drought had made in him some kind of madness, so that even his dreams have dried out. But he misses those places sometimes, if he lets himself. But also, he didn't miss them at all.

When he wakes he lies there in the silence until he realises that it must have been the rain stopping that woke him. A pale light is seeping in around the ill-fitting blind. He sits up, and the book he was reading before he fell asleep clatters to the floor. Sofia sleeps on. She is more tired with the pregnancy. The baby is not due until

January but already he feels the responsibility acutely. Three years ago it was just him. Now there are the two of them, and soon it will be three. He pulls on his boots and sets a coffee on the gas and pushes out the door into the day.

The sky is cloudless and the grass is sodden, and further down the valley the clouds are rising as though down there is where the clouds are brewed and formed. Viola and Pioggia, his two herding dogs, are up and turning circles round his feet, urgent with love. He grabs each dog roughly by the muzzle and kneads them behind the ears. He scratches his belly and looks up. There is a dawn wind blowing, but soon it will be hot again. That, then, is the end of the rain. The peaks, Castel Gaibana, Castel Malera, are already lit with sun. A defunct chairlift runs to the top of Gaibana, but no one has skied for years. No snow. He wanders away from the caravan to piss.

The sounds of the bells and the smells of the sheep cut through the clean, cold air. They are pressed within their electric fence, and a second fence encircling that. In the passage between the two fences are the four white Maremmano-Abruzzese, his guardian dogs – Bruma, Folco, Rollo, Pannolino – dozing in the nascent warmth like a pride of lions. He calls this construction his castle. Mostly the dogs bark at cows that pass by in the night, as though they've never seen one before, but he is yet to lose a sheep to a wolf.

There are 300 or so in the flock. There are the Bergamasca, your typical Alpine sheep, big and white and shaggy, with ears dangling like pigtails. And then there are the Brogna, smaller, coarser, with splotches like old tea stains, an ancient local breed that the Cimbri bred for the Venetian market and that was near extinction until a few shepherds undertook to pull it back. They're supposed to be good for milk, wool and meat, but really they're good for none of them. Another animal that the logic of capitalism had no use for. But then, if you cared that much for the logic of capitalism, you probably wouldn't be a shepherd in the first place.

By the time I arrive it is already hot. The sun climbs and the land sweats, a thin mist slowly rising. I drink a coffee with Mattia and Sofia and then we wander up the hill behind the flock. It was a waiter in a restaurant in Velo Veronese, where I first ate their lamb, who told me about them. They are unusual in Lessinia for keeping sheep, not cows, and they are unusual in being in their thirties, not their eighties. I got hold of Mattia and he invited me up to their summer pastures. By ten o'clock the whole mountain is bled of shadow and the three of us are up on the south-facing slope, sweating too and hazed by flies.

Sofia has a curved wooden earring, her hair sticking out of her bucket hat in plaits, an unflagging, infectious smile. Mattia is tall and bearded and wearing a bucket hat as well, both of them in old, weather-worn clothes. They are tough and lithe and built from the dailiness of hard work that the sheep demand of them. The flock moves and we move with them. The grass churns with grasshoppers. I forgot my own hat so they have lent me a spare. We will be out in this all day.

'Pioggia. *Vai sui. Vai sui. Passa avanti. Cerca cerca, vai vai. Vieni qua. Vieni. Cazo. Vieni qua. Porca dio! Vieni. Brava.*' Mattia's cries ring out like birdsong, the sonic rhythms of the landscape, directing his dogs to direct the sheep. 'Viola! Pioggia! *Titta titta titta titta!*' Small birds stir up from the scrub and flicker away as the herding dogs bolt this way and that. Just a couple mornings of rain have been enough to flush the grass with green. There is no better sight.

Mattia points out their boundaries to me. Looking east, they are permitted to move their flock to the gully bottom but no further. The EU pays subsidies to mountain farmers because it is not easy to make a living in a climate so harsh, doing a job that has not changed, in essence, for millennia. The higher and steeper the land, the more money you can draw, although it is a rare farmer who finds it enough to live on. But almost all the land in Lessinia is private, held for generations by a few big families, and they are only too happy to get hold of a landless shepherd and take the subsidies themselves. If you want to rent a *malga* of your own, they push up the prices accordingly. They are making, he reckons, around 40,000 euros for their landlord, just by being here.

'They live in Verona,' says Sofia.

'With a Ferrari or Lamborghini in the garage.'

'They might drive up here in a Cinquecento and a gilet, but you can see by their shoes that they have never done a real day's work. You find something similar everywhere in Italy. But in Lessinia especially.'

'When the guy showed us the land he didn't know his own borders,' says Mattia. 'I asked him where the other pond was and he said he didn't know.'

Mattia and Sofia met during Covid. Theirs is one of the good pandemic stories. Sofia had come to volunteer on the farm where Mattia was staying with his flock. She came for a fortnight and got locked down for three months, and then she stayed forever. Now they were halfway up a mountain with 300 sheep and a baby in her belly, and neither of them could imagine a life without the other that had any sort of meaning.

Sofia was from a small mountain town north of here, but she had been away for years. She worked at the Italian embassy in Congo before she understood that was no way to change the world, and she had quit and taken off travelling. She went to Togo, across North Africa, then on to the Middle East. She spent years in South East Asia. But in the end it was just one more routine – quitting places, quitting people, saying goodbye, over and over. A prisoner of your own paradise. In the end what she had been looking for was back where she began.

Between the autumn and the spring they move their flocks through the valleys near their house, grazing them on whatever ground their neighbours will permit them. The old people are moved by them, to see a young couple who love each other, still following the old ways. Someone will stand them a drink in the bar, or a woman will bring a bottle of grappa out to the fields to warm them.

'You have to try hard not to become an alcoholic,' Sofia grins.

And then summertime they come up here. These are the months they live for. Those same old valleys could start to weigh on the mind in the fifth month of winter, or the sixth; those old habits of wanderlust die hard. April, May, there's something that happens in your heart. The animals feel it too. The spring comes and they go crazy, raising their eyes up to the peaks. And one day the time is right, and all of them – the dogs, the sheep, the humans, the young lambs tucked in the donkeys' saddlebags, the baby in Sofia's belly – set off up into the hills on foot, pulled on their yearly cycle the way that the moon pulls on the tides.

'We are so lucky,' Sofia says. 'We are very independent. We can arrange the day according to how we feel. And we get to live like this.'

'It's amazing you spend so much time together,' I say.

'Every fucking minute!' Mattia laughs.

'We still enjoy it, though. Don't we, Mattia? Say yes!'

Mattia smiles and nods. They are clearly very happy together.

'You must spend a lot of time in silence.'

Mattia shakes his head. 'She speaks a lot!'

'*Ma dai!*' Sofia laughs, pushing at him. 'Sometimes we take a morning alone,' she says. 'We split the shift.'

'Everyone thinks that we're crazy,' smiles Mattia. 'They think I'm crazy because I live with my flock like an animal, and they think Sofia's crazy because she lives with me.'

They think they're crazy because they keep sheep, not cows, and they think they're crazy because they don't have a sworn vendetta against wolves. But everyone likes them too, more or less, because they are young, more or less, or at least a generation younger than almost anyone else up here. The brother and sister at the *malga* across the valley are in their seventies. They wake at five each morning and don't stop until eight at night and they have no other help. The man beyond the hill, sixty-five. Modesto, eighty-two. They like Mattia and Sofia because they are happy and in love. But they also know that they are different, that they have different opinions and they come from a different world, and difference is something that has never been welcomed in the mountains where the daily dangers are only manageable because of stability and constancy.

Mattia plants his crook in the hillside and leans back on it, looking out across his flock, gazing across the land as a kestrel might. He sees everything. He knows the tourists think he's simple. How can a man spend all day staring into space?

'You're a good shepherd if you have eyes,' he says. He points out members of the flock to me. 'This one is pregnant, due any day. I'm keeping my eye on her. This one has a problem with the foreleg. That one, a problem with the teeth.'

But then looking is what he has spent his life doing,

it's just that before he was holding a camera. He worked all over the Middle East. He spent a year and a half in Gaza. From Gaza he went to Syria. From Syria to Egypt, from Egypt to Turkey. The things he photographed, the things he saw, but he was fuelled by the adrenaline of it all. Everywhere he went, he saw shepherds. In Turkey he took a rubber bullet to the stomach documenting the protests in Gezi Park. He was bundled onto a bus, strip-searched, and held in a cell for two nights. He was looking at seven years until his embassy intervened. He was deported, and watched from Italy as eight people lost their lives and more than 8,000 were injured. Nine years later he is a shepherd up a mountain, and Erdoğan is still in charge of Turkey.

Mattia was twenty-six years old when he fell into advertising, because that was where the money was. By one metric he was a great success; at his peak he had fifteen assistants. And that was when he met his first goat. He was on one of his brief holidays, on a friend's farm in Liguria. At two in the morning his friend woke him to help with the milking. He sat there, his hands on this goat's udders, draining milk into a pail.

'And I was like, my God,' he says. 'This is what I want to do. With photography I'm creating nothing. Here I am creating life. I can look after myself.'

He wasn't the only journalist who had dirt under his nails now, or his hand up a sheep's arse. A friend who he had worked alongside in Palestine – a man who had won World Press Photo of the Year – had turned to farming.

He had his kids, his wife, his farm. Because what's the point, if you aren't happy?

'When I go to the city I go crazy,' Mattia says. 'It's not Rome, it's Verona. But still it's too much. I have to come back here and chop wood.'

At night they can see the city on the plain below, glowing like the embers of an exhausted fire.

'The only thing that affects people in the city is coronavirus,' Sofia says, from where she sits on the grass behind us. 'For people in the city it was terrible. But for us, if it's not raining, that's terrible. This is the most important political issue. We don't fight for right or left. We fight for water.'

'Does anyone represent your interests?' I say.

'No one puts climate change at the top,' she says. 'It's like that movie *Don't Look Up*.'

'The changes we have seen,' Mattia says. 'Not in six hundred years. In six.' There is something to be said for spending one's days looking. Back when he was a photographer, he once said in an interview, 'I want to feel part of this relentless history of ours.' Well, it certainly feels relentless now, and he is undeniably a part of it. To be out in it, in every weather, every day of the whole year.

'The farmers are killing their cows,' Sofia says. 'There is no water up here. If they take them back to the barns they cannot afford the hay, so what else can they do? A lot of farms will close this winter.'

They have been thinking about getting a Sardinian breed that is better adapted to drought. It means giving up the Brogna, but what good is the traditional if the world is no longer what it once was?

'I fear the future,' Mattia says. 'It changes too fast.'

The Maremmano-Abruzzese drift through the flock, great clouds of animal, but the sheep pay them no mind. Sofia pulls all four onto her and lies back, laughing. I lie back too, and listen to the gentle rhythm of the bells.

'Do you want your baby to have this life?' I say, after a time.

'It's a nice life for a kid,' she says. 'Not a vacation. A normal life. Maybe they will be passionate about sheep or maybe not. But the thing that really makes me happy is that he or she will have a tie with this for the rest of their life.'

For a while now we have not seen Pioggia and Viola, the herding dogs. It is not like them to run off. Mattia keeps raising his binoculars and scanning the horizon. One half of the flock is now down on the valley floor and is beginning to stray towards the neighbouring land. It is a long way down to get them back and he stares after them dispassionately. He is all too aware, at times like this, that without the dogs he is nothing. They are his ears, his legs, the projection of his will.

I look out, too, down the valley. There is a single bird, with a piercing song, flying high. It was Mattia's parents who first brought him up here. He left for a long time, but he came back. Sitting here in the grass I fairly ache for the life I think I want to give my children, however much I know that I romanticise it. Mattia and Sofia are people after my own heart. It is easy to imagine being friends. And in some way, I think, they romanticise it too. But is romance such a bad reason to do something?

'At university I studied cultural anthropology,' Sofia says. 'Sometimes I think that I became the study subject, instead of being the person who studied.' And if Mattia was to take photographs any more, he'd probably just take them all of sheep.

'I hear that there are lots of young people turning to shepherding,' I say.

'Really?' Sofia says, sitting up from where she is lying in the grass and looking around theatrically. 'Where are they?!'

But there are. Shepherding schools are popping up all over. This year there is a new one in the Abruzzo in the Apennines. Those in Spain have huge waiting lists. The Escuela de Pastoras del Siglo XXI, in Cantabria, is open only to women, and it is ten times oversubscribed.

Yes, there is something ludicrous about taking courses in how to be a shepherd. Mattia doesn't approve – it smacks of standardisation, regulation, paperwork, all the things that he is trying to escape. Once it might have been the youngest son who took the animals up to pasture for the summer, and he didn't need a qualification. All season he would have watched the flock, abandoned to the summer storms and his private thoughts and the occasional wolf. Payment was not part of the deal. Then those boys were forced into school, and they renounced an education handed down for generations in favour of their numbers and their letters. Today shepherding schools are all that remains to try to claw back the knowledge that has been lost.

That demand speaks to a need, and not just a need for shepherds. Not since Heidi has it been such an aspirational career move. Over the past few hundred years capitalism has freed us from the drudgery of a world that stinks of lanolin and sheep piss and delivered us into a clean, bright future of high-rises and Zoom calls, e-scooters and assorted nut milks, synthetic fibres and AI. And yet the end result is young people who want to throw it all away to go and live up a mountain with some sheep. In the Dolomites I had met a young man who was going through the training. He had worked in an old folks' home for ten years, but he had seen so many people die during the pandemic that he could no longer cope. 'Why do you want to work with animals?' I asked him. 'Because they don't lie,' he said.

Shepherds might not like wolves, but wolves are creating jobs. And yet who can afford to employ a shepherd? Max Rossberg of the European Wilderness Society, back in Tamsweg, Austria, suggested to me that we re-label a shepherd as a 'climate-change mitigator', paying him or her with the money raised from carbon taxes. It is a contentious subject. Regenerative agriculture has become something of a buzzword, promising everything from reversing climate change to improving the quality of topsoil. Regenerative grazing is claimed to have all manner of positive impacts, from reducing avalanche risk (cropped grass keeps the snowpack more stable) to providing natural fertilisers (through spreading manure) and enhancing biodiversity (by creating a patchwork of habitats), but its primary benefit is the sequestration of carbon. Grazing encourages grasses to put down deeper roots, the thinking goes, thus drawing carbon down from the atmosphere. Those who dispute this say that this carbon will only be locked away temporarily, and that livestock burp and fart out far more greenhouse gases than they will ever help to sequester. There is the argument, from an emissions-based perspective, that pastoralism is worse than animals raised intensively in feedlots, which will have much shorter, and therefore less polluting, lives.

The debate is as complex as it is polarised. Certainly industrial animal farming is one of the most destructive practices on earth, and viable alternatives are increasingly on the horizon. Yet worldwide there are still 300 million pastoralists, and in many places they remain a significant part of the economy, using animals to convert plants from otherwise unworkable land into protein. To demand their removal begs more questions than it answers. Italy's government has recently banned the import, sale or production of lab-grown meat in what it calls a defence of Italian tradition, although how much such decisions are taken in solidarity with pastoralists and how much they are influenced by the lobbying of agribusiness – what gets called Big Meat – is unclear. Certainly, for most of our settled history, up until the advent of industrial agriculture, domesticated animals were not a quantifiable technology with measurable datasets, but our primary connection to the natural world. Writer and activist Wendell Berry called farming a conversation with nature. Clearly, it has drifted far from that ideal. But up here with Mattia and Sofia, nature is not something other, as it was in the zoo or even in the woods, but something in relationship with us. Most of us will never live this life. But even so, observing the threads that bind human and sheep and dog and land and wolf, I cannot help but feel that we would be losing something profound if we were to lose all this.

Suddenly Mattia spots a flicker of movement, way down in the gully. He lifts the binoculars, but he knows already it is his dogs. He starts calling them, cursing them. He watches as they move at full pelt along the valley bottom and then on a diagonal uphill, rippling across the landscape. They slow as they near him, slinking in, their heads and tails low, profoundly guilty. They reach him and collapse at his feet, mouths agape. They are both panting like steam trains. He gives each one a full embrace, still cursing. He sniffs at the breath that comes pumping out of Pioggia.

'Pizza?' says Sofia.

Mattia shakes his head. 'Bones.'

He sends them back down to the flock to sort them out.

Later in the day Mattia gets a call. I walk down with him to the San Giorgio road and a few minutes later a battered Volvo pulls in. Two Moroccans get out, a father and son, and we shake hands and walk back up towards the flock. If it wasn't for the Muslims, Mattia says, there would be no shepherds left in Italy. Italians don't eat much lamb, but these guys will turn up and take several off to slaughter them halal. They are Italy's new working class and they have money to spend, especially on parties. They are now his biggest market.

'They can pick out the best lambs,' he says. 'There is no point trying to pass them off with anything else. I have no idea how they know, just by looking.'

I think of Hassan, working for Modesto, and of these men buying Mattia's lamb, and wonder what exactly the traditionalists are hoping to preserve as they try to hold back the change. The Moroccans select four sheep, and Mattia binds their legs and lugs them down the hill one by one and hefts them into the boot of the Volvo. They have another twenty-five sheep marked, which they selected in March and will be back for in September.

I will spend the whole day with Mattia and Sofia, and over the course of that long summer in Lessinia I will pay them several visits. I look forward to it each time. It is wholesome and peaceful to be up in the hills, doing nothing more than sitting and looking, going where the flock goes. Certainly I would not be able to do it every day. But stuck in the library, writing this book, these are the days that I think back to.

Late one afternoon, Sofia invites me to stay for dinner. While she cooks I help Mattia with the evening routine. The dogs corral the flock and he closes up the fences and connects up the solar-powered generator. One of the Brogna has bloat. Her left side is swollen like a mountain.

He wades into the flock and grabs her by a hind leg; she is too listless to run. He pins her beneath his leg and puts an ear to her stomach, and then invites me to listen.

'I can't hear anything,' I say.

'Exactly,' he says. 'Completely blocked.'

Sofia is in the caravan, singing in English as she cooks:

> 'Well, I know that you're in love with him
> 'Cause I saw you dancin' in the gym
> You both kicked off your shoes
> Man, I dig those rhythm and blu-ues!'

'Ten thousand years people have been keeping sheep,' Mattia says as he mixes a herbal extract and sucks it up into a syringe. 'There is no more ancient work. Nowadays people call the vet for everything. The old shepherds have tradition. Give them red wine. Give them coffee. Cut a vein here for a pain in the belly. Every problem, for me, is a problem. For them, it's a solution. Once I saw an Ethiopian kid hold his lighter to the arsehole of a sheep.'

'Why did he do that?'

Mattia shrugs. 'But after that she was right as rain.' He jams the syringe into the corner of the ewe's mouth and squirts the solution down her throat. He scribbles a blue mark on her back and lets her go. The animal startles away from him in a flurry of limbs. 'If that doesn't work then she'll be dead in two days,' he says.

> 'So bye-bye, Miss American Pie
> Drove my Chevy to the levee

But the levee was dry
And them good ol' boys were drinking
   whiskey 'n' rye
Singing, "This'll be the day that I die
This'll be the day that I die."'

Venus is up. A single candle burns in the caravan's window, a beacon in the dark. The sheep are settling down, chewing their cud, a quiet peace, the gentle tolling of their bells. We wash our hands and go inside and sit down. Sofia puts a plate of beans and rice in front of me. 'If you want something else, there isn't anything!' she says.

I have brought beers with me, and peaches for dessert. We sit around their tiny table, our knees pressed against one another. I ask them about the wolves.

'In theory, we are for them,' Sofia says.

For a long time they did not know what they thought. Mattia was from the city, and so were his family and all of his friends. He voted left. All that dictated that he should be for the wolf. And yet he was responsible for several hundred lives. They had never lost an animal to wolves but they knew plenty who had. This past winter a pack had been watching their flock. They never saw them, but they found plenty of sign, scat and spoor. But then he read a book that made up his mind.

'*Wolf Totem*,' he says. 'By a Chinese writer, Jiang Rong. It's about the nomads in Mongolia who keep animals on the steppe. It's about herders, like us. And it's beautiful, because it speaks about the work that the wolves do on the land, and how they serve us. It's incredible. They eat the wild animals and they eat our animals, but all the animals become stronger when they have a competitor. The wolf makes the land stronger. The Chinese want to get rid of the wolves, but the nomads know that getting rid of the wolf will kill the land as well. So he respects the wolf. It's beautiful.'

Mattia has a tattoo on his forearm of four parallel lines, like bracelets, the two in the middle close together and bracketed by two more. Once it had meant a road to him, the endless road that he was on as a photographer. But these days he reads it as a circle. You cannot cut the circle without it unravelling. That was what the wolf had come to mean to him. You only had to spend a bit of time in Lessinia to see that it wasn't the sheep that were dying here. It was the land.

'We are guests,' he says. 'If you make the choice to work in nature, you can't complain about nature. Nature gives us all this and we must give something in return. Two years ago, two eagles killed some of our lambs. So should I shoot every eagle? We cannot survive by killing everything. To have a good system you have to have every part of the system. We have taken too much from this planet, and now the planet it says fuck off.'

I finish my beer. I need to go soon. The whole of the caravan, the whole of these mountains, is focused around the candle burning on the table between the three of us.

'It is the sheep that give us power to create life,' Mattia

continues. 'Without the sheep there is no money. No dogs. Without the sheep, there is no Sofia. There is no baby. For ten thousand years we have shared our lives with animals. Without wool, we are nothing. Without meat. Without milk. We must stay together to survive against the nature. Not against,' he corrects himself. 'In nature. To survive in nature.'

'Every act is political,' Sofia says. 'You look after the land, you look after the future.' But the future is not what it used to be.

Outside, the dogs begin barking once again at something out in the night.

We are into the dog days of summer.

Slavc moves across the mountainside, over Lessinia's tired and yellow grasses. An eye that knew him well might see a stiffness to his hindquarters, but he appears as strong and sharp and powerful as he has been these last ten years. Animals do not fade away out here but only keep on going until they cannot, until one day they crawl off to die. He has been here a long time now. Does he remember what he came through to reach here? Does he remember the place of his birth? Does he remember how the land was with no wolves? The sun feels good in his old bones.

The pack moves with him. They pass a herd of cows that do not pay them any mind. Last night the pack killed again – a calf, on the far side of their range – and so for now there is no need to hunt. It is as though the cows know, that they can sense the wolves' particular quality of mind, and that for the time being there is enough space for them all.

This is the end of the easy times. There is food on these slopes all summer, but soon the last of the livestock will be gone and will not return again until the spring. Soon, the weather will turn. One by one the wolves walk a line in a loose column to higher ground.

It is not Juliet, but a different female that moves with Slavc. Orecchio Mozzo, she has been named – 'Bitten Ear' – for the defining tear that she has out of one ear. It is unclear where she came from; a descendant maybe, or another disperser from afar. She was first seen in the park last year. Her five pups follow on behind, their puppyish heads and feet still a little too large, moving with a loose and youthful energy. When the adults stop the pups lie down, stretching out in the late-afternoon sun like house cats.

Orecchio Mozzo is here because Juliet is not. Juliet has not been seen for a long time, not by Luca or Paolo or Gaetano or by any of the others. It is now believed that she died during the previous winter, killed in a fight with the Eastern Lessinia pack. A pack that would not have been here but for her and her journey, mortally wounded by one of her own. She would have been twelve, an astonishing age for a wolf in the wild. Months later there were rumours of some possible remains, but by the time they went to investigate nothing could be found. It was breeding season when she was killed; there was little time for grief. They had stayed together until the end, and the decade of their relationship came to a close as swiftly as it began, their lives once more shaped by fate. By the following month, Orecchio Mozzo was pregnant by Slavc.

One of their pups sees a marmot and gives chase, bounding gaily up the slope. A cow lifts its head, watches it go.

It is early October and chestnuts coat the ground, are ground by cars into the tarmac. The cherry trees flame like bonfires. For some weeks it has been cold and wet – still not wet enough, but wet – but now summer has returned once more, what they call an *estate San Martino*, an Indian summer in Italy.

On the drive up to Modesto's early this morning the hills were brushed with autumn, the stands of beech tan and sand and russet, and a mist hanging low in the valleys. The sky was scraped with contrails. The drinking ponds were full of rain at last, little pools of sky. Now, at ten, the sky is wholly blue, and Modesto is driving his cows down off the mountain before the winter can catch them unawares. He has invited me to join them.

The herd is ninety strong. We are all in T-shirts, and it is hard to believe that winter could be just around the corner. But among the men, and it is almost entirely men, there is muttering that snow is forecast for tomorrow. It comes that fast. The men walk with switches of hazel in their hands, grey stubble, camo caps and camo trousers, driving the cows before them. They have come from many places, from local villages and from as far away as Bergamo. And then there are families, out for a weekend walk, and photographers from the local papers, and teenage sons brought here by their fathers for an experience that they believe all men should have.

The cows are eager. I feel in pretty good shape now, walking-wise, but it is not easy to keep up. They know these paths as well as the men. Last year one got separated and she made her own way home days later. But they also want their last taste of these high pastures, and they stop to graze the verges while the men surround them, shouting, waving their arms as though signalling to a person far off. There are two herders on horseback, cantering after errant cows, and other herders lope across the grasslands, hemming them in, driving them downwards.

We walk among them. On the thin footpaths they nudge at your back, hot with breath. If I let myself, I can be nervous of animals this big, this close. I am surrounded by a cacophony of bells. High and low bells, rounded and sharp, minor and major. They are great bells that hang from the cows by thick collars, and in the midst of the herd, walking along at pace with the cows trotting around me, the din creates something uncanny. Within the deafening atonality a sort of harmony emerges, an additional music on the very edge of hearing, a drone built up of all the other bells, so that I am fairly washed by sound.

A buzzard wheels. We come down onto the mountain

road and pass by the abandoned ski resort of San Giorgio. On the rise above is where Mattia and Sofia's caravan was stationed until recently, but they left for the valleys a week ago. Old couples are parked up on the verges of the road, recumbent in deckchairs beside their cars, sacrificing themselves to the last of the season's sun. Modesto is in the truck, bringing up the rear, but Hassan is on foot, swinging a long switch and loping along and swiping at things as he walks. He greets me like an old friend. I fall into step alongside him.

'Last week it got very cold,' he says. 'It snowed. The cows wanted to leave. They'd come out from being milked and start heading down the hill.' He grins. '*Casino.*'

He is looking forward to being out of the mountains. He is looking forward to having Sundays again – he has not had a day off in months. From next week he will be working in a mechanic's in San Bonifacio, outside of Verona. He hopes to get enough money together to make a trip to Morocco. He has not been home in six years.

At Malga Pàparo di Sotto, just above Pozza dei Confini, they halt the herd for everyone to catch up. Modesto gets down from the truck and walks about, inspecting the cattle, shaking hands. The atmosphere is celebratory. And then we plunge off the road down into the Valle di Revolto. The cows sense home as we start to lose altitude, and the men must stop them from building up too much speed downhill in case they tumble and break a leg.

We come into the woods. There are drifts of chestnuts, and the beech leaves are blazing yellow in the late-autumn, early-afternoon light. The first of the leaves are falling. Somewhere, the gunshots of a hunter shooting birds. It is a shock to see cows trotting down switchbacks through autumnal woodland, as though they are some wilder sort of beast. The men herd them back from the edges, trotting along with them. A slip here would be fatal. The valley is steep and the path is ancient, hewn into the cliff; in one place it tunnels directly through the rock for a good distance.

It is unfathomable, the amount of effort that it would have taken to cleave this path into the mountain. These paths speak of tradition that is centuries old, a tradition now preserved by just one man who is nearing the end of his life. How quickly will this path be overgrown with trees? We built Lessinia, Modesto likes to say, but equally it is Lessinia that built him. I think back to Stane and Ivan and Lena and Michael and Enrico and Mattia and Sofia and all the rest of them. They would love this.

We emerge from the woods onto the valley bottom. Giazza is little more than a village surrounded by valley walls of tumbling forest, with the defiant finger of a church tower staking its place in the wilderness. Most of the townspeople are packing the narrow streets and watch as we go past. The old women and the men, appraising the animals. Others, holding up their phones. And the children, watching a life pass by that will never be theirs, which in truth vanished years ago. A pastel blue on a plaster wall is all that remains of a mural of the Virgin.

Beyond the square we pause and the cows bunch up and back up on the road. Rivulets of piss run down the tarmac and puddle in the gutters. The cows are hazed by flies and strings of drool swing from their lips, their mouths gaping, their tongues hanging. One mounts another half-heartedly. They are weary, we all are, and there are many kilometres still to go. Someone hands round espressos in small plastic beakers.

Stacked bales of silage in the fields. We follow Strada Provinciale 10 along the valley bottom and the camper vans and coaches back up behind us. And at last we leave the road and climb towards Campofontana.

The cows know they are approaching home. They pick up the pace and shoulder their way through the open gates into the fields and straightaway begin to graze. The men sort the cows from the calves, and by the time that has been done and the troughs filled and the animals watered, it is late in the afternoon. None of us have eaten since breakfast, many hours ago. We have covered thirty-two kilometres in six hours.

Outside Modesto's house, tables have been set with tablecloths. One of the men lifts scaffolding boards from the construction site next door and sets them across the chairs to create benches. The women cook and serve. There is an abundance of food. I wolf down two plates of pasta before I discover that was just the *primo*. There is a *secondo* of beef *spezzatino* and polenta, cabbage, salad, and then cheese, bread, wine, coffee laced with grappa, and wild cherries dripping with liqueur. Food has never tasted better.

We sit together, laughing and chatting, listening to stories of transhumances past, all getting joyously drunk. Hassan does not eat with us. I cannot see Modesto either. Someone tells me he has gone to bed already. Tomorrow he will be up at four-thirty, as he is every morning of his life.

The Italian washes over me. How much longer will these ways of life last? The mountains have long been the last strongholds not only of predators, but also of culture. Just as we are suffering a biodiversity crisis, so we are suffering an equivalent collapse in cultural diversity, and I have long believed that their regeneration must go hand in hand if we are to make sense of our place upon this planet.

Each extinction is a story of great violence. Britain's last great auk was stoned to death on St Kilda in 1840, so uncanny and unexpected that it was believed to be a witch. We cannot efface anything from the webs that bind us all without wider consequence. Ecosystems unravel, societies falter, imaginations become bland. Yet it is easier to imagine resurrecting mammoths than changing how we live.

After these years of thinking about wolves, of following their path back into Europe, I have come to see them as disruptors. They move fast and they break stuff. They are provocative, as symbolic as they are ecological. They demand answers. Can we cede space? Can we sanction risk? Can we cope with change? Can we permit ourselves to fall back in love with the world? If we are to relinquish at least some of our grip on the land, as we must, then it is the wolf that asks us whether we really think we can. If wolves have shown us anything during their million years on the planet, it is that *they* are supremely adaptable to change. As the great migrators on this planet have always known – people and animals alike – movement is an existential necessity. That in times of crisis, nothing can be contained. That in times of need, we move.

What does conservation mean these days, when so much is unravelling? We are not going back to a time when there were wolves. We are moving forward towards something new, something not yet determined. We find ourselves on the brink of disaster, and that is not a place we can remain. What the future looks like is by turns terrifying and brimming with possibility, and it remains up to us to facilitate it. I have been wary of the wolf as a symbol of hope, but I realise now that is only true for those of us interpreting the wolf's resurgence as a sign that the world is healing. For the wolf, this is clearly a time of hope. How could they ever have expected this? That we have opened our doors to what was once the most vilified of creatures, and permitted it to forge new lives in old lands, is perhaps the most startling aspect of all.

The meal is nowhere near to wrapping up. There is more wine, great three-litre bottles of it. I am tired. At last I leave them to it and head off, walking the paths that we came in on. It is hours since we first passed through, and the lanes still smell of cows.

Epilogue

Italy, 2023

Slavc is dead, and I am back in Lessinia.

It is another spring, it has come again. It is March and eleven years to the day since Slavc first set foot in this place. The latest report, published this month, recorded two packs in the park and another two, the Carega pack and the Giazza Forest pack, overlapping Lessinia's borders. A total of perhaps thirty-six wolves. There are at least fifteen packs in the entirety of Veneto, covering one-fifth of the whole region. The legacy of the two of them, filling these mountains in ever-expanding orbits – wolves that sire wolves that sire wolves. Over the ten years they stayed together Slavc and Juliet had, at best guess, forty-two pups. Last year there were 207 predations in Lessinia: 157 cattle, forty-five sheep, four donkeys and a llama. Since October 2022 Giorgia Meloni, leader of the far-right Brothers of Italy, has been prime minister of Italy.

I am meeting Gaetano Pimazzoni, the photographer, once again. I am yet to see a wolf in the wild. It is an hour before dawn, and I am climbing the narrow mountain road above Branchetto. The headlights pick out patches of snow still lying across the hills, the messiness

EPILOGUE

of in between the seasons. An electric candle gutters in a roadside shrine. I pull into the large car park at Rifugio Bocca di Selva. There is no one else about. It is Sunday and in a few hours the place will be full, but for now there is just a single camper van parked up in a far corner. I roll back the seat and close my eyes.

The last photo of Slavc is from the morning of 13 August 2022. In it, he is standing in a steep forest of beech, his head bowed. But no further sightings in itself did not mean much. Gaetano warned me on the phone last night that he has not seen any wolves since November, and he is out several mornings every week. Not for the first time I find myself in awe of his commitment to a species other than his own. That for all our failings, humans still have a capacity to be attentive to the lives of other species in ways that are unparalleled.

But then came a sighting of Orecchio Mozzo, Slavc's new mate, with another, younger male that was behaving like the dominant male of the pack. Later came news that in the autumn a hunter had found wolf bones out in the woods. Two weeks ago that news made its way to Paolo Parricelli, the park ranger. Paolo went to the spot and collected what remained. The genetic analysis confirmed what his gut already knew: Lessinia's pioneers were dead. This past Tuesday *Arena*, the Verona paper that has chronicled Slavc's and Juliet's lives like a gossip magazine for the past decade, ran his obituary.

Slavc had been twelve years old, the same age as Juliet. As a centenarian's life spans a scope of human history,

EPILOGUE

I think of these two wolves in the same way. When they were born, wolf numbers had only recently begun to pull back from the brink. Along the entire length of their two vast journeys there was not a single pack. Today, in Europe, the wolf is listed as a species of 'Least Concern'. Slavc and Juliet are both dead, but their purpose is not, their journeys are not. As two of Europe's pioneers, their lives have mirrored the history of the wolf.

I open my eyes as Gaetano's Fiat pulls in beside my car. I get out and shake his gloved hand, and watch while he sorts his equipment. Then we set off, walking fast. It is good to see him, although we have only ever met like this and we have never shared more than a few words. We are following a track that in the winter is used for Nordic skiing, the gravel a pale-grey ribbon in the dark. The night is cloudy and there are no stars to speak of.

We descend into a thin gully and climb up the far side, and then Gaetano veers from the path and climbs steeply. At the crest I follow him back down into a fold of the hills that narrows gradually towards the valley's wooded floor. Beside a tree, in front of a rock, we stop. There is snow on the ground and he lays out a tarp. And then we sit down to wait.

Piece by piece the land takes on hue, eases into relief. Below is the forest and beyond it, above it, another naked hill, and the variegated stripes of snow and rock of the mountain range behind. Hunkered in the dark, a *malga* and its outbuildings. We sit. We watch. We wait.

A roe deer walks across the scene, picking each one

of its feet high up out of the snow. It is charged with the same tension that we are, and although it does not see us, in that moment we are all part of the same world. Around the base of each small spruce is a halo of melted snow. Later I will read in the paper that down near Badia Calavena wolves are killing sheep tonight.

It is becoming easier to do this. The chill is less insistent. I notice that I am not making lists of things I must do today, or counting off the quarter-hours. Sometimes I forget what we're doing here at all and just . . . look. To watch like this is to be an animal oneself. I scan the hills with the binoculars, sucking in all available light. Birds pass overhead; I can hear their individual wing beats. In the woods, the hammering of a woodpecker. Single grasses rise like snorkels from the snow.

And then, suddenly, I see something, a whisper, below the distant *malga*. A grey shape against the grey land, moving swiftly and diagonally downhill. I steady the binoculars and hold my breath. There are no cows up here this time of year, no sheep. It is larger than a fox. It is not moving like a deer. It is . . . I hardly dare to think it. I so want it to be what I hope it is that it feels it cannot be. '*Gaetano*,' I hiss. '*There.*'

In the time it takes to point it out it is gone, below the treeline, into the woods that clog the valley at our feet.

It is in there. I fix my binoculars on the stand of trees. It is *in there*. And the light comes up and the trees brighten, and of course I do not see it again. Half an hour passes. An hour. It could be anywhere. Did I even imagine it? But I find that in fact, this morning, I do not care so much. That urge, that desperation to stare into a wolf's eyes — it isn't there today.

At last, the sun high, we stand up. We stretch. We piss. We walk back up the hill. Gaetano points out to me some wolf prints, a week old now and ruined by the sun, each one melted to the size of a dinner plate.

On the path back to the car we find old wolf scat, full of hair like severed plaits. The day is coming up. It will be a fine one, and as we walk the sun breaks through the dawn's blanket of cloud and flares on what is left of the snowpack on the Carega. It feels like we are on the way home from a party — that moment after staying up all night when you feel that you could stay awake forever — and we chat with an easy familiarity. We chat about the death of Slavc, and the death of nature, and how nice it is to get up early and just sit and look at things for a while.

'Do you think it was a wolf?' I say.

'Could be,' Gaetano says. 'It could be.'

There is a man coming towards us, up early for his Sunday hike, dressed head to toe in bright, primary colours. 'Any luck?' he says, gesturing to Gaetano's tripod.

Gaetano shrugs. 'Nothing,' he says. 'Still nothing.'

'I saw a wolf just back there,' he says. He points in the direction of the road. 'From the car. Twenty metres off.'

'*Complimenti*,' says Gaetano, graciously. 'Enjoy your walk.'

And the man strolls off, swinging his sticks. The two

EPILOGUE

of us reach the car park and shake hands and drive off our separate ways.

The tiredness hits me as I drive back down the road, winding down out of the hills towards the plain. My flight is not until midday. I do not know when I will be back again. I think I will stop for a coffee and a brioche at the first bar that I find. And in my mind I go back to those few seconds of movement on the hill. I had imagined that my sighting of a wolf would be dramatic and profound. That my eyes would lock with its amber eyes. That I would close my book with it, of course. At the very least, that I would be sure it was a wolf. And yet the wolf remains as mysterious today as the day that I first set out to follow it.

But then a suggestion, I think, is appropriate. A suggestion is all we ever really seem to get. And it is from the suggestion that we will make the wolf into whatever we want it to be.

Slavc: 2010–2022
Juliet: 2010–2022

Postscript

Ramsgate, England, February 2025

'I put it to him that a change in EU law will not come about because one corner of Austria wishes it so.' Few words I have written have aged faster than these. They are from my interview with Edwin Angerer, provincial party chairman of FPÖ Carinthia, addressing his conviction that the only way to alleviate Europe's so-called wolf problem was a change in the animal's level of protection. I thought his vision was fanciful. What I had not foreseen back then was quite how many other corners of Europe also wished it so.

GW950m, the wolf that allegedly killed Ursula von der Leyen's pony, set in motion a long chain of events. The investigation ordered by von der Leyen, president of the European Commission, led to a proposal to downgrade the wolf's protection status, and in September 2024, after a last-minute change of heart by Germany, it was agreed on by a majority of EU member states. The Bern Convention's Standing Committee voted it through in December. The changes will come into effect next month, and the EU will then go through the process of updating its Habitats Directive.

GW950m remains at large.

We're not talking about a free-for-all. The wolf's new category is equivalent to a chamois, say, or a golden jackal, 'protected' rather than 'strictly protected'. Plenty of people, wolf biologists included, have suggested to me that making it easier to manage populations is not necessarily a bad thing. Around Verona, wolves are approaching the city, and perhaps they need an injection of fear. As I have argued, it is the farmers' felt impotence in the face of the wolf threat that has often seemed to me the biggest danger of all.

And yet. While wolves are flourishing from a continental perspective, populations are in 'unfavourable or inadequate conservation status' in all but one of Europe's biogeographical regions. It is questionable whether allowing people to kill things just a little bit is a good way to protect what remains, or whether, once something sacred is profaned, it only justifies further rollbacks. Last week, four wolves, probably poisoned, were found dead by a bike path in Trentino. Downgrading the wolf is part of an ongoing trend of watering down EU environmental protections in the wake of farmers' protests, further lurches to the right, playing catch-up all the time.

'If we could count on logic and rationality and scientific rigour, this decision is not dangerous,' said Luigi Boitani, Italy's pre-eminent wolf expert. But this, as I have seen in a long walk across Europe, is rarely how we reason.

POSTSCRIPT

Once again, it is illuminating to understand the wolf's world as a mirror to our politics. In September 2024 the FPÖ took the highest share of the vote in Austria's general election. If they can form a coalition, it will be the first time a far-right party has led Austria since the Second World War. Giorgia Meloni has consolidated her power to become one of the most influential politicians in Europe. Elections in Germany and France loom. And as for the United States, well . . . it is not a good time there to be a wolf, nor anyone trying to forge a life outside of the dominant paradigm.

Another world is possible. Soon after my walk, Slovenia elected a left-leaning coalition who immediately began dismantling the fence along the Slovene/Croat border. Slavc's natal territory was whole once more. If we can learn anything from Slavc's life, I think it is that even in the face of hopeless odds, even when what lies over the horizon is unknown, it still makes sense to get up and go searching for it at first light.

There are others out there, doing the same, looking for you.

Acknowledgements

Writing this book would have been impossible without the help of several grants. I am deeply grateful to the Society of Authors and the K Blundell Trust; the Oppenheim-John Downes Memorial Trust; and the Royal Literary Fund, which gave me the J. B. Priestley Award. Broughton Sanctuary provided a place to write as I began a second draft.

Several companies were very generous in providing equipment for the walk. Thank you to Varg (clothing) and Klean Kanteen (water bottles) for supporting me once again, and also to Klättermusen for other clothing and bags; Meindl for the hiking boots; Olympus for binoculars and camera equipment; and the ever-obliging map room at Stanfords.

Many people who supported the journey feature in the book and I am grateful to you all for showing me around your homes, providing beds when they were most welcome, and for trusting me with your stories. There are many others who, for one reason or another, aren't mentioned in the text, but were just as important for how this book was shaped:

I would like to thank Adela Pukl for several long conversations about the carnival culture of Slovenia; Christa Tuczay for her expertise on werewolves; and Joel Pullin

ACKNOWLEDGEMENTS

for having watched every werewolf film out there so that I didn't have to. Thanks to Toby Jones and family for showing me Parma and keeping me up to date with Italian wolf titbits; and to Jacques Willemen for being my lupine eyes and ears in Holland. Lisa Zaffuto and Saqib Rehman helped me understand the asylum system in Veneto; Silvia Montanaro and Silvana Fasoli explained nuances of pastoralism in Lessinia; and Max Rossberg of the European Wilderness Society did the same for me in Austria. Emma Marris answered all my questions about the Yellowstone wolves. Don McLean let me use the lyrics of 'American Pie'. And huge thanks to Paola Selva for translating in Italy, to Eva Lems in Austria and to Blažka Čemažar in Slovenia.

Francesco Romito and Alessandro Brugnoli patiently fielded my questions about wolves on the Italian side of the border. The team at the Biotechnical Faculty at the University of Ljubljana did the same for Slovenia. I want to particularly mention Hubert Potočnik, who has been immensely supportive of the project from its inception – this book would not exist had it not been for your unwavering enthusiasm and help.

The kindness of certain people along Slavc's trail made several places in the Alps feel so much like a home that I almost started marking out a territory. Annika Lems and Paul Reade in Millstatt; Manuela Ponmari, Massimo D'Agostino and the rest of the family at Pizzeria Lessinia; Kate Cozza in Verona – this journey would have been much harder and much less fun without you.

ACKNOWLEDGEMENTS

I want to extend a special thank-you to Emma Barana Sartori and Giacomo Cristiano, for translations, risottos, Italian lessons, mountain hikes, mysterious liqueurs and your warm and generous friendship.

It takes a pack to write a book. Helen Conford, Amanda Betts and Madhulika Sikka have all poured their time, wisdom and energy into every page to make this story as good as it could be, and I'd also like to thank Francis Geffard for his enduring support. The team at C&W, including Kate Burton and my superlative agent, Sophie Lambert, dispersed *Lone Wolf* far and wide and found it a home each time, and many thanks also to Sarah Fuentes and Veronica Goldstein at United Talent. To those who have read drafts and discussed endless details – Effie, Claude, Ulli, Gareth, Harry, James and my family – I value your insights so much. Thanks to Amber, Chris and everyone else at Faith in Strangers, where I've written this from the beginning to the end – I would have gone quietly mad without your company and humour. And to Mum and Dad and Nan: I am so very lucky to have your unfailing love and support.

Lastly, to my wonderful kids, Leika and Svalan – I've finished it! And to my wife, Ulli, whose love, energy, imagination, belief and unwavering conviction that art matters made it possible to write this with everything else going on. On a small mountain road in Slovenia it became obvious to me that we should get married, and I could not be happier. Let's do the next journey all together?

Selected Bibliography

I'd like to acknowledge here some of the books, articles and websites that I relied on most heavily while researching and writing *Lone Wolf*. A full list of references can be found at www.adamweymouth.com.

Books and articles

Aesop, (1894), *The Fables of Aesop* (trans. Joseph Jacobs)
Aesop, (1919), *The Aesop for Children*
Arnds, P. (2021), *Wolves at the Door: Migration, Dehumanization, Rewilding the World*
Berger, J. (2009), *Why Look at Animals?*
Berizzi, P. (2020), *L'Educazione di un fascista*
Bismara, C. (2020), *'Lupi e "lupesse" a Verona fra medioevo e Rinascimento'*
Cason, D. and Nardelli, M. (2020), *Il monito della ninfea: Vaia, la montagna, il limite*
Cesco-Frare, P. (2000), *'Tunin e il Lupo'*
Chatwin, B. (1987), *The Songlines*
Cheshire, J. and Uberti, O. (2016), *Where the Animals Go*
Dundes, A., ed. (1989), *Little Red Riding Hood: A Casebook*
Eckert, A. M. (2019), *West Germany and the Iron Curtain: Environment, Economy and Culture in the Borderlands*

SELECTED BIBLIOGRAPHY

Ehrenreich, B. (1997), *Blood Rites: The Origins and History of the Passions of War*

Eisler, R. (1948), *Man into Wolf: An Anthropological Interpretation of Sadism, Masochism and Lycanthropy*

Girard, R. (1982), *The Scapegoat*

Gow, D. (2024), *Hunt for the Shadow Wolf*

Graves, W. (2007), *Wolves in Russia*

Grimm, J. and Grimm, W. (1812), *Grimms' Fairy Tales*

Heywood, W., trans. (1906), *The Little Flowers of St Francis*

Jiang, R. (2004), *Wolf Totem*

Johnson, H. (2020), *Cry Wolf: Inquest into the True Nature of a Predator*

Jones, T. (2003), *The Dark Heart of Italy*

Köhler-Rollefson, I. (2023), *Hoofprints on the Land*

Krange, O. and Skogen, K. (2011), 'When the lads go hunting: The "Hammertown mechanism" and the conflict over wolves in Norway'

Kranjc, A. (2011), 'The Origin and evolution of the term "Karst"'

Kurlander, E. (2017), *Hitler's Monsters: A Supernatural History of the Third Reich*

Lems, A. (2023), 'Cultures of unwelcome: Understanding the everyday histories of exclusionary practices – A view from across the German border'

Leser, J. and Pates, R. (2021), *The Wolves Are Coming Back*

Linnell, J. et al. (2002), 'The fear of wolves: A review of wolf attacks on humans'

Lopez, B. (1978), *Of Wolves and Men*

Macfarlane, R. (2019), *Underland*

McGillicuddy, M. (2020), 'NEW from 1928: the Vatican gifts a live Capitoline wolf to Mussolini's Rome'
Marris, E. (2018), 'A good story: media bias in trophic cascade research in Yellowstone National Park'
Marris, E. (2021), *Wild Souls*
Marvin, G. (2012), *Wolf*
Mazzoni, C. (2010), *She-wolf: The Story of a Roman Icon*
Mech, L. D. (2019), 'Unexplained patterns of grey wolf *Canis lupus* natal dispersal'
Mech, L. D. and Boitani, L., eds (2003), 'Wolves: Behavior, Ecology, and Conservation'
Meyer, C. J. et al. (2022), 'Parasitic infection increases risk-taking in a social, intermediate host carnivore'
Monbiot, G. (2013), *Feral*
Monbiot, G. (2024), 'What do angry farmers in Nevada and Germany have in common? They're being exploited by the far right'
Mott, A., ed. (2012), *Carnival King of Europe II (2010–12)*
Natterson-Horowitz, B. and Bowers, K. (2019), *Wildhood*
Nicholls, H. (2014), 'Incredible journey: one wolf's migration across Europe'
Pangrazio, A. (2022), *Lupi A Nordest: Antiche paure, nuovi conflitti*
Perri, A. (2020), 'Prehistoric dogs as hunting tools: the advent of animal biotechnology'
Rowlands, M. (2008), *The Philosopher and the Wolf*
Safina, C. (2015), *Beyond Words: What Animals Think and Feel*
Sax, B. (2000), *Animals in the Third Reich: Pets, Scapegoats, and the Holocaust*
Schenkel, R. (1947), *Expressions Studies on Wolves*

SELECTED BIBLIOGRAPHY

Scheutz, M. (2001), 'Bettler – Werwolf – Galeerensträfling. Die Lungauer "Werwölfe" des Jahres 1717/18 und ihr Prozess'

Serpell, J. (2008), *In the Company of Animals: A Study of Human–Animal Relationships*

Spyri, J. (1880), *Heidi*

Wodak, R. (2015), *The Politics of Fear*

Yong, E. (2016), 'A New Origin Story for Dogs'

Websites

Alta Lessinia – www.altalessinia.com
L'Arena – www.larena.it
Io Non Ho Paura Del Lupo – www.iononhopauradellupo.it
Lessinia Bolf – www.lessiniabolf.it
Storia della Fauna – www.storiadellafauna.com